Experiencing Social Research

THE DORSEY SERIES IN SOCIOLOGY

Advisory Editor
Robin M. Williams, Jr.
Cornell University

Consulting Editor
Charles M. Bonjean
The University of Texas at Austin

Experiencing Social Research

Revised Edition

JOHN F. RUNCIE
Development Analysis Associates, Inc.
Cambridge, Massachusetts

1980

THE DORSEY PRESS   Homewood, Illinois   60430
Irwin-Dorsey Limited   Georgetown, Ontario   L7G 4B3

© THE DORSEY PRESS, 1976 and 1980

ISBN 0-256-02304-2
Library of Congress Catalog Card No. 79–53962

Printed in the United States of America

2 3 4 5 6 7 8 9 0 ML 7 6 5 4 3 2 1

For Libby

Preface

As I noted in the preface to the first edition of *Experiencing Social Research* (1976), I am convinced that one of the most important lessons anyone can learn about conducting social research is that Murphy's law ("If a thing can go wrong, it will") and its corollary ("When a thing goes wrong, it goes wrong at the worst time") always apply.[1] My recent research projects, one involving participant observations on the assembly line of an automobile factory and another involving survey research in another country, have both been affected by the actions of Murphy's law. For example, in the cross-cultural research project, I was approximately 10,000 miles from home when I learned that all my questionnaires had been lost (not destroyed, but lost) in a freak rainstorm in one of the driest Middle Eastern countries.

I am of the opinion that the only way students can learn to deal with the problems that beset research is to do the research and learn to live with the problems as they happen. Sitting in a classroom, listening to an instructor describe the problems of research (the instructor's own or someone else's) does not prepare the student for the experience. Nor, I might add, do descriptions of research prepare the student to design research. One must be involved in the research to appreciate how it is done and why.

Sending our graduates out with little real experience in research does them a great disservice, especially when Murphy's law operates. In addition, sending students out trained as "researchers" without real research experience does a disservice to sociology. We fool ourselves into thinking our students are trained in research when in fact they have been talked at about it but they have not experienced it.

In the course of one's undergraduate and graduate career, one is

---

[1] Murphy's Second Law states: A piece of bread with jelly on it, that falls from a table, will always land jelly side down.

exposed to many forms of social research techniques and theories, but one rarely gets to do any research on one's own. My first chance to do empirical research on my own came when I was an undergraduate and involved in a course of independent study. I decided that the best way to write a paper for the course was to do a "study" of some social "thing" and then write it up. At the time I had taken no course in either research methodology or in statistics. I "ran" a study using some fraternity members, friends and other students as my subjects, discovered a number of rather strange results, and eventually had enough "data" for a paper. I wrote the paper over a Christmas vacation (as do many undergraduates) and handed the paper in. The paper had no statistics, there was no real methodology to the paper other than what I had concocted. The sampling of the subjects had seemed logical at the time but was, in the words of the paper, a "semirandom sample," and on it went. It is to the credit of the professor that I earned only a B for the course, at least based on the methodological content of the paper. At the same time, if I could have been graded on what I learned about the research process, I should have been given an A+.

The point of my experience as an undergraduate is not the grade I received nor the fact that I "conducted" research. The important point is that I went out and experienced the doing of social research. It is the doing of the research that is most important. One cannot ever really know what a "probe" is until he or she has tried one and found that it did or did not work. One cannot know what an evasive answer to a question on income is until one asks a question and receives a vague answer. Likewise, reading about another person's experience, one popular approach for learning research strategies, is clearly not as good as actually doing research oneself. The best technique, of course, would be to combine the various approaches. It would be most preferable if we could give the student insight into the theory behind the doing of social research, show the student what scientists have done in terms of social research strategies, and finally and most importantly have the student go out in the field and conduct research as he or she proceeds through the course. Such a course of study would combine the learning of research with the doing of research. In this book we will attempt to do just that, combine the doing with the learning.

In revising the earlier edition of this book, a number of major changes, and many minor changes have been made. The major changes have been the addition of two new chapters and the updating of material in existing chapters. Chapters were added which deal with sampling and also the analysis of data in order to "round out" the coverage of survey research. In the other chapters the changes have been designed to show the evolutions in approaches to research which have taken place since the publication of the first edition.

I would like to acknowledge once again some of my teachers whose ideas I am no doubt using in this book, albeit without footnotes at each spot. A. George Gitter was the instructor who did not discourage me from doing research when I had no idea what I was doing. He "pushed me from the nest" and I found out the fun (and pain) of doing research. Arthur L. Wood, Gerald Heiss, and Matilda White Riley also tried to teach me research methodology. I think they succeeded, but their judgments are still to be awaited. I also want to again acknowledge the debt I owe to Edward G. Stockwell and J. David Colfax. Their friendship and guidance helped me to stay in a field that I otherwise might have left. I would also like to thank all the people who have worked with me on this book, particularly Randy Hyman and June Lipnoski for their able typing of the revisions. I am also indebted to David Knoke, Sheldon Olson, and Rodney N. Friery for their comments on my early drafts of the manuscript. I owe a particular debt to Robin Williams, whose ability to suggest extremely useful improvements where I see only perfection, never ceases to amaze me. Finally, I want to thank Jonathan H. Simonson for his comments and suggestions on using and describing various statistical approaches to sampling and data analysis. Although all of these people (and many others) were responsible for shaping my ideas, I alone am responsible for any faults in this book.

December 1979   *John F. Runcie*

Contents

Summary of Problems to Be Done

Chapter 2

A.   Go to the library and find an article that was written in a sociology journal. The article must be a report of some empirical study that was done. For this exercise you are to review the article: We want you to describe how the study was done, what theory was used to "ground" the study, what the choice of the sample (if there was one) entailed, and so on. In other words, we want a review, or a précis, of the article that you read. In addition, we also want you to criticize the article that you read.

B.   As an exercise in understanding and interpreting tables of data, compute percentages for one table and explain the relationships shown in a second, using tables included at the end of Chapter 2.

Chapter 3

Observe a person engaged in a repetitive cycle of action *and* social action. The observation should cover at least three to four cycles of the behavior. Consequently, the cycles should be of relatively short duration. In your observation you should record all that you see. Write up the notes of your experiences, including in your report the rough notes that you took in the field.

Chapter 4

Observe a relatively large area in which various types of social behavior are occurring simultaneously. The "large area" could be an area such as a shopping center. The time period for the observation should be of such duration that you can see regularities in behavior patterns. Record all that you see. Include in the report of your research your field notes, analyses, and conclusions.

Chapter 5

Conduct a participant observation of some group of which you are a member. The group to be observed should be one in which you interact frequently and in which you are a "member in good standing." Try to observe in such a manner that you cover the entire period of one of the group's meetings (preferably of one to two hour's duration). In your report include your analysis of the group situation as well as any field notes that you may have made.

Chapter 6

Construct a sociogram and a sociomatrix using preference choices made by persons living in a coed dormitory section at a large midwestern university (the data are included at the end of the chapter). In addition to the construction of a sociogram and a sociomatrix, describe and analyze the patterns shown in the choices made by the students.

Chapter 7

Draw a 10 percent random sample of the persons in your social research class. Ask the subjects their ages and, based on your sample, compute the average age. Using the data from each person's sample of the class, compare the data from the samples taken with the real population value. How right (or wrong) were you? Why?

Chapter 8

Using a questionnaire designed in class or using the questionnaire supplied in the text, interview five people (students or others). The questions in the interview schedule should be primarily closed-ended (that is forced-choice alternatives) although they do not all have to be so. Submit the completed questionnaires and any comments you may have on the design or the responses. For example, which questions "worked" and which did not?

Chapter 9

Analyze the data from the questionnaire designed in class or the questionnaire supplied in the text. In your analysis include your hypotheses as well as tables showing the relationships you tested and your conclusions concerning these relationships. If time does not permit a complete analysis, you should prepare the hypotheses to be tested as well as the rationale for the hypotheses. Further, you should submit dummy tables showing the variables you would use to test relationships.

Chapter 10

Using the techniques that you began to develop in the previous chapter, interview someone in depth about his or her relationships with brothers and sisters. In this interview, record as completely as possible what the subject said about the relationships. The interview should be a "focused" interview rather than one in which a definite schedule must be followed. Include in your report both your notes on the interview and your analysis of the individual's relationship with his or her siblings.

Chapter 11

Using prudence and good judgment violate certain rules that are commonly understood in social situations to see what those around you do about the violation. As an experiment you may (1) pretend for a day to be a boarder in your home, or (2) you may go to a church of a different faith than the one in which you were raised. In the first problem, the violations of the rules will be yours as they are interpreted by others and in the second, the violations of the rules will be by others as they are interpreted by you. Write up the notes of your experience(s) stressing the tactics you used, the unwritten rules that were violated, and your observations of what transpired.

1

Introduction: Why Experience Research?

Most definitions of "science" indicate that the word means both a body of knowledge *and* a method of gathering that knowledge. Science, then, might be considered as both a knowing *and* a doing. To be a scientist means that one understands something about a body of knowledge that is at the base of a particular discipline and also that one understands how to gather that data. As a background to a discussion of the techniques for gathering the data of sociology, we must examine sociology and sociological statements in order to try to answer the question raised above: "Why experience research?"

SOCIOLOGY AS AN ENTERPRISE

In order to more clearly understand social research methods it is important to spend time dealing with the material that forms the background for research. We must outline what sociology is so that we can then determine what we must do in order to conduct sociological research. In addition to defining sociology, we want to examine statements made by sociologists which have led us to the argument that one ought to *experience* social research. There are, it would seem, two reasons for experiencing social research: (1) Experience is really the only way to learn the techniques; and (2) the concept of experience is at the base of much sociological thought concerning the "nature" of social life. Through experience one gets practice *and* insight into social and sociological life.

1

Sociology (at least from our point of view) seems to suggest to different sociologists different ways of looking at society. Sociology can be a science of large-scale things (macrosociology) or of small things (microsociology). Sociology can be a study of many people or of a few. What is most important in all of this is agreement on the more general level that sociology is the study of human beings in interaction with other human beings.

Sociologists are interested in the many ways in which people interact with other people. We want to know what people do in their spare time; what people do in the privacy of their own homes; what people are willing to do in public; and what people are willing to do in groups that they would not do if they were alone. The crucial aspect of human behavior for the sociologist is that the person (or persons) we are studying are interacting and it is the nature of interaction with which we are concerned. While sociologists are interested in the interaction of persons, the sociologists are also interested in the ways in which people experience their social worlds through this interaction. Because the concept of experience is so important in sociology as well as in the social world, we will spend some time examining it by looking at a few (selected) theoretical statements.

The argument for experiencing research begins, for us, with Weber's argument that the technique of the sociologist ought to be that of *verstehen*. For Weber, *verstehen* meant that the social scientist ought to "understand on the level of meaning." The scientist should examine the actor's motives and try to find out the meaning of the act *for the actor*. Sociologists ought not to put their own meanings into an act, but should let the actor define the meaning. Weber wanted to look at what he called action (Weber, 1947:88); that is, human behavior whether overt or not to which the acting individual attached subjective meaning. It is the notion of the subjectivity of the action that has received much critical comment in recent years. Weber argued that it was important to note the meaning of the action *to the person doing the act*. According to Weber the *verstehen* approach was accomplished in one (or both) of two ways: (1) either observational understanding of the subjective meaning of the other's act, or (2) an understanding of the motive behind the act. The process by which this was to be accomplished for Weber was as follows. First, the researcher should imagine the emotion aroused in people by the impact of a given situation. Second, the researcher should imagine the motive behind the action. Third, the researcher should construct some explanation of the action that shows clearly that the "feeling state" of the actor is caused by the act or the event. The problem is that the subjectivity involved here may not only be that of the actor, it may also be the subjective feelings of the sociologist. It is, unfortunately, entirely possible that the sociologist may put his or her own emotions into the situation and not ever get to the emotional feeling state of the actor.[1]

In the strictest sense of the meaning of *verstehen*, Weber is not describing a method of social investigation. Rather as Schutz (1963:239) points out, Weber is arguing for ". . . the particular experimental form in which common-sense thinking takes cognizance of the social cultural world." It is precisely at this point that many sociologists feel that the subjective world of the observer enters in and ruins the data being collected. We are, as scientists, always intruding our own personal emotions into anything we do (even our choice of topics of study is dictated, in part, by our own feelings states), so this worry on the part of many social scientists seems more like crying wolf to hear oneself "holler" than to stave off an attack. Thus, we cannot always eliminate our own emotions from the research but as we will show later, it is not always that crucial to do so (even if it were possible, which it is not).

Weber is arguing that sociologists must go to the people they are interested in and find out what it is that social actions mean to them. We may not, as scientists, intrude our meaning into or onto the acts of people in social situations. However, at the same time it is important that we experience what they are experiencing and feel what they feel in order that we may understand why people do what they do.

A similar approach to the study of social phenomena was taken by W. I. Thomas. Rather than deal with an actor in a social action situation who is doing a social act, Thomas dealt with the consequences of the situation as a whole. Thomas (1928:572), describing subjective feeling states, indicates that "if men define situations as real, they are real in their consequences." We must accept the fact that the person who imagines a burglar in the living room will act as if there really is a burglar in the living room whether or not the burglar is there. If we are unable to understand the situation giving rise to the belief, we will also be unable to understand the subsequent behavior. Once again we must "get into the other's head" and understand the subjective meaning of the situation. We must imagine what the other person is going through so that we can see how that person is reacting. The approach of Thomas sounds suspiciously like the approach of Cooley in his discussions of the "looking-glass self" and in a research sense it is. Cooley (1956:184) wanted us to imagine our appearance to another person, imagine another's judgment of our appearance, and then we would react with a feeling of either pride or mortification. In a research context, the first two of Cooley's steps are the most crucial. As a researcher we would imagine the other person's judgment of the impact of some

---

[1] We will deal with values and the sociologist later in this chapter.

occurrence, and at the same time, imagine the other's reaction. As an additional tool for understanding, of course, we also have all of the available research techniques so that we may ask people what is going on. For both Thomas and Cooley then, one must experience what the other experiences in order to know what it means.

The meaning of social science to Thomas has been outlined by Volkhart (1951) and bears investigation for a moment. According to Volkhart (1951:2), the essential features of a study of human behavior for Thomas were:

1. The goal of social science is to obtain verifiable generalizations about human behavior.
2. Human behavior occurs only under certain conditions, which in the abstract may be represented by the concept of "situation."
3. The human situation often included some factors common to both the observer and the actor, such as the physical environment, relevant social norms and the behavior of others. The implication of this is that social science requires first-hand empirical description of the observable or "objective" aspects of the situation.
4. The human situation also includes some factors that exist only for the actors, i.e., how they perceive the situation, what it means to them, what their definition of the situation is. This implies that the subjective aspects of human life must be grasped by the investigator as much as the objective aspects. Moreover, the subjective must be understood in its real first-hand character as opposed to the imputed ideas of those factors (as represented by concepts of "needs," "wishes," "attitudes," etc.)
5. The methods of social science, therefore, must provide for the systematic analysis of both the objective and the subjective (experiential) aspects of human life.
6. Such a methodology requires the joint efforts of all the social sciences, including special techniques of obtaining data, such as the life history.
7. The social goal of this approach is to make available the kind of knowledge necessary and useful for the rational control of behavior.

Note once again that one must experience the social situation of the other actors in order to understand and "control" behavior.[2]

The question still remains: Is it necessary that one go out into the field to experience things when one can simply send out a questionnaire and have the answers returned for analysis? Were it not for the observer going into the field to do research he[3] might never be able to

---

[2] I am not certain that Thomas and I are in agreement on the notion of the need to control behavior. If he means the personal control of one's own behavior as based on this approach then I would agree. Any additional control from external sources (such as the state) would not be acceptable.

[3] It is understood that researchers and others mentioned in the text may be male or female. The common pronoun "he" refers to persons of either sex and is not intended to be masculine or feminine but simply "human."

notice the latent consequences of human action; that is, the unintended and unforeseen consequences of all human action (as Weber suggested long ago). Asking a truck driver why he stops at a particular rest stop may elicit the response that the law says one must take a break every so many hours. If one received such a response on a questionnaire it might be taken at face value. However, if one were present when the driver stopped, the unintended or latent consequences of stopping at that place might be so that the driver could see the waitress, see friends; or simply see other drivers to obtain information about conditions on the road ahead. Likewise, asking a resident of a ghetto what kinds of city services are liked and disliked may elicit the response that the city does little to remove abandoned cars. If, however, one walked the streets of the ghetto, the real reason for the persons' displeasure might become more apparent: for example, heroin dealers could be seen using the cars as permanent offices in the streets.[4]

Assuming that one does research, what is it that the analyst of the social situation must do when in the field? According to Lofland (1971:7), "The qualitative analyst seeks to provide an explicit rendering of the structure, order, and patterns found amongst a set of participants." It is safe to say that the above dictum is what any social scientist ought to do in any research context. Even survey research is setting out to give a complete account of the information it is designed to elicit. Lofland, of course, restricts himself to the qualitative analyst of the social scene and indicates that this person should include a description of all relevant action that has gone on, should include direct quotes from those participating, and finally, should attempt to explain and analyze what he or she has seen. There is, in other words, an attempt on the part of Lofland's social scientist to experience the world much as the participants are experiencing the world. When the analyst puts the field notes together, then, the true analysis of the data begins. In the field one is a collector and experiencer of the happenings. It is in the analysis of the data that the social scientist comes through the reporter's disguise. It is in the analysis that the data are analyzed *both* from a sociological point of view and also from the point of view of the participants.

An analogous approach is used by the ethnomethodologists who study human society by examining the actor's subjective feelings concerning behavior. One of the techniques used by the ethnomethodologists is to examine a social situation when the common expectations

---

[4] Realize that alternative means for "teasing" meaning from data also exist. The analysis of data through multivariate techniques available on computers is another means for "teasing" meaning from data. Any technique that aids understanding is an acceptable one for the sociologist.

of the participants have been violated. The notion held by the ethno-methodologists is that we, as human beings, do not consciously define for ourselves what the common norms underlying our actions are. Human beings use the common values without really thinking about them. It is not until a situation comes up where values are somehow violated that we actually bring them to the conscious level. Once the values are brought to a level of consciousness they can be discussed and analyzed by the astute observer (not usually by the person in-volved in the situation). One example of the method used by the ethno-methodologists is a common game that we all have played at one time or another: tic-tac-toe. After indicating that student experimenters try to get as wide a range of subjects as possible, Garfinkel (1967:71) outlined the ethnomethodological rules of the game as:

> After drawing the tic-tac-toe matrix [experimenters were to invite] the subject to move first. After the subject made his move the experi-menter erased the subject's mark, moved it to another square and made his own mark but without giving any indications that anything about the play was unusual.

We all "know" how to play the game and here are Garfinkel's students sending 4,000 years of civilization "down the drain." The intriguing fact is that most of the people do not even realize that there are rules to the game until someone violates them—at the point of violation some good sociology can be done (assuming of course, that one is not having to protect himself from an outraged tic-tac-toe player at that time.)[5] For us, the importance of the ethnomethodological approach is that when the students are doing experiments, they are doing soci-ology. In order to find out about society these students are out doing things designed to locate hidden meaning in and about the social structure. They are, to return to Weber's discussion, trying to under-stand the other's behavior on the level of meaning. We are back where we began: We want to go out and find out what it is that society means to those persons who are involved in society. The only way to find out is either ask to or watch. At the same time it is important to note that when one watches or when one asks it is important to do so scientifically.

Another approach that argues for experiencing the world is to use Berger's phrase, humanistic sociology. While not explicitly arguing for research experience, Berger sees the sociologist as one who is 'in-terested in the doings of men." Berger's feelings about sociology are

---

[5] Other experiments have included bargaining for a better price at a super-market checkout counter and repeatedly (and insistently) asking for clarification of statements in conversation.

clearly indicated (1963:13) in a statement on methodology where he argued that:

> . . . it is quite true that some sociologists, especially in America, have become so preoccupied with methodological questions that they have ceased to be interested in society at all. As a result they have found out nothing of significance about any aspect of social life, since in science as in love a concentration on technique is quite likely to lead to impotence.

His argument suggests that there are many sociological studies that have forgotten that we are studying human behavior (the "doings of men") and not only the statistics that represent the behavior in question. In what may be one of the best passages in modern sociology, Berger (1963:18) defines a sociologist, and, at the same time, shows the importance of experiencing the social world:

> . . . The sociologist . . . is a person intensively, endlessly, shamelessly interested in the doings of men. His natural habitat is all the human gathering places of the world, wherever men come together. The sociologist may be interested in many other things. But his consuming interest remains in the world of men, their institutions, their history, their passions. And since he is interested in men, nothing men do can be altogether tedious for him. He will naturally be interested in the events that engage men's ultimate beliefs, their moments of tragedy and grandeur and ecstasy. But he will also be fascinated by the commonplace, the everyday. He will know reverence, but this reverence will not prevent him from wanting to see and to understand. But this also will not deter him from wanting to have his questions answered. The sociologist, in his quest for understanding, moves through the world of men without respect for the usual lines of demarcation.

For Berger (and for us) the sociologist is no "ivory-tower academic." The sociologist is the one who is out watching people, asking questions, listening to voices, and opening doors to see what is going on. Sociologists do not sit back and wait for results, they go out and gather data. In addition, the data that sociologists go after are not always data that are particularly pleasant. Sociologists study race riots, poverty, ghettos, strippers, prostitutes, and pimps. True sociologists balk at nothing that will give them a better insight into human conditions (whatever these might ultimately turn out to be).

For Berger (1963:167), the basic sociological question is: What does it mean to be a human being in a particular situation? We are not to ask about things and then draw our own conclusions; we are to find out what it means to the persons involved. Such an approach is, of course, what we have been discussing. One of the ways to find out what others think is to imagine oneself in the same situation and then ask if the imagination is correct. We cannot, however, ask questions of the persons in the situation if we happen to be in our offices within the confines of academia.[6]

VALUES AND SOCIOLOGICAL RESEARCH

The question of the intersection of values and science (or from the other direction, the question of neutrality) alluded to above is important enough to warrant some additional discussion. The problem concerns the area where or when the values of science[7] and the values of the scientist overlap. Such an overlap would be less likely in the natural sciences because it would be difficult to be too closely involved with the problems of the liverwort plant or the comings and goings of an ion. At the same time the scientist experiences difficulty divorcing oneself from the problems of the ghetto, from the problems of race relations, from the "blue-collar blues," and so on. Problems of value conflict can arise not only within ourselves but also when values are the subject of study. In an interview that I conducted, the first statement made by the subject was "I am a racist, what are you going to make of that?" My values being somewhat different from the subject's I was somewhat at a loss for words. I resolved the problem, and an interesting interview was gained, when I chose to say nothing and simply continued as if nothing had changed. Thus, while the examination of the values of a society is a legitimate area of social scientific study, one may not suggest what the values of the society ought to be: examining values is a legitimate undertaking for scientists; pushing their own values as a cure-all is not.

The examination of values leads also to the problem that all social scientists must face at one time or another and it is one that they must solve in their own minds or not be effective. The question is simply: To what extent ought scientists be value free in their dealings with the world? Obviously, the ideal would be for social scientists to remain absolutely value free; to allow none of their own values to sneak through and intrude on their research. It is unfortunate, but true, that there have yet been few saints and as far as we know no sociologist has been canonized. We waste our time by going around and proclaiming that we are free of all values in our research.[8] No human being can be totally value free about any subject, so why

---

[6] This statement does not imply that our questionnaires might not be out in the "real world" while we are in academia, however. One can venture into the "real world" in many ways.

[7] For discussions of the values of science, see Bierstadt (1963); Lundberg (1961); Olsen (1968); and Parsons (1962).

[8] In graduate school one of my professors and I went "round and round" on the subject of value-free sociology. He wanted the ideal and I suggested that the ideal was unreachable. Neither convinced the other.

bother to pretend. Consequently, the social scientist should not pretend to be something that he is not. The best approach for social scientists (and probably anyone who has hopes of doing science) is to admit that as living, breathing human beings they have values and these values affect what they do. As a procedure one could simply sit down and examine one's own value structures and decide what they are. Since we cannot remove them we might as well examine them *in situ* and thus deal with them should they become problematic. We are suggesting, then, that we examine our own values and then take them into account whenever we design and conduct research projects. Because someone is a racist is no reason why that person cannot conduct research on race—all that is necessary is to say that the research will be conducted as honestly as possible realizing that the researcher has a "hang-up" about race. Such an honest appraisal of one's values doesn't guarantee that what is done will be "good" research but it helps to remove any values that might get in the way of *potentially* good research. A little soul-searching on the subject of one's values never hurt anyone and may do a world of good. On this point, Berger's comment (1963:5) is relevant. Berger says ". . . within the limits of his activities as a sociologist there is one fundamental value only—that of scientific integrity."

We are suggesting here that one should not become overly attached to any one theory or approach. One should be open-minded and willing to admit that one is wrong. If we might be allowed to anthropomorphize "science" for a moment we might also argue that science suggests as its basic philosophy of life "It is better to know than not to know." Science would also say (if it could) that "It is better to know than not to know whatever the outcome." The scientists should *attempt* to remain value free and thus they should take no moral, ethical, or other value position concerning their (or any other person's) data. The controversy raging in certain quarters concerning the recent studies of racial (genetic) differences in IQ is one that is "raging" simply because the people involved are not neutral (see Bodmer and Cavalli-Sforza, 1970; Herrnstein, 1971). Both sides are arguing the "rightness" of their own findings and the "wrongness" of the data presented by the opponents. It is interesting to note that the persons suggesting the genetic imbalance hypotheses are being denied publishing rights in journals because their opponents *feel* the findings are wrong rather than being allowed to publish and then being shown empirically to be wrong. There is no neutrality in this conflict; the protagonists are using the studies to bolster private points of view. We should note that just as there is no neutrality here, there is no real science either. The "value freeness" of science has been lost because of the feeling on the part of some of the "combatants" that "it is better not to know."

As researchers we must pursue all avenues toward the answers posed by the research questions. We must demonstrate "scientific integrity" as we attempt to discover relationships between variables in the "real" world. We must try to discover the relationships between variables without at the same time intruding our own values and ideas into the study. To restate our basic scientific maxim from above: "It is better to know than not to know, whatever the outcome."

WHY DO RESEARCH?

The question of why scientists of whatever discipline do research is not a simple question to answer. While there are many reasons for conducting research, the primary one seems to be to further the knowledge of the subject matter that is claimed by the discipline. Thus, psychologists do research that will further the knowledge they have of the mental and cognitive processes. Political scientists do research into the techniques of attitude manipulation so that they will know more of how the advertising of candidates works. Sociologists may investigate the living arrangements of persons in a area to see if there is a relationship between residential segregation and social class. Thus, for all disciplines, one must do research if the discipline is ever to be anything more than speculation based on guesswork.[9]

When scientists conduct research on a subject, the work moves in a number of directions at once. First, scientists examine the existing theories about the phenomenon they wish to investigate to determine if there is any direction they can take from another person's work on the same subject. From the other's theory or theories, the scientists may also derive their hypotheses, those testable guesses that lead to the tentative confirmation or rejection of theories. Once the research project is completed and the researchers know the results, they may return to the theories and feed the results back into them, modifying them in the process.[10] Between the theory and the research project, there are extremely complex and important feedback mechanisms at work:

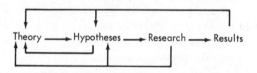

[9] On the subject of sociologists doing research, see Adams and Preiss (1960); and Hammond (1967). General discussions of doing research include: Denzin (1978); Phillips (1971); Selltiz et al. (1959 and 1976); and Simon (1978).

[10] More on this subject later—see Chapter 8.

Any piece of the research process that is incorrectly (or even badly) designed will influence what the researcher can, and should, say about the theory on which the research is based. For example, the results of one study are fed back into the accumulated body of empirical knowledge that the discipline has and may be used to adjust the theory (or world view) held by members of the discipline, and in their turn to be used as ideas for further research projects whose results are then fed back into the accumulated body of knowledge, and so on and on. To separate theory from the methods of research, then, is to make a false separation because the two go inextricably together. One influences the other which in turn influences the first. As Kaplan (1964: 302) has argued:

> Theory . . . functions throughout inquiry, and does not come into its own only when inquiry is successfully concluded. It has a greater responsibility than that of an accessory after the fact; it guides the search for data, and for laws encompassing them.

At the same time, such a relationship can lead to a paradox, as Kaplan has suggested (1964:53): a good set of concepts is needed to arrive at a good theory at the same time that a good theory is needed to arrive at a good set of concepts. Feedback systems between the methods and theories of any science are important and must never be overlooked: We must not sacrifice one part for another. Scientists are constantly working back and forth from one level to another in order to do the best job possible in their researches.[11]

All research both causes and is caused by the theory of the discipline in which one is located. The feeding back into itself helps develop extended theories about human behavior without which the discipline would not (or could not) grow.

THE RESEARCH PROCESS

Within the social sciences there are a number of research approaches that one can take: (1) A social survey asking the same questions of several hundred or several thousand persons; (2) an observational research project in which questions are not asked by the researcher but which is conducted only through the watching of the behavior of the subjects (and the subsequent interpretation by the researcher); and (3) an experiment with human subjects carefully controlling the effect of some independent variable to see what its effect is on some supposed dependent variable. Whatever a social researcher

---

[11] On this subject we might note in passing that the good methodologist should also be a good theorist.

does, however, there are commonalities in all research projects. In other words, no matter what type of research is being undertaken, there are certain features that will (should) always be present.

One of the most important features common to all research projects is the attempt to show how one variable is the "cause" of another. Sociologists interested in the area of work and occupations are interested in the "causes" of job satisfaction and alienation; sociologists interested in the study of juvenile delinquency are interested in the "causes" of deviant behavior; and so on. While we are seeking the causes of items in the social fabric, we also want to be certain that we have located a time sequence that is accurate at the same time. If we assert that some variable, A, is the cause of another variable, B, then variable A cannot happen next week while variable B is occurring now. The search for "cause" permeates social science as well as other types of research.[12]

Even when you think you have discovered a causal variable, you may find that another explanation is just as reasonable as yours. There are, unfortunately, always rival interpretations for relationships between variables in social research projects. The fact that there are rival interpretations for relationships leads to the last warning we want to give you about research (for now). Be sure to design your research so that your assertions are testable. If you hypothesize that "the gods will punish evil behavior," you will have some difficulty testing your assertion (unless you can interview one of the pantheon to discover his/her predisposition toward punishment).

Science is a series of feedback systems that we use to try to determine the influence of one variable on another. Our theory tells us what to expect, our methods tell us how to go about our research, and our results show us what we have found which feeds back into the first two. Causal analysis is not as easy as one might first imagine—one is never sure of causation no matter how hard we work. We must control our methodologies so that we gather the best possible data. By "best" we mean data that help us to show causal relationships with the greatest certainty.

Before moving to the doing of research, we should examine the notion of "the research process" a bit more closely. Figure 1–1 is an elaboration of the earlier discussions of feedback systems. One does not just think up a question and go out and ask people what they think. There is a series of steps that ought to be followed if one wants to improve the odds that the project will be successful. The steps should be followed whatever the type of research you are going to do—participant observation, systematic observation, or survey research. There

---

[12] We will have more to say on causality and hypothesis testing in Chapter 9.

FIGURE 1–1
Flow Diagram for Social Research

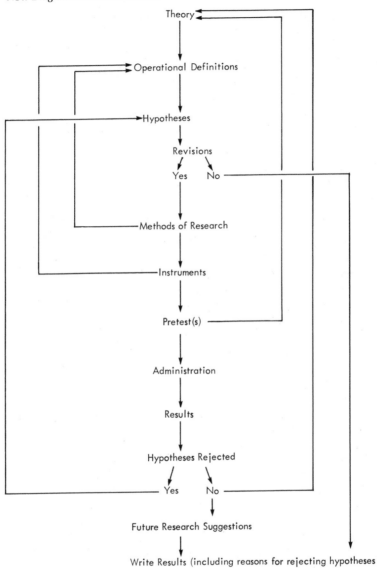

may be reasons for not following this general design, but you do so at your peril.

The sociologist begins, as we have noted, with a theory. Obviously, before you get to the point of beginning your research project, there must be some notion that a facet of the sociocultural world needs examining. Once you have decided on your subject matter you will want to see if others have already dealt with the subject. In your search through the literature you will (should) be able to find aspects of social theory to support your rationale for conducting your study.

Once your theory is "in place" you can move to the operationalizing of your concepts. This move involves determining the operations that you will use to measure whatever it is you want to look at in the world. The operational definitions logically lead you to your hypotheses. These hypotheses, or "educated guesstimates" about real world relationships, are what you really want to examine. As you conceive your research, your hypotheses will go through a number of revisions: you will find that some are true by definition, some are untrue, some are untestable, and some will be the ones that you use in your research project. As you will discover, how you define what you think are the real world relationships will, to a great extent, determine the methods you will use.

The determination of the methods should lead you in two directions. First, you should go back to the beginning and make certain you are doing what your theory says you should be doing. Second, defining the methods takes you to the creation of the instruments you will use. Will you get at your data through interviews, questionnaires, videotapes of behavior, or what? What method you use is up to you, but you should certainly test it before you commit yourself to your "real" research project.

Pretests are a useful means for seeing if you are even near to where you should be in terms of the results you think you should get. If the instruments you have so carefully designed do not produce pretest results similar to what you think you should be getting, it had better mean that you go back to the beginning and start over. While this logic may sound like defeatism, consider that it is better to redesign than to spend a lot of time, energy, and money to find out that your research is worthless. Spending a little time, money, and energy early can save you a lot later.

Once you are satisfied that all is ready, go ahead with the research. We assume that you have cycled through the feedback loops enough so that you are confident you have done all the preparatory work that you can. Murphy's first law ("If a thing can go wrong, it will.") may still operate, but at least you will improve your odds for success by being careful in following the steps.

When your data have been gathered you can move to the analysis and the write-up. Once again, we think that you must go back through what you have done in the design process in order to show how your data relate to your theory, hypotheses, and so on. Have you shown your educated guesses to be right or wrong? Whatever the case, tell your reader about what you have done.

The research process, as outlined here, is the method of design that you *should* follow. As we suggested, there may be times when you short-circuit the process, there may be times when you go over and over and over the same ground until you are satisfied. Whatever the problem you are researching, you should keep this flow chart in mind. The steps outlined may well keep you from making serious mistakes and, at the least, if we can suggest an analogy, they may work like chicken soup for a cold. They may not help, but they can't hurt.[13]

Science as we have shown, is both a technique and a body of knowledge that is accumulated through the use of that technique. Science and scientists indicate that they would rather know the answers to questions about man's existence than not to know the answers. To the end of finding the answers, the scientists investigate. They attempt to control as much nonrelevant information as possible in order to isolate the variables that are responsible for the condition being investigated. It is possible that the scientist is manipulating the variables mentally rather than physically, but that really does not matter. The scientist is pursuing the end with logical and methodical means. The scientist is doing the science; that is, not simply sitting back and being told that it is possible to do research if one wishes. The scientist, rather, is experiencing what research is all about. For the practitioner in the *social* sciences it is even more crucial to experience society. How could one possibly write about the demonic possession of a person if one had not been there to see all the physiological changes that take place? How could one write about an occupational culture had one not seen intentional production delays in action?

Because people in society define situations differently, it is important for the social scientist to be on the spot at the places where these differing definitions of the situation are made. Be a researcher, go out and ask, go out and watch, go out and listen. A course of study in social research ought to be like a road map: we give you the directions, but you have to get there. The remainder of this book will be what might be called a "forced road map." The problems are designed to get you into research situations. How hard you work and, consequently, how much you learn are up to you.

DESIGN OF THE BOOK

While the book is designed to be read in sequence, individual projects can be used or done in almost any order, given sufficient background information. Each of the chapters builds on the one before

---

[13] We will have more to say about these steps in the design of research as we move through the development of the research skills. You may well want to refer back to this diagram a number of times as you proceed through the book.

and incorporates material from preceding chapters into it; albeit, sometimes implicitly rather than explicitly.

In Chapter 2, the student researcher is asked to read articles in scientific journals as a prelude to doing research in the field. The "library research" involved will lead the reader toward an understanding of the process involved in not only the writing-up of the research project but also that of generating hypotheses. In addition, Chapter 2 shows how to read tables, an important skill both for the writing and the reading of scientific articles.

Chapter 3 begins the process of observations. In this chapter, a small-scale observation is indicated which is designed to sharpen the observational, or watching, skills. In this chapter also, we suggest some of the means for investigating aspects of social life and some of the ways to test our assertions.

Chapter 4 extends the observation to a larger area than in the previous chapter. Here, again, some hypotheses are suggested that can be tested in the observation of the large-scale area.

Chapter 5 takes the researcher into a smaller group but this time the research involves more than the observation of the behavior of the participants. In this exercise, the researcher is both a participant in the group and also the observer of that group. Because of the dual nature of this particular research exercise it is a pivotal one for the development of the various research skills.

Chapter 6 is, in one sense, a step backward from the skills utilized in Chapter 5. In Chapter 6 we ask that the research problem be thought of in terms of a structured situation where there is absolutely no possible interaction with the subjects of the research. In this chapter a sociometric problem is analyzed suggesting a technique that might be used in conjunction with other methods rather than necessarily a technique that ought to be used by itself (although it certainly could be used alone).

Chapter 7 requires the researcher to utilize a number of statistical formulas to create a random sample of a population. Using techniques outlined in the chapter, students are expected to randomly sample a population as preparation for exercises in the following two chapters.

Chapter 8 requires the researcher to conduct a survey of attitudes using either a questionnaire designed in the class or the one included in this book. The survey gathers responses to closed questions rather than forcing reliance on observational data (and thus one's own interpretations of the goings-on in the "real" world). By asking structured questions, the researcher begins to get some ideas of the complexities of surveying attitudes.

Chapter 9 requires the researcher to analyze the data that have been gathered for the exercises in the previous two chapters. Through the processes of hypothesis testing and table construction (as described in Chapter 2), the researcher begins to realize his/her abilities as a data analyst and also the opportunities and limitations of the social scientist in the analysis of data from research.

Chapter 10 requires the interviewing of persons about what may turn out to be rather "touchy" information. In this problem the researcher is given only rough guidelines, rather than set questions to ask, and is forced to rely on his or her own interviewing skills to elicit the required information.

Chapter 11 attempts to put all the knowledge of the previous chapters together and requires the researcher to conduct an experiment where broken rules of social behavior lead others to examine their own value structures. The researcher in such an "experiment" is forced to use all the various techniques of research to extract meaningful information from the welter of information that will be available.

Throughout the course of the book we stress the acquisition of skills to be used in research along with the reasons for doing research in a particular way. We cannot stress too strongly, therefore, that a theoretically oriented textbook in research methodology should be used along with this book, because this book combines features of textbooks with those of problems manuals. Thus we are combining a more theoretical approach with a more applied approach to the learning of research skills. Through this combined approach we feel that you will, at the very least, be aware of research and its problems and be able to understand and to conduct research projects on your own.

2

Reading Articles

THE PROBLEM

Go to the library and find an article that was written in a sociology journal. The article must be a report of some empirical study that was done. For this exercise you are to review the article: We want you to describe how the study was done, what theory was used to "ground" the study, what the choice of the sample (if there was one) entailed, and so on. In other words we want a review or précis of the article that you read. In addition, we also want you to criticize the article that you read.

THE APPROACH

One of the most important sources of ideas about research is the work that has been done by other persons on a subject. If, for example, you have an idea about a research project that you would like to do, it will serve you well to look through the various journals in the social sciences to see if the subject has already been examined. If you have examined all the journals in the area and discovered that your topic has already been extensively investigated, are you in trouble? Not necessarily. You might be able to show how other investigators neglected to examine an important relationship. You might also be able to show how the other investigators had incorrectly assumed certain aspects of some relationship to be true when in fact the aspects did not hold true. You might be able to find an interesting approach to the analysis of the data that the other investigators had not thought of. You might also discover that you wish to replicate (or redo) the study you find written up in an article. While there is less replication in sociology than in most other sciences, redoing another person's work is one way to "advance" the discipline. As suggested, the only way to discover the possibility of replicating another's works is to first read the study. Whichever the case, you will not be able to do much with your research project until (and unless) you have examined the available literature to see what has already been done on the subject. As Selltiz et al. (1976:92) have suggested: "One of the simplest ways of economizing effort in an inquiry is to review and build upon the work already done by others."

There are a number of procedural reasons for investigating the available literature before starting one's own research project and the most important one is to see if another investigator has already done your work for you. Discovering whether or not you are too late, however, is not the only reason for searching the literature. As we suggested above, other studies on subjects similar to the one you are pursuing may suggest hypotheses for your study. You may discover a valuable way to organize your data after you have seen how another person has organized similar data. Finally, it is possible that you will find that no other work has been done on your subject and that the "field" is open for you.

In addition to procedural reasons for investigating the available literature, there are also what might be called intellectual reasons. For the student unfamiliar with research, the articles in the social science journals may serve as valuable resource material about how to write a scientific article that summarizes one's research project. By examining the existing literature, the student can see not only how to write a scientific article but can also discover how to organize one's results to put them into some kind of meaningful order in the article. Finally, the student can also see what to communicate to a reader about one's research. Suggesting that one learn what to communicate suggests that not all that one knows at the end of a research project will necessarily be included in the report about the research. For example, in the report of your research you will want to show which hypotheses were confirmed and which were rejected but you may not want to include the codes you used to transfer the data from your questionnaires to your data cards for input to the computer.

The reading of articles before you begin a research project is, then, not simply an intellectual exercise. There are important reasons for immersing yourself in the literature other than to simply read journals (which by the way, is not a bad idea in itself).

One of the major problems faced by students in their early years in the field of sociology is to discover exactly what and where the sociology journals might be. While there are numerous journals that are of a social science orientation, the following are some of the more common journals that sociologists "call their own":

Administrative Science Quarterly
American Journal of Economics and Sociology
American Journal of Sociology
American Sociological Review
British Journal of Sociology
Canadian Review of Sociology and Anthropology
Current Sociology
Demography
Human Organization
Journal of Applied Psychology
Journal of Marriage and Family
Journal of Social Issues
Pacific Sociological Review
Rural Sociology
Social Forces
Social Research
Sociological Inquiry
Sociological Quarterly
Sociology and Social Research
Sociology of Education
Sociology of Work and Occupations
Sociometry
Urban Life and Culture

Since these are the more common journals it would seem logical that most libraries would have them. How many are in your college library? I frankly have no idea but that is one thing you should find out at your earliest convenience.

Once you have located the sociological journals, you might sit down and go through them at your leisure. While you could locate an article to review in about two minutes, it would be better to find one that you want to read and review, rather than reviewing the first one you come across. While you are looking for this article to review, you will discover a number of facts about the journals that will save you time and energy next time: do they use an index in the front of the journal, or is it at the back; do they use an abstract at the beginning of each article so that you can know the subject matter without reading the article; do they have footnotes at the bottom of the page, or do they put all the references at the end of the article; and so on?

Let us for the moment assume that you have located an article and have decided that you like it well enough to do a review of it (it may be that it is simply the article that you dislike the least but for the moment we will not comment on that). What are the kinds of information that ought to be included in a review of an article?[1] First of all, assume that the person who reads your review has no idea what was in the original article. If you write your review with this assumption clearly in mind, there will be much less chance of a misunderstanding between the writer and the reader of the review. As you read through the article to find material to include in the review, define terms for yourself (and for your reader) that may not be clear to you. Examine in some detail the logic behind the article: How does the author get from his theory to his hypotheses to his conclusions?

In order for any review to adequately cover the material in a scientific article, it should contain—at the very least—information on the following subjects:[2]

Theory. What theory was used as the basis for the study conducted in this article? Where does the theory come from? Who else has written on the same subject? What justification is there for doing the study in the way that it was done?

Hypotheses. How are the hypotheses derived from the theory that is used in the study? To move from the theoretical level to the empirical level of the study, what other theories are brought in? How are the concepts put into working order? How are the working definitions arrived at?

Sample. How is the sample of persons used in the study chosen? What are the techniques for defining the universe of people from whom the sample is chosen? What is the strategy used for picking the sample? What is the "no response" rate for the sample; that is, how many persons refused to be interviewed, questioned, watched, and so on?

Methodology. How does the author go about doing what he said he would do? What are the methods used to uncover the findings reported later in the paper? Does the author use a questionnaire? Does he use an in-depth interview? Does he just stand around and watch? What techniques are then used for analyzing the data that has been gathered? Are simple tabular representations used? Are path analyses used to explain relationships? What sort of statistics are used to show that the findings are "legitimate"?

Results. What does the author find from using his sample and methods? Does the author confirm his hypotheses or does he fail to find data to support them? If he seems to have trouble confirming his hypotheses, does he find support for some of the hypotheses but not

---

[1] On this subject, see Knop (1967).

[2] At this point you may want to reread sections of Chapter 1 where the "basics" of research were described. How does the author of the article deal with these aspects of research?

others? What does he say if he is shown to be partially right and partially wrong?[3]

Conclusions. When the author of the article finishes his presentation what are the sorts of things that he says about the study just completed? Does the author generalize his findings to other areas within the field of sociology? While the results of a study may confirm hypotheses (or at least not disprove them) it may be that the generalizability of the findings may be limited. What does the author have to say about this problem?[4]

The following pages present an example of an article from the *American Sociological Review*.[5] As a prelude to reading an article that you may have chosen, read the article below and follow through the analysis of it. In your review or précis, pay particular attention to the means used for alerting the reader of a review to various pitfalls the author might have fallen into. In addition, pay attention to the development of the argument in the review: What aspects of the article are dealt with first? Are the comments in the review in a parallel form to those in the article? As you read the article, make notes on it in line with the outline presented earlier.

When you get to the review which follows the article see if your comments are similar to those of the reviewer.

NORMS AND COUNTER-NORMS IN A SELECT GROUP OF THE APOLLO MOON SCIENTISTS: A CASE STUDY OF THE AMBIVALENCE OF SCIENTISTS*

IAN I. MITROFF
University of Pittsburgh

This paper describes a three and a half year study conducted over the course of the Apollo lunar missions with forty-two of the most prestigious scientists who studied the lunar rocks. The paper supports the Merton-E.

[3] On the subject of results, see the section of this chapter which discusses reading and interpreting tables of data.

[4] For a more detailed discussion of the formulation of research, see Selltiz et al. (1976), chapter 1; Kerlinger (1964), chapter 2; and Denzin (1978), chapter 1.

[5] The *American Sociological Review* is the official journal of the American Sociological Association. It is in this journal that the presidential address (the address of the president of the American Sociological Association) is printed each year.

* The work for this paper was partly supported under a grant from the National Aeronautics and Space Administration, NGL 39011080. I should like to acknowledge the great influence of Robert K. Merton in the writing of this paper. Professor Merton not

Barber concept of sociological ambivalence, that social institutions reflect potentially conflicting sets of norms. The paper offers a set of counter-norms for science, arguing that if the norm of universalism is rooted in the impersonal character of science, an opposing counter-norm is rooted in the personal character of science. The paper also argues that not only is sociological ambivalence a characteristic of science, but it seems necessary for the existence and ultimate rationality of science.

INTRODUCTION

The sociology of science owes a debt to Robert Merton for his many substantive contributions and for his continual suggestion of important, unsolved problems. This paper addresses one of these problems.

This paper considers three aspects of Merton's work: (1) his earliest (1949) attempts to codify the norms of science; (2) his later ideas (1957, 1963a, 1963b, 1969) regarding the norms of science; and (3) his developing ideas about the nature of social or institutional norms and the concept of sociological ambivalence (summarized in Merton and E. Barber, 1963). We begin with the last, the notion of sociological ambivalence. Consider the following:

> [We must] consider, first, how potentially contradictory norms develop in every social institution; next, how in the institution of science conflicting norms generate marked ambivalence in the lives of scientists; and finally, how this ambivalence affects the actual, as distinct from the supposed, relations between men of science (Merton, 1963a:80).
>
> From the standpoint of sociological ambivalence . . . , the structure of [for example] the physician's role [consists] of a *dynamic alternation of norms and counter-norms.* These norms call for potentially contradictory attitudes and behaviors. For the social definitions of this role [the physician's], as of social roles generally, in terms of dominant attributes alone would not be flexible enough to provide for the endlessly varying contingencies of social relations. Behavior oriented wholly to the *dominant norms* would defeat the functional objectives of the role. Instead, *role behavior is alternatively oriented to dominant norms and to subsidiary counter-norms in the role.* This alternation of subroles *evolves* [italics in original] as a social device for helping men in designated statuses to cope with the contingencies they face in trying to fulfill their functions. This is lost to view when social roles are analyzed only in terms of their major attributes (Merton and E. Barber, 1963: 104, major italics added).

Starting in 1942 from a conception of a single dominant set of norms (1949), Merton has come to perceive science as reflecting conflicting sets of norms. While Merton and others (B. Barber, 1952; Hagstrom, 1965; Storer, 1966), have tried to codify the "dominant norms of science," these

only gave me valuable criticism on the substantive ideas but offered valuable suggestions for improving the paper's style and organization. I should also like to thank Paul F. Lazarsfeld and Burkart Holzner for their helpful comments. Thanks are also due to two unidentified reviewers of this paper who made extensive valuable comments. Whatever errors of interpretation remain are of course solely mine.

Source: American Sociological Review 1974, Vol. 39 (August): 579–595.

Note: The article is reprinted, except for minor corrections, exactly as printed in the original.

efforts represent only half the total effort. Despite Merton's attempt to explicate the "subsidiary norms" (1961), the second half of the effort has yet to be accomplished. Indeed, the language and manner of the first set of norms (and their Zeitgeist) may have impeded work in explaining the subsidiary norms.[1]

This paper focuses on the intense personal character of science. Whereas the impersonal character of science was central in early studies, the reverse is true in later writing. The following from Merton and Barber presents the case for the impersonal character of science:

> Universalism finds immediate expression in the canon that truth claims, whatever their source, are to be subjected to *preestablished impersonal criteria:* (italics in original) consonant with observation and with previously confirmed knowledge. The acceptance or rejection of claims entering the lists of science is not to depend on the personal or social attributes of their protagonist; his race, nationality, religion, class and personal qualities are as such irrelevant. *Objectivity precludes particularism.* The circumstance that scientifically verified formulations refer to objective sequences and correlations militates against all efforts to impose particularistic criteria of validity . . . *The imperative of universalism is rooted deep in the impersonal character of science* (Merton, 1949: 607, italics added).
>
> Emotional involvement is recognized to be a good thing even in science—up to a point: it is a necessary component of the moral dedication to the scientific values and methods. But in the application of those techniques of rationality, emotion is so often a subtle deceiver that a strong moral disapproval is placed upon its use.
>
> This is not to say that strong emotions are entirely absent in the relations among scientists themselves. . . . In all their specialized fields, scientists have been something more than bloodless automatons. The ideal of emotional neutrality [as an instrumental condition for the achievement of rationality], however, is a powerful brake upon emotion anywhere in the instrumental activities of science *and most particularly in the evaluation of the validity of scientific investigation* (Barber, 1952:126–7, italics added).[2]

These earlier passages stand in marked contrast to later views:

> No one who systematically examines the disputes over priority can ever again accept as veridical the picture of the scientist as one who is exempt from affective involvement with *his* ideas and *his* discoveries of once unknown fact (Merton, 1963a:80, italics in original).

Michael Polanyi (1958) argues with even more force that the personal character of science infuses its entire structure. The testing and validating of scientific ideas is as governed by the deep personal character of science as

---

[1] I am not suggesting that these speculations suffice to explain the lack of widespread investigations by sociologists on the subsidiary norms of science. The entire phenomenon is certainly a fitting topic for investigation. Indeed, it would constitute an appropriate topic in the sociology of sociological knowledge. Such an investigation would undoubtedly shed light on why we have been loath to study science (cf., Merton, 1963a: 84).

[2] Note that the idea of the impersonal character of science, particularly as it relates to validating scientific statements, enters into two distinctly different norms. For Merton (1949), it is deeply rooted in the imperative or norm of universalism; whereas for

the initial discovery of the ideas. In sharp contrast to the views of Popper (1961, 1971), Polanyi (1958) argues that not only is this the case, but it ought to be the case. That is, science ought to be personal to its core. Science is not thereby reduced to a state of hopeless subjectivism. Indeed, it is the interplay between personal and impersonal forces that makes for the rationale and ultimate rationality of science. This paper is a case study of sociological ambivalence and the personal nature of science.

This paper seeks (1) to reevaluate the initial set of dominant norms proposed by Merton, and subsequently refined by Barber, Hagstrom, Storer, and West (1960), (2) to propose a tentative set of subsidiary norms based on the results of an empirical and theoretical case study, (3) to examine the relationship between these two sets, and thereby, (4) to raise the question whether a sense exists in which both sets of norms are primary or dominant as, for example, in a dialectic where neither side or position is "superior" or "inferior" but merely "different from" and "maximally opposed" to the other (Churchman, 1971; Mitroff and Betz, 1972; Mitroff, 1973, 1974a).

THE CASE STUDY

Almost three months to the day of Apollo 11's landing (July 20, 1969), a series of extensive interviews were begun with forty-two of the most eminent scientists who studied the moon rocks. Each scientist was interviewed intensively four times over a span of three and a half years; the interviews were conducted between the completion of one Apollo moon mission and the start of another. The scientists were thus interviewed between Apollo 11 and 12, 12 and 14,[3] 14 and 15, and 15 and 16. The interviews ranged from open-ended discussions in the opening round to written questionnaires in the subsequent rounds. The open-ended discussions were designed to explore a range of issues connected with the lunar missions and to establish rapport with the scientists. The written questionnaires, given in person to encourage the scientists to talk about and even criticize the questionnaire items, focused on specific attitudes towards issues raised in the opening discussions.

All interviews were conducted by the author. Each interview was tape-recorded for several reasons: One, tape-recording permitted a detailed analysis of the substantive and affective content of the interviews as manifested in the emotions and vocal inflections displayed by the scientists. Two, the taped interviews are an oral-history record of some of the most impor-

Barber (1952), it is rooted in the norm of emotional neutrality. The difference may be due to the fact that for Merton the very notion of becoming a scientist implies commitment to the norms of science (Merton, 1949:605). In this sense, it is nonsense to speak of the idea of the emotionally uncommitted scientist. However, since this notion seems so deeply ingrained (Taylor, 1967:3–5), I believe with Barber that it is worthwhile to consider the idea of emotional neutrality as a separate norm (see also Storer, 1966: 80). Doing so will allow us to challenge this norm and make the case for the existence of an opposing counter-norm.

[3] Apollo 13 is not listed since it did not influence the scientific beliefs of the scientists during the period. It was the ill-fated mission that failed to land on the moon.

tant scientists in the Apollo program, worth preserving for the archives.[4] All in all, approximately 260 hours of interviews were recorded.[5] In addition to these interviews conducted in private, the public behavior of the scientists was also monitored (for comparison with their private responses) at such scientific conferences during the interim period of the study as the first three Apollo Lunar Science Conferences held in Houston, Texas, plus various national meetings of the American Geophysical Union, the American Meteoretical Society, and the American Association for the Advancement of Science. The results and conclusions which follow are thus based on observations and inferences from behavior and expressions of attitude made on repeated occasions and cross-checked over a period of almost four years. The stability and consistency of the responses over time and over different methods of measurement gives added credence and significance to the results.

Rationale

The Apollo moon scientists were chosen for study for various reasons. A major initial premise (later confirmed) was that the Apollo program would be an excellent contemporary setting in which to study the nature and function of the commitment of scientists to their pet hypotheses in the face of possibly disconfirming evidence. A review of the scientific and popular literature before the landing of Apollo 11 found that various scientists had strongly committed themseves in print as to what they thought the moon would be like, and in a few cases, what they ardently hoped the moon would be like.[6] Furthermore, in some cases, these scientists' views were in direct conflict. Coupling this with the drama surrounding the landing of Apollo 11 and the competitiveness in the community of Lunar scientists, it appeared that the Apollo program had many of the same ingredients aptly described by Watson (1968) in the race for the discovery of DNA. In short, the Apollo program offered an interesting setting[7] in which to study the "Resistance by Scientists to the Scientific Discoveries of Other Scientists" (cf. B. Barber, 1961) plus "the Commitment of Scientists to their Pet Hypotheses."[8] Most important of all was the chance to study the possible

---

[4] Preliminary arrangements have been made to deposit the materials in the library of the American Institute of Physics, New York City, to make them available to interested and qualified scholars.

[5] The average recorded length of the first set of interviews was 2¼ hours; the second, 1½ hours; the third, 1⅓ hours; and the last, 1 hour. Thus, for 3½ years an average of 6.1 recorded hours was spent with each scientist. This was supplemented by an average of another four hours of unrecorded time. This does not include the time spent in informal conversation at various conferences.

[6] As desirable as it would be to give examples (for one thing to show that such expressions were not isolated and infrequent), to preserve the anonymity of the respondents, some of whom were members of this group, I cannot cite this literature. The reasons for such stringent constraints will become apparent.

[7] In Merton's terms, the Apollo program constituted a "strategic research site" for observing counter-norms. See Merton (1963b:239) on the importance of "strategic research sites" in the sociology of science.

[8] The fact that some scientists had publicly and repeatedly declared their scientific positions in print was important. Kiesler's work (1971) suggests that "the explicit and forceful declaring of one's commitment has the effect of increasing the degree of com-

normative value of such behavior instead of assuming it to be dysfunctional, unscientific, or irrational.[9]

The notion of commitment was central to the study in other ways. For example, much of it concerns what the body of scientists thought about their fellow scientists. Who were perceived as most committed to their pet hypotheses? What did they think of such behavior? What did the scientists think of the abstract idea of commitment itself? While they might differ in the degree and nature of their commitments, did they believe that every scientist had to have a certain amount of commitment to do good science? If so, how did the scientists then react to the notion of the disinterested observer? Is that notion as deeply ingrained in the beliefs of scientists as the conventional portraits of science would have us believe?

The study also asked how did the scientists' ideas about the moon change from mission to mission? What were the significant results from Apollo? Which scientists were credited with producing these results? Were serious errors committed in selecting lunar landing sites? After Apollo 11, did they continue to think the moon trip was worthwhile? Why? Why not? Are there lessons to be learned from Apollo for planning future missions?

As for methodology, what did the moon scientists believe about the relationship between theory and data? Did they believe that observations were independent of theory, or as increasing numbers of philosophers of science (Churchman, 1961, 1971; Feyerabend, 1965, 1970a, 1970b) were asserting, that observations were theory-laden? Further, what did the scientists believe about the notion of the hypothetico-deductive method as an accurate and fruitful representation of scientific method? Countless philosophers and methodologists of science have examined such issues, but there are few (cf, Hagstrom, 1965) systematic studies of what scientists themselves think about such issues. No matter how idealized the concept of scientific method and however far removed from real concerns, it should be compared with the reality of everyday practice and the beliefs of practicing scientists (cf, Maxwell, 1972:133). One way to do this is to submit methodological statements for the scrutiny and responses of scientists.

The Sample

Table 1 gives the breakdown by institutional affiliation of the scientists interviewed in round I (the time period of the Apollo 11 mission) who were either (1) principal investigators (PI's) or (2) co-investigators (Co-I's), (3) those who were neither but who had access to or contact with the lunar samples (Access), and finally, (4) those scientists who had no contact at all with the lunar samples (No-Access). The term PI is the official designation that NASA (like other granting agencies) uses to denote the officially desig-

---

mitment to one's position." The Apollo program thus presented the rare opportunity to study the commitment of scientists to their ideas and the change in their ideas, or lack of it, in the face of strong prior beliefs.

[9] Such behavior is not "irrational" from every standpoint. Certain theories or philosophies of science (Churchman and Ackoff, 1950; Laudan, 1965) maintain that it is rational for scientists to act in accord with the principle of tenacity; i.e., a scientist ought to do everything "legitimately" (excluding cheating, falsifying evidence) in his power to present his hypotheses in the best possible light and to defend them. This point will be discussed later when we deal with an alternative normative structure for science.

TABLE 1
Form of Involvement in Lunar Program and Institutional Affiliation of Scientists

Institutional Affiliation	Form of Involvement in the Lunar Program				Total
	PI's	Co-I's	Access	No-Access	
University or university affiliated research labs	15	2	4	5	26
NASA** installations	0	2	4	3	9
USGS*** plus related Govt. agencies	1	0	1	− 1	3
Govt. research**** labs, institutions plus foreign counterparts	1	0	0	0	1
Private industry	1	0	1	1	3
Total	18	4	10	10	42

```
    **   = National Aeronautics and Space Administration.
    ***  = United States Geological Survey.
    **** = For example, like the Brookhaven National Lab.
    PI's      = Principal Investigators.
    Co-I's    = Co-Investigators.
    Access    = Neither a Principal nor Co-investigator, but had access to Lunar materials.
    No-Access = Had no form of access to Lunar materials, but interviewed because of his-
                torical importance.
```

nated principal researcher (or proposer) of a project or experiment. Every experiment whether it had a co-experimenter or Co-I had a principal investigator or PI. Access refers to those scientists who were neither PI's nor Co-I's but who had legitimate access to the lunar materials as members of a PI's research team. The Sample Access scientists contributed directly to the study of the lunar samples experimentally or theoretically, as the remaining category of scientists did not. Although many were indirectly involved, the No-Access scientists were not directly involved in analyzing lunar materials. They were included because they had played an important historical role in our understanding of the moon, or had significant insight into the lunar missions or their fellow scientists, or finally, because they had been recommended for inclusion by their fellow scientists.

Table 1 shows that the majority of the scientists interviewed were based in universities (26) and that an even larger number of PI's were university scientists (15). To appreciate the full significance of these percentages plus the remaining percentages, it is necessary to discuss how the sample was formed.

Like the total population of scientists selected by NASA to be PI's and Co-I's for Apollo 11 (see Table 2), almost two-thirds of our sample were university scientists. The sample is a snowball sample (Sjoberg and Nett, 1968). It began with a few key scientists willing to lend their names to draw others into the sample. Two questions were asked of everyone interviewed, *Which scientists would you recommend that I ask these same (interview) questions of next?*, and, *For which reasons do you recommend that I see these persons?*

The sample was formed this way for the following reasons: (1) Not only were the scientists inordinately busy, but they had been besieged by reporters for interviews. They had to be induced to give time and thought to the study. (2) Some of the interview questions were sensitive in that they asked the scientists to express their feelings about their colleagues. However, the investigation was given legitimacy by the support of their peers.

TABLE 2
Form of Involvement in the Lunar Program of Total Population of
Scientists Selected by NASA to be PI's and Co-I's for Apollo 11 and
Institutional Affiliation

	Form of Involvement		
Institution Affiliation	PI's	Co-I's	Total
University or university-affiliated research labs plus foreign counterparts	96	101	197
NASA installations	9	23	32
USGS plus foreign counterparts	20	23	43
Govt. research labs, institutions plus foreign counterparts	7	12	19
Private industry	10	13	23
Total	142	172	314

NOTE: The numbers in this table were compiled from several sources, published PI lists in technical magazines and internal NASA documents. Since the various lists are not always in complete accord, the numbers reported above can only be taken as approximate. However, they would seem to be in the right range since the number that was commonly bantered about to denote the number of Apollo 11 PI's was of the order of 140.

(3) Some scientists in the system were so important that no study of the Apollo missions could ignore them, whether or not they appeared in a random sample. (4) The social organization of the system was of basic interest. Asking the respondents who should be interviewed not only formed the sample but also generated vital information about this organization. (5) Forming the sample thus tends to offset some of the objections (Lakatos and Musgrave, 1970) raised against studying the "average" scientist, or in Kuhn's (1962) terms, the "normal" scientist. The argument is that a sample composed entirely of "average" scientists is a poor one on which to base conclusions about the nature of science. It can be an even worse basis for concluding about the ideal practice of science. Why base ideas for the superior or improved practice of science on the behavior of average or mediocre scientists? Selecting a sample in the above manner tends to counter this objection, since such a sample will tend to contain the elite scientists in the system under study.

If the general population of Apollo 11 scientists represents an elite to begin with, then the sample is best described as an elite of elites (cf. Zuckerman, 1972). It contains some of the most distinguished geologists and scientific analysts of the Apollo missions. Two of the forty-two have the Nobel prize; six are members of the National Academy of Scientists; thirty-eight have their Ph.D.; thirteen are major editors of key scientific journals in the field. Nearly all are at prestigious universities or a top-ranked government research lab.

The sample was not expressly generated by asking for elites. The scientists based their recommendations of others on one or more of three criteria: (1) that they should be important or eminent; (2) that they should be included if the study were to represent many scientific points of view (most recognized that they represented only one viewpoint of the scientists and hence recommended that I see at least one whose views were opposed to theirs); and (3) that the study should include several "typical" or "average" scientists. Many asserted: "You should see some of the average stiffs, not just the stars," or, "If you see only those guys, you've got a sample of all chiefs and no Indians." Despite their warning, the snowball sample contains "many more chiefs than Indians."

The sample also includes data on age and scientific discipline. As of July, 1969 (the time of Apollo 11), the mean age was 47.0 years with a standard deviation of 9.3 years. This is indicative that these are largely established scientists. Only six in the first round of interviews were under forty and only three in the entire study were under thirty-five. In this regard, the sample differs markedly from the general population of Apollo scientists. In their summary of the Apollo missions, Levinson and Taylor (1971) note that "a surprisingly large number of the scientists are in their 30's; only a small percentage are over 50 years (Levinson and Taylor, 1971:2)." The sample almost exactly reverses the trend in the larger population of Apollo scientists. Finally, nearly all the scientists are located in an academic department or institutional setting that corresponds closely to the academic discipline in which they received their degree (see Table 3).

CONDUCT OF THE INTERVIEWS

The opening interviews explored the scientific issues connected with Apollo and assessed the scientists' positions on these issues before and just after Apollo 11. They were asked: What theories for the origin of the moon are you familiar with? Can you rate how plausible you felt each theory was before the Apollo 11 data? Can you rate how plausible you feel each theory was after the Apollo 11 data? Other technical issues, such as the temperature of the moon and the origin of mascons (Muller and Sjogren, 1968) were also explored in this way.

These questions elicited needed information and were natural interview openers. They were designed to get the scientists talking about an area of interest to them in which they were the experts. They avoided personal issues and focused on supposedly neutral technical issues. They did not ask which scientists were most committed to their pet hypothesis. I assumed that such an issue, especially reference to particular scientists by name, would be far too sensitive to approach directly. These fears turned out to be entirely unfounded. The scientists themselves raised the question of commitment.

TABLE 3
Scientific Disciplines Represented in the Sample*

Scientific Discipline	Number of Scientists
Geology (general)	7
Geophysics	4
Geochemistry	16
Chemistry	5
Physics	4
Astronomy	4
Engineering	2

* Based on discipline in which received highest degree.

SOME GENERAL FINDINGS

All the interviews exhibit high affective content. They document the often fierce, sometimes bitter, competitive races for discovery and the intense emotions which permeate the doing of science.

No matter what the topic—for example, the status of some technical physical theory—the scientists moved the discussion toward intensely personal matters. They could not discuss the status of a physical theory and the scientific evidence bearing on it in purely impersonal or "objective" terms (see footnote 13). Some scientists or group of scientists were clearly associated in the minds of the sample with each theory, serving as its personal advocates and defenders. Hence, the scientists could not react to a theory without reacting simultaneously to its proponents.

After *The Double Helix* (Watson, 1968), these observations are no longer novel. As Merton (1969) pointed out, only our naïveté about science and our lack of historical awareness of past priority disputes caused this aspect of *The Double Helix* to make news. Bitter competition and acrimonious disputes have been more nearly the rule in science than the exception.

What was surprising in my interviews was the ease with which the scientists recognized the commitment of their peers to certain doctrines, their willingness to talk about it openly and to name names. Even more surprising was the extent to which most of them had considered the effect of commitment. The term "commitment" was used in three distinct (but related) senses. The first expressed the notion of intellectual commitment, that is, that scientific observations were theory-laden. In order to test a scientific hypothesis, one had to adopt or commit oneself, if only provisionally, to some theory so that the phenomenon could be observed. The second sense expressed the notion of affective commitment. More often than not scientists were affectively involved with their ideas, were reluctant to part with them, and did everything in their power to confirm them. The third sense expressed the notion that the entire process of science demanded deep personal commitment. Deep personal emotions were not merely confined to the discovery phases of scientific ideas but to their testing as well. In the words of the respondents, it took "as much personal commitment to test an idea as it did to discover it." The context of the interviews generally made clear which notion was being invoked.

In response to the opening interview questions on the relative plausibility of various scientific hypotheses associated with the moon, three scientists were overwhelmingly nominated as most attached to their own ideas.[10] The comments referring to these scientists were peppered with emotion. The following is typical:

> X is so committed to the idea that the moon is Q that you could literally take the moon apart piece by piece, ship it back to Earth, reassemble it in X's backyard and shove the whole thing . . . and X would still continue to believe

---

[10] These same three scientists were nominated in open-ended conversation and also in response to the direct questions: "Which scientists are in your opinion most committed to their pet hypotheses?" and "Which scientists do you think will experience the most difficulty in parting with their ideas?" These questions were asked at each interview in the 3½ year period. No matter how they were asked or when, the responses are the same.

that the moon is Q. X's belief in Q is unshakeable. He refuses to listen to reason or to evidence. I no longer regard him as a scientist. He's so hopped up on the idea of Q that I think he's unbalanced.

The three scientists most often perceived by their peers as most committed to their hypotheses and the object of such strong reaction were also judged to be among *the* most outstanding scientists in the program. They were simultaneously judged to be the most creative and the most resistant to change. The aggregate judgement was that they were "the most creative" for their continual creation of "bold, provocative, stimulating, suggestive, speculative hypotheses," and "the most resistant to change" for "their pronounced ability to hang onto their ideas and defend them with all their might to theirs and everyone else's death." Because of the centrality of these scientists, the perception of them by their peers was studied over the course of the Apollo missions. The perceived intensity of commitment of these scientists to their pet ideas was systematically measured in terms of various attitude scales. Every scientist in the sample was asked to locate the scientific position of each of the three scientists with respect to a number of possible positions and to rate the intensity of their commitment to their position. *There was virtually no change in the perceived positions and the perceived intensity of their commitment to their ideas over the three and a half year period.*[11]

The Emergence of Counter-Norms

The concept needed to make the transition between the interview material and the first counter-norm is provided by the following criterion for recognizing the existence of a norm:

> . . . as we know from the sociological theory of institutions, the expression of disinterested moral indignation is a signpost announcing the violation of a social norm (Merton, 1957:639; see also Parsons, 1949:368–70, and Merton, 1949:390–4).

---

[11] It is beyond the scope of this paper (cf. Mitroff, 1974b) to report on this aspect of the study in detail. Measuring and assessing the differences in psychology between the scientists in the sample was a major focus of the study. Various typologies of different kinds of scientists were constructed from their comments. At the one extreme, are the three highly committed scientists who "wouldn't hesitate to build a whole theory of the solar system based on no tangible data at all; they're extreme speculative thinkers." At the other is the data-bound experimentalist who "wouldn't risk an extrapolation, a leap beyond the data if his life depended on it." Whereas the three highly committed scientists are perceived as biased, brilliant, theoretical, as extreme generalists, creative yet rigid, aggressive, vague, as theoreticians, and finally as extremely speculative in their thinking, the opposite extremes are seen as impartial, dull, practical, as specialists, unimaginative yet flexible, retiring, precise, as experimentalists, and extremely analytical in their thinking. It is also beyond the scope of this paper to show (cf. Mitroff, 1974b) that these psychological differences can be used, contrary to Merton (1957:638–40), to argue for a psychological explanation for the contentious behavior of scientists involved in priority disputes. This is not to say that such behavior must be explained purely psychologically or sociologically. Indeed, it is due to the interaction of both factors in that individual scientists react differently to the social institution of science. In other words, science probably does not attract contentious personalities more than other institutions. However, some kinds of scientists are more contentious than others and thus quicker to initiate and press their claims for priority.

If moral indignation towards a certain kind of behavior₁ announces that a social norm₁ has been violated, then moral indignation towards a class of opposing behavior₂ announces the violation of an opposing norm₂ (cf., Mitroff, 1973, 1974a).

The intense reactions of the scientists towards the behavior of the three scientists perceived as most committed to their ideas suggests strong support for the notion of the impersonal character of science. The behavioral characteristics which produced the most intense reactions were those most in conflict with the impersonal character of science. In this regard, the scientists affirmed precisely the norms of universalism and emotional neutrality in science (Merton, 1949:607–10; Barber, 1952:126–7); hence, one can infer that these particular norms of science are accepted. Further, although this conclusion is based on an inference, it is strengthened repeatedly since it arises directly out of the scientists' open-ended responses. Early in the study, I deemed it important to avoid references to the norms of science that might put socially desirable responses in the mouths of the scientists. I quote from some of the scientists regarding the three scientists perceived as most committed to their pet hypotheses: "They have no humility;" "their papers are public relations jobs;" "X relishes the spectacular and has a craving for power;" "Y is a good salesman: that's why he gets attention;" "Z tried to put words in the astronauts' mouths; he tried to get them to see what he wanted them to find;" "X has a curious if not perverted pattern of reasoning that goes something as follows: Hypothesis—If the moon were P, then Q would be true; Premise—I WANT Q to be true; Conclusion—therefore, P IS true;" "X and Y don't do science, they build personal monuments to themselves; I no longer regard them as scientists."

On the other hand, if the preceding can be interpreted as moral indignation indicating support of the dominant norms of emotional neutrality and universalism, then some equally strong responses from the scientists suggested the existence of two equally strong counter-norms. Immediately after the responses to the opening questions, two follow-up questions were raised: "Given your strong reaction to the behavior of the particular scientists you've mentioned as being most committed to their ideas, is there any positive role that you see that commitment has to play in science? If so, what is your opinion of the concept of the disinterested observer?" Again, in many cases I need not have raised these questions since the scientists raised them in the course of their comments. Also, the context made clear that the scientists used the term "emotional commitment" in two of the three senses referred to earlier: in the sense of an individual scientist's deep affective involvement with his ideas and in the sense that science was a personal enterprise from beginning to end.[12]

Every one of the scientists interviewed on the first round of interviews indicated that they thought the notion of the objective, emotionally disinter-

---

[12] The norm of "disinterestedness" was not raised in the sense originally formulated by Merton (1949:612–14) and Barber (1952:131–3), i.e., as the idea that a scientist is expected to achieve his self-interest in work-satisfaction and prestige through serving the community.

ested scientist naïve.[13] The vocal and facial expressions that accompanied the verbal responses were the most revealing of all. They ranged from mild humor and guffaws to extreme annoyance and anger. They indicated that the only people who took the idea of the purely objective, emotionally disinterested scientist literally and seriously were the general public or beginning science students. Certainly no working scientist, in the words of the overwhelming majority, "believed in that simple-minded nonsense." Because they actually did science and because they had to live with the day-to-day behavior of some of their more extreme colleagues, they knew better.

What was even more surprising was that the scientists rejected the notion of the "emotionally disinterested scientist" as a prescriptive ideal or standard. Strong reasons were evinced why a good scientist *ought* to be highly committed to a point of view. Ideally, they argued, scientists ought not to be without strong, prior commitments. Even though the general behavior and personality of their more extremely committed colleagues infuriated them, as a rule they still came out in favor of scientists having strong commitments. The following comments are typical:

Scientist A.   Commitment, even extreme commitment such as bias, has a role to play in science and it can serve science well. Part of the business [of science] is to sift the evidence and to come to the right conclusions, and to do this you must have people who argue for both sides of the evidence. This is the only way in which we can straighten the situation out. I wouldn't like scientists to be without bias since a lot of the sides of the argument would never be presented. We must be emotionally committed to the things we do energetically. No one is able to do anything with liberal energy if there is no emotion connected with it.

Scientist B.   The uninvolved, unemotional scientist is just as much a fiction as the mad scientist who will destroy the world for knowledge. Most of the scientists I know have theories and are looking for data to support them; they're not sorting impersonally through the data looking for a theory to fit the data. You've got to make a clear distinction between not being objective and cheating. A good scientist will not be above changing his theory if he gets a preponderance of evidence that doesn't support it, but basically he's looking to defend it. Without [emotional] commitment one wouldn't have the energy, the drive to press forward sometimes against extremely difficult odds. You don't consciously falsify evidence in science but you put less priority on a piece of data that goes against you. No reputable scientist does this consciously but you do it subconsciously.

Scientist C.   The [emotionally] disinterested scientist is a myth.[14] Even if there were such a being, he probably wouldn't be worth much as a scientist. I still think you can be objective in spite of having strong interests and biases.

---

[13] The notion of objectivity was not defined for the scientists because the context of the interviews and their comments made clear that it was most typically taken to mean facts "uncoloured by, [or] independent of, the feelings or opinions of the person making them (Graham, 1965:287)." As Popper (1972) put it:

> Knowledge in this objective sense is totally independent of anybody's belief, or disposition to assent or to assert, or to act. Knowledge in the objective sense is *knowledge without a knowing subject* (Popper, 1972:109).

The scientists generally rejected this notion of objective knowledge.

[14] See Imagination and the Growth of Science (Taylor, 1967:3–5) for a forceful presentation of the myth of science: "Scientists must be immediately prepared to drop a theory the moment an observation turns up to conflict with it. Scientists must have an absolute respect for observations, they must hold scientific theories in judicial detach-

Scientist D. If you make neutral statements, nobody really listens to you. You have to stick your neck out. The statements you make in public are actually stronger than you believe in. You have to get people to remember that you represent a point of view even if for you it's just a possibility. It takes commitment to be a scientist. One thing that spurs a scientist on is competition, warding off attacks against what you've published.

Scientist E. In order to be heard you have to overcommit yourself. There's so much stuff if you don't speak out you won't get heard but you can't be too outrageous or you'll get labeled as a crackpot; you have to be just outrageous enough. If you have an idea, you have to pursue it as hard as you can. You have to ride a horse to the end of the road.

Scientist F. The notion of the disinterested scientist is really a myth that deserves to be put to rest. Those scientists who are committed to the myth have an intensity of commitment which belies the myth. Those scientists who are the movers are not indifferent. One has to be deeply involved in order to do good work. There *is* the danger that the bolder the scientist is with regard to the nature of his ideas, the more likely he is to become strongly committed to his ideas. I don't think we have good science because we have adversaries but that is in the attempt to follow the creed and the ritual of scientific method that the scientist finds himself unconsciously thrust in the role of an adversary.

And finally,

Scientist G. You can't understand science in terms of the simple-minded articles that appear in the journals. Science is an intensely personal enterprise. Every scientific idea needs a personal representative who will defend and nourish that idea so that it doesn't suffer a premature death. Most people don't think of science in this way but that's because the image they have of science only applies to the simplest, and for that reason, almost non-existent, ideal cases where the evidence is clear-cut and it's not a matter of scientists with different shades of opinion. In every real scientific problem I've ever seen, the evidence by itself never settled anything because two scientists of different outlook could both take the same evidence, and reach entirely different conclusions. You eventually settle the differences, but not because of the evidence itself but because you develop a preference for one set of assumptions over the other. How you do this is not clear since there's not always a good set of reasons for adopting one rather than the other.

Note that in this part of the discussion the scientists partly reversed themselves and praised their more committed colleagues precisely for their extreme commitments:

> The commitment of these guys to their ideas while absolutely infuriating at times can be a very good thing too. One should never give up an idea too soon in science—any idea, no matter how outrageous it may be and no matter how beaten down it seems by all the best evidence at the time. I've seen too many totally disproven ideas come back to haunt us. I've learned by now that you never completely prove or disprove anything; you just make it more or less probable with the best of what means you've got at the time. It's true that these guys are a perpetual thorn in the side of the profession and for that reason a perpetual challenge to it too. Their value probably outweighs

ment. Scientists must be passionless observers, unbiased by emotion, intellectually cold" (Taylor, 1967:4). Also see Taylor (1967) for an argument as to why the preceding view of science though false is not a straw-man (see also Merton [1969:2–3] and Mitroff [1972]).

their disadvantages although I've wondered many times if we might not be better off without them. Each time I reluctantly conclude no. We need them around. They perpetually shake things up with their wild ideas although they drive you mad with the stick-to-itiveness that they have for their ideas.

The comments illustrate clearly the variety of reasons for the belief that scientists should be emotionally committed to their ideas. Above all, they reveal the psychological and sociological elements that permeate the structure of science. Psychologically, the comments indicate that commitment is a characteristic of scientists. The comments strongly support Merton's ideas on scientists' affective involvement with their ideas (1963a:80). Sociologically, the comments reveal the social nature of science. Scientist E, for example, says there's so much "stuff in the system" that if one wants to be heard over the crowd, one must adopt a position more extreme than one believes in.[15] Scientist F continues that this inevitably thrusts scientists into the midst of adversary proceedings, a highly significant observation.

In recent years, considerable work in the philosophy of science, for example, the work of Churchman and Feyerabend, has explained science as resulting as much from conflicts between scientists as from agreements. They argued that disagreement between scientists is as natural as agreement between them, and that such disagreements are as necessary for the growth of science as their agreements (see also Kuhn, 1962). Feyerabend has consistently expressed the view that science depends on intense opposition between at least two theorists who disagree strongly about the same phenomenon. In Feyerabend's theory, the proliferation of contesting views on any subject is fundamental to the progress of science. The implications of Feyerabend's thesis for the present discussion are as follows (Mitroff, 1974a, 1974b): If every scientist were committed to the same idea to the same degree as every other scientist, there would be nothing positive in commitment per se. Indeed, if all men shared the same commitments, the terms "commitment" and "bias" would have no meaning since they would be undetectable. The fact that men differ greatly in the make-up and degree of their commitments and biases enables scientific objectivity to emerge from conflict and passion.[16] Furthermore, science can always afford a few men of deep commitments. Although they run the risk of being labeled crackpots and being ignored (Davis, 1971), the comments of the respondents suggest that they serve a positive function in science. Finally, Scientist G's comments indicate that the personal character of science pervades its entire structure (Merton, 1957, 1963a; Polanyi, 1958).

In the second round of the study a semantic difference related to the concept of the ideal scientist was administered to check on the strength

---

[15] Scientist E's statement is interesting for a variety of reasons. For one, it corresponds almost exactly with Murray Davis's provocative notions of what makes a theory in social science interesting. According to Davis (1971), if a theory is to be interesting, then it must differ substantially from our ordinary common sense expectation, but not too much or "you'll get labeled as a crackpot."

[16] This of course requires a different concept of scientific objectivity than the one stated in footnote 13. Churchman (1971) has developed a dialectical notion of objectivity which does not depend for its existence and operation on the presumption, as Popper's (1972) does, of knowledge without an opinionated knower.

and consistency of the beliefs expressed in the first round. A full discussion of the results would take us too far afield (cf., Mitroff, 1974b). Therefore, we will report the results of the one scale (impartial-biased) of twenty-seven scales most relevant to our concerns.

The semantic differentials were administered in person to encourage the scientists to state freely what the scales and their end adjective pairs meant to them. Each of the twenty-seven scales on the semantic differentials were used to gather quantitative scale responses and verbal protocols. I adopted this technique to maximize the information gained by collecting both qualitative and quantitative responses and to balance the weaknesses of the structured instrument with the strengths of the open-ended or projective interview and vice versa (Sjoberg and Nett, 1968). A t-test performed on the quantitative responses to the scale impartial-biased shows that the scientists reject the notion that their ideal scientist is completely impartial at a high level of significance (p < 0.001).[17]

The verbal responses are even more instructive. They parallel those of the first round of interviews and exhibit new aspects as well. The comments indicate that the scientists know that "impartiality is the commonly accepted norm or ideal of scientific life," and that they deliberately reject it as a fact of scientific life and as an ideal. Even more important, their responses indicate a deep ambivalence. They reflect not a simple either/or choice between complete impartiality or complete bias but a complex tug-of-war between two opposing norms operating simultaneously. The following are representative responses:

Scientist A. The concept of the completely impartial observer is as much an absurdity as the completely disinterested scientist. I can't recall any scientist I've ever known who has made a fundamental contribution that was impartial to his discoveries or to his ideas. You not only don't discover anything by being impartial but you don't even test it by being impartial. The severest test of an idea occurs when you've done everything in your power to make the best possible case for it and it still doesn't hold water. Nowhere in all of this are you impartial. This doesn't mean that you ultimately don't discard your ideas. You do, but with reluctance.

Scientist B. It's all right for a scientist to be rather strongly biased while he's pursuing an idea; he should not be indifferent to the various alternatives he's trying to decide between, but he has to be objective enough to discard an alternative that runs into difficulty. This means he has to be able to switch back and forth between being biased and being impartial. Within the constraints of this questionnaire, I'd check a 3. However, scientists should be around 6 part of the time and then be able to switch back to 1. Even better, I'd like to check near both ends of the scale, say 2 and 6, at the same time because in reality you have to have both of these things going on in you simultaneously. It's not as black and white as this questionnaire makes it to be.

---

[17] Again see Taylor (1967) for why the notion of the completely impartial observer (Mitroff, 1971) is not a straw-man argument. The persistency with which this notion appears in accounts of science destroys the contention that it is a straw-man. If anything, the concept deserves analysis not dismissal. Indeed, labeling such an image a straw-man seems more defensive than analytical. As Merton put it: "The practice of seeking to trivialize what can be shown to be significant is a well-known manifestation of resistance" (Merton, 1963b:251).

In short, if scientific knowledge were the product of uncommitted or weakly committed observers, its understanding would be trivial. Given the presumption of untainted, unbiased observers, it is a trivial matter to explain how objectivity results. It is also a trivial matter to justify the concept of objectivity as knowledge "uncoloured by, or independent of, the feelings or opinions of the person making them" (Graham, 1965:287). The problem is how objective knowledge results in science not despite bias and commitment, but because of them. As Churchman and Ackoff put it:

> Pragmatism does not advocate a scientist who removes all his emotions, sympathies, and the like from his experimental process. This is like asking the scientist to give up being a whole man while he experiments. Perhaps a man's emotion will be the most powerful instrument he has at his disposal in reaching a conclusion. The main task, however, is to enlarge the scope of the scientific model so that we can begin to understand the role of the other types of experience in reaching decisions, and can see how they too can be checked and controlled. The moral, according to the pragmatist, should not be to exclude feeling from scientific method, but to include it in the sense of understanding it better (Churchman and Ackoff, 1950:224).

In summary, this section has offered theoretical and empirical support for the following proposition: if there exist serious reasons why the concepts of emotional neutrality and universalism ought to be considered as norms of science, then serious reasons also exist for positing emotional commitment and "particularism" as opposing counter-norms of science (see Table 4).

Some Additional Counter-Norms

Similarly, for every norm proposed by Merton (1949) and Barber (1952) one could seriously consider an opposing counter-norm. Table 4 represents the outcome of such an effort.

As important as it would be to go through Table 4 in detail, space requires that we treat only one additional norm.

Consider the conventional norm of communism:

> "Communism," in the non-technical and extended sense of common ownership of goods, is a second integral element of the scientific ethos. The substantive findings of science are a product of social collaboration and are assigned to the community. They constitute a common heritage in which the equity of the individual producer is severely limited (Merton, 1949:610). The institutional conception of science as part of the public domain is linked with the imperative for communication of findings. *Secrecy is the antithesis of this norm; full and open communication its enactment* (Merton, 1949:611, italics added).

On the face of it, it would seem absurd to contend that there could be an opposing norm having some positive function in science. Still, the idea that such a norm might exist came out during the interviews. While it was by no means universally acknowledged as a problem, approximately a fifth of the

TABLE 4
A Tentative List of Norms and Counter-Norms

Norms	Counter-Norms
1. *Faith in the moral virtue of rationality* (Barber, 1952).	1. *Faith in the moral virtue of rationality and nonrationality* (cf., Tart, 1972).
2. *Emotional neutrality* as an instrumental condition for the achievement of rationality (Barber, 1952).	2. *Emotional commitment* as an instrumental condition for the achievement of rationality (cf., Merton, 1963a; Mitroff, 1974b).
3. *Universalism:* "The acceptance or rejection of claims entering the list of science is not to depend on the personal or social attributes of their protagonist; his race, nationality, religion, class and personal qualities are as such irrelevant. Objectivity precludes particularism. . . . The imperative of universalism is rooted deep in the impersonal character of science" (Merton, 1949:607).	3. *Particularism:* "The acceptance or rejection of claims entering the list of science is to a large extent a function of who makes the claim" (Boguslaw, 1968:59). The social and psychological characteristics of the scientist are important factors influencing how his work will be judged. The work of certain scientists will be given priority over that of others (Mitroff, 1974b). The imperative of particularism is rooted deep in the personal character of science (Merton, 1963a; Polanyi, 1958).
4. *Communism:* "Property rights are reduced to the absolute minimum of credit for priority of discovery" (Barber, 1952:130). "Secrecy is the 'antithesis' of this norm; full and open communication [of scientific results] its enactment" (Merton, 1949:611).	4. *Solitariness* (or, *"Miserism"* [Boguslaw, 1968:59]): Property rights are expanded to include protective control over the disposition of one's discoveries; secrecy thus becomes a necessary moral act (Mitroff, 1974b).
5. *Disinterestedness:* "Scientists are expected by their peers to achieve the self-interest they have in work-satisfaction and in prestige through serving the [scientific] community interest directly" (Barber, 1952:132).	5. *Interestedness:* Scientists are expected by their close colleagues to achieve the self-interest they have in work-satisfaction and in prestige through serving their special communities of interest, e.g., their invisible college (Boguslaw, 1968:59; Mitroff, 1974b)
6. *Organized scepticism:* "The scientist is obliged . . . to make public his criticisms of the work of others when he believes it to be in error . . . no scientist's contribution to knowledge can be accepted without careful scrutiny, and that the scientist must doubt his own findings as well as those of others" (Storer, 1966:79).	6. *Organized dogmatism:* "Each scientist should make certain that previous work by others on which he bases his work is sufficiently identified so that others can be held responsible for inadequacies while any possible credit accrues to oneself" (Boguslaw, 1968:59). The scientist must believe in his own findings with utter conviction while doubting those of others with all his worth (Mitroff, 1974b).

sample, of their own accord, brought up the fact that stealing ideas was a minor, and sometimes a major problem in science (cf., Gaston, 1971). By stealing, the respondents did not mean conscious stealing. Such stealing was felt to be so rare as not to constitute a problem. The problem was the unconscious, unintended appropriation of another's ideas—the fact that one often could not trace the origin of one's ideas and hence properly credit one's peers (cf., Merton, 1963a:91). If only as a protective device, it makes sense to consider secrecy as a working "norm-in-use" (Sjoberg and Nett, 1968). However, the more interesting question is whether secrecy is a rational standard or ideal norm of science and not merely a crude protective device.

As a norm opposed to communism, secrecy (or "particularism") can serve various positive functions in science: (1) Rather than detracting from its stability and progress, under certain circumstances secrecy can be seen to serve the ends of science. With no protective counter measures at its disposal, the social system of science would be continually racked by the kinds of open internal disputes for priority so aptly described by Merton. Without secrecy, science would degenerate into a state of continual warfare. A certain amount of secrecy *is* rational since scientists are not always able to acknowledge the source of their ideas. Until we can develop better social safeguards, we may have to learn to live with some secrecy. (2) Perhaps its most interesting and important function is as a before-the-fact acknowledgment to oneself and others that one has something in the works worth protecting. A certain amount of stealing or appropriation may be both tolerable and beneficial as long as it doesn't reach epidemic proportions. While stealing may be more difficult than secrecy to make into a counter-norm, even it can serve some positive function. As perverse and potentially dangerous as they are, stealing and appropriating may be important ways of informing a scientist and his peers that his work is significant. As one respondent put it:

> It was only when I began to do something significant and important that people began to *steal* [italics added] from me. When I began to manage a big research program and all the big, important people began to visit me, they would rush home and try to outdo our results. *You know you're doing something significant when people want to steal it* [italics added].

Science typically measures the significance of a piece of work by its statistical significance. Perhaps the social test of the real significance of a scientist's work is whether it is worth stealing or not. Whatever the ultimate implications of the study, it has long been an unwritten rule of science that you don't divulge what you're up to until you're 99% sure that you've got the competition beat in the race to print (cf. Merton, 1957).

I would not make secrecy an unrestricted ideal of scientific life. If science were to follow the norms of commitment and secrecy exclusively, commitment could cause it to degenerate into complete subjectivity and secrecy could breed solipsism. If science were exclusively founded on secrecy, I doubt it could exist as we know it. The public communication, sharing, and testing of ideas would all but vanish (Ziman, 1968). But the key word is exclusively. For if science were also exclusively founded on the norms of disinterestedness, universalism, and community, I doubt science could have arisen as we know it. The point is that each norm is restrained and if any were unrestrained, science would probably collapse.

CONCLUDING REMARKS

This paper has argued that science contains norms and counter-norms. Both, however, do not operate equally in every situation. Indeed, the concept of sociological ambivalence supposes that one set of norms is dominant and the other subsidiary. However, as this study reveals, the actual situation is more complicated. Norms dominant in one situation can be subsidiary in another. Dominancy is not an invariant property of a set of norms. The dependence of dominancy on situations undoubtedly derives from a host of factors (cf. Mitroff, 1973) such as the paradigmatic structure of a science (Kuhn, 1962). Understanding such dominance is a problem for future research in the sociology of science.

A previous paper (Mitroff and Mason, 1974) examined one of the factors on which dominance depends. The class of scientific problems can be arrayed along a continuum whose underlying dimension is "ease of definition" (Churchman, 1971; Mitroff, 1973, 1974a). At the one extreme are "well-defined" problems, at the other are "ill-defined" problems. Well-defined problems (like the chemical composition of the lunar samples) are amenable to solution in that they can be clearly posed and hence solved by relatively clear-cut, standard, analytic techniques; they are "consensible" (Ziman, 1968) in that a relatively wide degree of consensus can be obtained regarding the "nature of the problem;" in short, they are easily formulated. Ill-defined problems (like the origin of the moon) are almost defiantly elusive; they seem to defy a common "consensible" formulation (Mitroff and Betz, 1972). Because of their widespread consensible nature, well-defined problems seem independent of the personality of their formulators; they appear to be impersonal. Ill-defined problems, on the other hand, appear to be the intensely personal creations of their creators. Whereas the conventional norms of science are dominant for well-structured problems, the counter-norms proposed here appear to be dominant for ill-structured problems. An information theoretic analysis of the shift in the beliefs of the scientists over the course of the Apollo missions with respect to key scientific hypotheses reveals that the more well-structured the problem or hypothesis, the more it was felt to be settled. Conversely, the more ill-structured the hypothesis, the less it was felt to be settled by Apollo (Mitroff and Mason, 1974), and hence, the more it was felt to be subject to the counter-norms described in this paper.

The study of the ambivalence of scientists remains one of the important, unsolved problems in the history, philosophy, psychology, and sociology of science (Holton, 1973). It deserves much more systematic study. The results of this paper, while tentative, are hopefully a step in this direction.

REFERENCES

Barber, Bernard
   1952   Science and the Social Order. New York: Collier.
   1961   "Resistance by scientists to scientific discovery." Science 74:596–602.
Boguslaw, Robert
   1968   "Values in the research society." Pp. 51–66 in E. Glatt and M. W. Shelly (eds.), The Research Society. New York: Gordon and Breach.

Churchman, C. W.
   1961   Prediction and Optimal Decision: Philosophical Issues of a Science of
            Values. New Jersey: Prentice Hall.
   1968   Challenge to Reason. New York: McGraw-Hill.
   1971   The Design of Inquiring Systems. New York: Basic Books.
Churchman, C. W. and Russell L. Ackoff
   1950   Methods of Inquiry: An Introduction to Philosophy and Scientific Method.
            Saint Louis: Educational Publishers.
Davis, Murray
   1971   "That's interesting: towards a phenomenology of sociology and a soci-
            ology of phenomenology." Philosophy of the Social Sciences 3 (Decem-
            ber):309–44.
Feyerabend, P. K.
   1965   "Problems of empiricism." Pp. 145–260 in Robert G. Colodny (ed.), Be-
            yond the Edge of Certainty. Englewood Cliffs, N.J.: Prentice-Hall.
   1967   "On the improvement of the sciences and arts and the possible identity of
            the two." Pp. 387–415 in Robert S. Cohen and Marx W. Wartofsky (eds.),
            Boston Studies in the Philosophy of Science. Dordrecht, Holland: D.
            Reidel.
   1970a   "Against method: outline of an anarchistic theory of knowledge." Pp.
            17–130 in Michael Radner and Stephen Winokur (eds.), Analyses of The-
            ories and Methods of Physics and Psychology, Minnesota Studies in the
            Philosophy of Science. Bloomington, Minnesota: University of Minnesota
            Press.
   1970b   "Problems of empiricism, part II." Pp. 275–354 in Robert G. Colodny
            (ed.), The Nature and Function of Scientific Theories. Pittsburgh, Pa.:
            University of Pittsburgh Press.
Gaston, Jerry
   1971   "Secretiveness and competition for priority in discovery in physics."
            Minerva 9 (October):472–92.
Graham, E. C.
   1965   The Basic Dictionary of Science. New York: Macmillan.
Grunbaum, A.
   1963   Philosophical Problems of Space and Time. New York: A. Knopf.
Hagstrom, Warren
   1965   The Scientific Community. New York: Basic Books.
Holton, Gerald
   1973   Thematic Origins of Scientific Thought. Cambridge, Mass.: Harvard Uni-
            versity Press.
Kiesler, Charles A.
   1971   The Psychology of Commitment, Experiments Linking Behavior to Belief.
            New York: Academic Press.
Kuhn, Thomas
   1962   The Structure of Scientific Revolutions. Chicago: University of Chicago
            Press.
Lakatos, Imre and Alan Musgrave (eds.)
   1970   Criticism and the Growth of Knowledge. Cambridge, England: Cam-
            bridge University Press.
Laudan, Laurens
   1965   "Discussion: Grunbaum on the Duhemian argument'." Philosophy of
            Science 32 (July-October):295–9.
Levinson, A. A. and S. R. Taylor
   1971   Moon Rocks and Minerals. New York: Pergamon.

Maxwell, Nicholas
  1972   "A critique of Popper's views on scientific method." Philosophy of Science 39 (June):131–52.
McClelland, David
  1970   "On the dynamics of creative physical scientists." Pp. 309–41 in Liam Hudson (ed.), The Ecology of Human Intelligence. England: Penguin.
Merton, Robert K.
  1957   "Priorities in scientific discovery: a chapter in the sociology of science." American Sociological Review 22 (December):635–59.
  1961   "Singletons and multiples in scientific discovery: a chapter in the sociology of science." Proceedings of the American Philosophical Society 105 (October):470–86.
  1963a "The ambivalence of scientists." Bulletin of The Johns Hopkins Hospital 112 (February):77–97.
  1963b "Resistance to the systematic study of multiple discoveries in science." European Journal of Sociology 4:237–82.
  1968   Social Theory and Social Structure. Enlarged edition. New York: The Free Press.
  1969   "Behavior patterns of scientists." American Scientist 57 (Spring):1–23.
Merton, Robert K. and Elinor Barber
  1963   "Sociological ambivalence." Pp. 91–120 in E. A. Tiryakian (ed.), Sociological Theory, Values, and Sociocultural Change. Glencoe: The Free Press.
Mitroff, Ian I.
  1971   "Solipsism: an essay in psychological philosophy." Philosophy of Science 38 (September):376–94.
  1972   "The myth of objectivity, or, why science needs a new psychology of science." Management Science 18 (June):B–613–B–618.
  1973   "Epistemology as general systems theory: an approach to the design of complex decision-making experiments." Philosophy of the Social Sciences 3 (June):117–34.
  1974a "Systems, inquiry, and the meanings of falsification." Philosophy of Science 40 (June):255–76.
  1974b The Subjective Side of Science: A Philosophical Inquiry into the Psychology of the Apollo Moon Scientists. Amsterdam—The Netherlands and San Francisco: Elsevier and Jossey-Bass.
Mitroff, Ian I. and Frederick Betz
  1972   "Dialectical decision theory: a meta-theory of decision-making" Management Science 19 (September):11–24.
Mitroff, Ian I. and Richard O. Mason
  1974   "On evaluating the scientific contribution of the Apollo moon missions via information theory." Management Science. (n.p., n.d.).
Muller, P. M. and W. L. Sjogren
  1968   "Mascons: lunar mass concentrations." Science 161 (August):680–4.
Parsons, Talcott
  1949   The Structure of Social Action. Glencoe: The Free Press.
Polanyi, Michael
  1958   Personal Knowledge: Towards a Post-Critical Philosophy. New York: Harper and Row.
Popper, K.
  1961   The Logic of Scientific Discovery. New York: Basic Books.
  1972   Objective Knowledge. Oxford: The Clarendon Press.
Roe, Anne
  1961   "The psychology of the scientist." Science 134 (August):456–9.

Sjoberg, G. and R. Nett
    1968   A Methodology for Social Research. New York: Harper and Row.
Storer, Norman W.
    1966   The Social System of Science. New York: Holt, Rinehart, and Winston.
Tart, Charles
    1972   "States of consciousness and state—specific sciences." Science 176 (June):
            1203–10.
Taylor, A. M.
    1967   Imagination and the Growth of Science. New York: Schocken.
Toulmin, Stephen
    1972   Human Understanding. Princeton, New Jersey: Princeton University Press.
Watson, James D.
    1968   The Double Helix, A Personal Account of the Discovery of DNA. New
            York: Atheneum.
West, S. S.
    1960   "The ideology of academic scientists." IRE Transactions on Engineering
            Management EM–7 (June):54–62.
Ziman, John
    1968   Public Knowledge. Cambridge, England: Cambridge University Press.
Zuckerman, Harriet
    1972   "Interviewing an ultra-elite." The Public Opinion Quarterly 36 (Summer):
            159–75.

We have now both read the paper and we have both taken notes on its information. Let us now see if we agree on what sort of information ought to be included in a review of the article:

In an article entitled, "Norms and Counter-Norms in a Select Group of the Apollo Moon Scientists: A Case Study of the Ambivalence of Scientists,"[6] Ian Mitroff examines two aspects of science and scientists: (1) norms and counter-norms and (2) ambivalence. Rather than doing a massive study of all scientists, Mitroff chose instead to do a case study of the 42 most eminent scientists who studied the moon rocks that were brought back to the earth by the Apollo astronauts. According to Mitroff, he used what he calls a "snowball sample" in which he asked a number of key respondents whom else should be interviewed and thus the sample snowballed (grew in size). Both the initial respondents and the members of the "snowball sample" were chosen to see if the material or information that was found from the analysis of the moon rocks would cause conflict between themselves and other scientists. Because of the snowballing nature of the individuals questioned, the sample that finally resulted was, according to Mitroff, "an elite of elites" (584). In other words, elite members of science mentioned other elite members of the scientific community and thus the sample was chosen.

The first discussion centered on the problem of the Merton-Barber theory of sociological ambivalence where it is suggested that "institu-

---

[6] *American Sociological Review*, 39 (August, 1974):579–595.

tions reflect potentially conflicting norms" (579). Mitroff documents the fact of high amounts of competition in science. At the same time, Mitroff finds different types (and degrees) of commitment on the part of scientists. Thus, scientists questioned see three types of commitment on the part of their colleagues: (1) intellectual commitment to the norms of science; (2) affective commitment or emotional attachment to ideas and finally; and (3) personal commitment to certain doctrines. While it is shown by Mitroff that there are certain impersonal norms of science that affect what a scientist does (universalism and emotional neutrality), it is also shown that there are strong counter-norms operating in the scientific community. Scientists are shown to see science as a personal enterprise and they are shown to be emotionally involved in their work. As Mitroff indicates, "Psychologically, the comments indicate that commitment is a characteristic of scientists. The comments strongly support Merton's ideas on scientists' affective involvement with their ideas. . . . Sociologically, the comments reveal the social nature of science" (589).

Closely related to the notion of conflicting norms is that of ambivalence. In order to test the concept of ambivalence, the author used a semantic differential series of questions. Among those used in the semantic differential was the impartial-biased dichotomy. On the basis of this differential, Mitroff indicates that ". . . the scientists reject the notion that their ideal scientist is completely impartial . . ." (590). In terms of the ambivalence of the scientists, Mitroff stated that their comments

> . . . indicate that the scientists know that "impartiality is the commonly accepted norm or ideal of scientific life," and that they deliberately reject it as a fact of scientific life and as an ideal. Even more important, their responses indicate a deep ambivalence. They reflect not a simple either/or choice between complete impartiality or complete bias but a complex tug-of-war between two opposing norms operating simultaneously (590).

In addition to the counter-norms of impartiality-bias, the author also discusses a number of others. In all these he also discovers a series of counter-norms for all the "do's" of science. As Mitroff argues, "whereas the conventional norms of science are dominant for well-structured problems, the counter-norms proposed here appear to be dominant for ill-structured problems" (594).

While the research appears to be well thought out and well done, there are nonetheless a number of areas in which it may be criticized. First, we must question the use of a "snowball sample." The author admits the sample is not a random one and with this we must agree. In addition, however, the question arises as to how much the snowball effect is related to actual "eliteness" of the respondents and the others and how much the snowball effect might be related to one of the sub-themes being examined, that of jealousy between competing scientists and competing viewpoints. Does a scientist suggest another because that person actually is an important person or because that person holds a competing viewpoint about the sample of rocks? In addition, we might ask whether or not the inclusion of Principal Investigators (PI) *and* scientists who are not involved in the examination of the rocks will bias the research? The PIs may have too much emotional in-volvement and the scientists who are not involved have too little. Fi-nally, we would want to add that the entire notion of competing value systems has been investigated in other areas than that of the sociology of science and that this other research might have usefully been dealt with here. For example, Tumin in his book *Social Class and Social Change in Puerto Rico* (1961) demonstrated the presence of two com-peting value systems among the residents of Puerto Rico. The presence of two competing value systems among the Puerto Ricans apparently causes trouble only for the researcher, the people themselves have little trouble adapting to what appears to be ambivalence. For the people of Puerto Rico, the ambivalence is more apparent than real and they easily deal with the fact of two value systems existing simultaneously within their society. While the study by Tumin is outside the realm of the "sociology of science" there are important implications for the Mitroff study.

Putting aside the problems mentioned above, the Mitroff study adds an interesting dimension to the study of science and the scientist. The existence of counter-norms in science (as in other professions and occupations?) is clearly of import and, as Mitroff indicates, is in need of additional investigation.

While some persons (including the author of the article) might dis-agree with the conclusions drawn from (and the criticisms of) the above article, such an outline as just provided is the essence of a re-view. As mentioned earlier, it is necessary to present what the author says he or she will do, what the author does, and what you feel about the article; a review of an article, or a précis, must indicate to an unin-formed reader what has transpired in the article *and* what criticisms can be made about it.[7]

We did not deal with the tables and numbers in the preceding article primarily because conclusions could be drawn from the author's dis-cussion alone. It is, however, necessary to be able to understand and interpret tabular presentations. It is necessary simply because the

---

[7] On this subject, see Hagedorn and Labovitz (1973), chapter 3.

great majority of articles and monographs that are published are empirical in nature and spend great amounts of time discussing their statistical findings. The following section of this chapter discusses the nature of "table reading."

READING AND INTERPRETING TABLES

As sociologists, one of the major aspects of the research process is both the constructing and the interpretation of data in tabular form. While this is one of the more fundamental aspects of the sociologist's craft, it is also one of the hardest to learn. There are many students who shy away from the entire concept of numbers and who, when confronted with a table, go into uncontrollable panics. While there are tables that will bring on a panic in even the most seasoned sociologist, the majority of tables are reasonably easy to understand if sufficient time is taken. In the following pages, a number of tables are presented in hopes that you can be persuaded to examine them and to learn how to read them. At the end of the chapter are examples that will require you to read and interpret data tables.

Analyzing tables and tabular presentations of data is important for the sociologist for a number of reasons. First, by reading and interpreting tables presented by others, the researcher can see how it might be done in his or her own research project. (Obviously at the same time that one can see how to construct and interpret tables, one may also learn the way not to construct and interpret tables—not all sociologists each and every time build tables that accurately reflect their data.) Closely examining the data in an article or research report will also allow the reader to draw his or her own conclusions about the results of a study. If one ignores the tabular presentations in a report, one must rely on the author of the report to present and interpret the data honestly. If you examine the data yourself, you can decide whether the conclusions drawn by the author of the report are justified and legitimate in light of the data presented.

As a prelude to reading a table, examine one closely. What do you see in the table? First, there is a heading which describes the content of the table. As you can see in Table 2–1, the content of the table is the distribution of the ages and the races for students at the university. If you examine the other tables you will see that they too are distributions of the ages and races of the students. At the same time, you will see that the tables look somewhat different; that the tables, while showing the same (are you certain?) data show it differently.

What else can you see in the table? There are, at least, two variables represented in the table. One is normally constructed across the top

TABLE 2–1
Age and Race for Students at the University

	Age				
Race	18–19	20–23	24–27	28–35	35 and over
White	90.4%	90.7%	85.2%	86.9%	94.3%
Black	6.4	6.4	13.6	10.9	5.7
Native American	0.0	0.8	0.0	0.0	0.0
Mexican-American/ Chicano	1.7	1.4	0.6	0.7	0.0
Oriental	0.4	0.4	0.0	0.0	0.0
Other	1.1	0.4	0.6	1.5	0.0
Total	100.0	100.0	100.0	100.0	100.0
(N)	(543)	(514)	(176)	(137)	(105)

of the table (horizontally) and the other is shown vertically. For each category of each variable there will be a separate column or row. There will be, then, at the intersection of each column and row a separate cell that shows the data that fits those two coordinates. For example, in Table 2–1, for the intersection of the "24–27"-year-old age group and the "Black" race there is exactly one set of numbers that apply. If you find that the number "13.6 percent" is in this cell, then we are in agreement to this point. At the bottom of the column there are two figures: a total for the column and also an (N). If you were to add up the percentages in the columns you would find that they will sum to 100.0 percent (or a close approximation if the numbers are rounded off). The other figure, the (N), is the number of persons for the column on which the percentages are based. In other words, for the column headed by age 20–23, the total number of persons included in the percentages is 514. This figure, the total number of persons included in the calculation of the percentages, is useful if you want to convert from percentages to the actual numbers. Thus, if you wanted to know how many persons were actually black and who were 20–23 years of age, you would simply multiply the percentage (converted to a decimal) by the total number of persons in the column.

Black *and* 20–23 years of age = .064 times 514 = 32.8 = 33

We must round off the answer to the nearest whole number since there are very few fractional people wandering around this campus (although there are some of the students and faculty we are somewhat worried about). Before we begin an analysis of the tables, it is important to describe what might be called "conventions" in table construction in sociology. Whenever and however you construct a table, you always calculate the *percentages within the categories of the independent variable*. When a table is constructed, figuring the percentages of the variables is not done randomly; there is always a reason for the direction in which the percentages move. Thus, whatever variable you are using as your independent (or causative) variable is the one in which the percentages are given. By arriving at percentages within the categories of the independent variable, one is then able to compare across the categories of the independent variable to see what effects the independent variable has on the dependent variable.

A second convention follows from the first. Generally, when you construct a table it is customary to *place the independent variable across the top of the table* (in the horizontal plane) *and the dependent variable vertically*. The categories of the independent variable will, then, be spread across the table and the categories of the dependent variable will be located on the side. While the second "convention" is not quite the absolute that the first is, you should follow it unless you have an extremely good reason for changing. When, and if, you change from the standard way of presenting your data, be sure that you inform your readers that you are changing. Never leave your reader in doubt as to what you are doing in the presentation of your data in your report.

Table 2–1 presents the distribution of the students at the university by age and race, but it also does something more. In Table 2–1, we can determine the racial distribution of the students for each age category. *In Table 2–1 we cannot determine the age distribution of the students for each racial category.* We do know from Table 2–1 that 90.4 percent of the 18–19-year-old students at the university consider themselves white, that 6.4 percent of the 18–19-year-old students consider themselves to be black, that 1.7 percent of the 18–19-year-old students consider themselves to be Mexican-American/Chicano, and so on. For Table 2–1, in other words, one must read *down* the columns. At the same time, it is possible to make comparisons across the columns. In this way we can determine that the age group with the highest percentage of white students is the 35-year-old and over group. At the same time, we note that the age group with the largest concentration of blacks is ages 24–27. *For a table where the data are shown in columns, you read down the columns and you compare across the rows.*

In Table 2–2, the data are arranged in rows so that one must read the table from left to right. In Table 2–2, we can determine the age distribution of the students at the university within any of the racial groups. For the Mexican-American/Chicano students, we see that 50.0 percent are 18–19 years old, 38.9 percent are 20–23 years old, that 5.6 percent are 24–27 years old, and that 5.6 percent are 28–35 years old. As in Table 2–1, comparisons can be made across the groups but in this case, the comparisons must be made within a column. In other

TABLE 2–2
Age and Race for Students at the University

| | | | *Age* | | | | |
Race	18–19	20–23	24–27	28–35	35 and over	Total	(N)
White	37.1%	35.2	11.3	9.0	7.5	100.0	1,325
Black	31.0%	29.2	21.2	13.3	5.3	100.0	113
Native American	0.0%	100.0	0.0	0.0	0.0	100.0	4
Mexican-American/							
Chicano	50.0%	38.9	5.6	5.6	0.0	100.0	18
Oriental	50.0%	50.0	0.0	0.0	0.0	100.0	4
Other	54.5%	18.2	9.1	18.2	0.0	100.0	11

words, we can see that 37.1 percent of the white students are 18–19 years old, while only 31.0 percent of the black students are this age. We can also show, for example, that for the age group 28–35 years old, the most heavily represented racial category is that labeled "Other" with 18.2 percent, followed by the black group with 13.3 percent in this category. We might also point out that for a table where the data are arranged in rows, the totals for each row and the number of persons on whom the percentages are based should be shown in the last row, most often at the right side of the table. You should keep in mind that *for tables where the data are shown in rows, you read across the row and you compare down the columns.*

Table 2–3 takes yet a different approach to the presentation of the same data. In Table 2–3, each cell shows the percentage of all the students at the university who fall within it. In other words, the percentages are based on a total figure for the table as a whole rather than on a row or a column total. In Table 2–3, then, we can see that 33.2 percent of all the students at the university are 18–19-year-old white students. In the same vein, 0.4 percent of all the students at the university are black students who are 35 years old or over. Finally, as a part of the example, we can show that 0.5 percent of all the students at the

TABLE 2–3
Age and Race for Students at the University

| | *Age* | | | | |
	18–19	20–23	24–27	28–35	35 and over
White	33.2%	31.6%	10.2%	8.1%	6.7%
Black	2.4	2.2	1.6	1.0	0.4
Native American	0.0	0.3	0.0	0.0	0.0
Mexican-American/					
Chicano	0.6	0.5	0.1	0.1	0.0
Oriental	0.1	0.1	0.0	0.0	0.0
Other	0.4	0.1	0.1	0.1	0.0

Total for table: 100.0
N for table: 1,475

TABLE 2-4
Sex of Students at the University by Age and Race

Race	Age									
	18–19		20–23		24–27		28–34		35 and over	
	M	F	M	F	M	F	M	F	M	F
White	88.7	91.7	90.8	90.6	90.9	72.7	86.1	87.9	82.6	97.6
Black	6.3	6.6	6.3	6.5	8.3	25.5	11.4	10.3	17.4	2.4
Native American	0.0	0.0	0.8	0.7	0.0	0.0	0.0	0.0	0.0	0.0
Mexican-American/Chicano	2.5	1.0	1.3	1.4	0.8	0.0	1.3	0.0	0.0	0.0
Oriental	0.4	0.3	0.0	0.7	0.0	0.0	0.0	0.0	0.0	0.0
Puerto Rican–American										
Other	2.1	0.3	0.8	0.0	0.0	1.8	1.3	1.7	0.0	0.0
Total	100.0	100.0	100.0	100.0	100.0	100.0	100.0	100.0	100.0	100.0
(N)	(240)	(303)	(238)	(276)	(212)	(55)	(79)	(58)	(23)	(82)

university are Mexican-American/Chicano who are also 20–23 years old. As in the previous tables, it is possible to convert the percentages back to the actual numbers by converting the percentage to a decimal and multiplying it by the total number of persons included in the table (in this case 1,475 students). In Table 2–3, rather than comparing one row or one column against another, we are comparing each cell of the table against all other cells.

For tables where the data are presented as percentages of the total, you may read across rows or down columns and you may compare each cell against each other cell.

In Table 2–4, we have added an additional variable, the sex of the students. By including an additional variable we can examine the orginal relationships to see if they still hold. If the orginal relationship between age and race holds in this table (as it should since we are discussing biographical factors of students rather than the more "normal" types of independent and dependent variables), we can suggest a causal relationship between the two. However, should the relationship disappear with the introduction of a third variable, we will be able to show that the original relationship was a spurious one. The relationship between age and race of the students at the university is not materially changed by the addition of the third variable except in two places. Among the 24–27-year-old black students, we find a greater proportion who are female, and among the 35-year-old and over blacks we find a greater proportion who are male than we would find if sex made no difference. In the other relationships shown in the table, however, there are no major changes in the percentage distribution in the various categories after the additional variable of sex is introduced. The original relationship between age and sex seems to hold in the great majority of the cases shown in the categories of the table.

As an exercise in understanding and interpreting tables, percentage the following table, Table 2–5, both vertically and horizontally.

In the space of one page describe the relationships shown in Table 2–6. How, for example, do the variables affect each other? Which is the dependent variable and which is the independent variable?

TABLE 2–5
Area of Study by Class Standing of Students at the University

	Class Standing				
	Freshman	*Sophomore*	*Junior*	*Senior*	*Other**
Business administration	45	53	87	63	1
Education	65	94	144	152	6
Humanities	43	29	28	28	2
Physical science/Math	96	85	67	42	2
Social sciences	22	166	118	77	5

* Includes persons taking classes but who are not working for a degree.

TABLE 2-6
Amount of Money Available as a Factor in Decision to Attend This School, by Religion and Marital Status

Importance of Money	Protestant		Catholic		Jewish		Other[1]	
	Married	Not Married[2]	Married	Not Married	Married	Not Married[2]	Married[2]	Not Married[2]
Very important	57.2%	66.7%	62.2%	69.1%	50.0%	57.1%	67.5%	76.1%
Important	29.0	22.6	28.6	22.1	50.0	42.9	20.9	12.8
Unimportant	1.4	1.2	1.0	0.8	0.0	0.0	0.0	1.7
Very unimportant	9.1	7.8	7.1	6.1	0.0	0.0	9.3	5.1
Undecided	3.3	1.7	1.0	1.9	0.0	0.0	2.3	4.3
Total	100.0	100.0	100.0	100.0	100.0	100.0	100.0	100.0
N	(276)	(421)	(98)	(262)	(4)	(14)	(43)	(117)

[1] Includes members of all other religions as well as persons indicating no religion.
[2] Includes all persons who were single, widowed, divorced, or separated.

3

Observation of
Cycles of Behavior

THE PROBLEM

Observe a person engaged in a repetitive cycle of action *and* social action. The observation should cover at least three to four cycles of the behavior. Consequently, the cycles should be of relatively short duration. In your observation you should record all that you see. Write up the notes of your experiences, including in your report the rough notes that you took in the field.

THE APPROACH

Sociologists use a great number of techniques to gather data on social action. We use techniques that range from the in-depth questioning of our subjects to techniques that require us to watch what persons are doing and record their behavior. It is this latter technique that we will be working on in this chapter (and in this exercise).

One of the difficulties of sociology as a social science is that many persons feel that if *all* sociology does is watch people then it cannot be all that scientific. Most persons, in other words, feel that since they watch people they must be doing what the social scientist does when he or she watches people. Hopefully, your observations will be more systematic (and thus more "scientific") than the observations of the untrained.

Before we begin a discussion of the specific problem(s) to be dealt with in this chapter, we feel it important to discuss generally the whole notion of observation. We want to discuss some of the other possible roles the field observer might play, looking not only at the present but also to the future.

Methodologists distinguish a number of roles that the social researcher may play in doing field research of the observational type. Gold (1969), as well as others,[1] suggests a number of possible field roles that may be taken by the researcher. At one extreme is the role played for the present assignment, that of the complete observer (as complete as you can make it). As a complete observer, there is as little interaction with the participants as is possible.[2] The field role of the observer is defined by Gold (1969:36-37) as a role which:

> entirely removes a field worker from social interaction with informants. Here a field worker attempts to observe people in ways which make it unnecessary for them to take him into account, for they do not know he is observing them or that, in some sense, they are serving as his informants.

At the other extreme is the complete participant; the person who has lost some of the scientific objectivity that he or she had when beginning the research project and who has, to some extent, "gone over to the other side," or who is said to "have gone native." In such a situation, the researcher is no longer acting as a researcher but has become a member of the group being observed. By compromising one's objectivity, the researcher loses the ability to go where he or she might normally go—the researcher is now bound by the same taboos as the other members of the group. The researcher who is identified as a researcher, on the other hand, is less bound by the group's taboos and is often able to gather information not easily found by using other methods. Gold adds, however, that it is occasionally useful to consciously make the choice to be a hidden observer and thus become what is, in terms of outward appearances, a "complete participant." As a hidden observer, the researcher is deceiving the subjects into thinking that he or she is one of them. The "double life" is hard to play, as Gold points out, and in fact may turn into the situation mentioned above: the researchers find they have great difficulty keeping their objectivity and end up "going native."[3]

---

[1] In addition to the Gold article, see Jacobs (1970); Adams and Preiss (1960); McCall and Simmons (1969); and Schwartz and Schwartz (1955). Each of these details both methodological considerations and possible problems involved in participant observation. The topic of participant observation will be dealt with more fully in Chapter 5.

[2] In Chapter 6, we detail a situation where the observer has no contact whatever with those being observed during the course of the observation.

[3] While Gold indicates this type of research (of leading a double life) would be called the "complete participant," we would be inclined to include this as simply

The two extremes of research roles are just that, extremes. In this chapter we have you do the one (observer) and eventually we will get you to try the other (complete participant). For the moment, however, we want to concentrate on the possible research roles intermediate to the extremes. If we can assume that there is a continuum along which the possible roles can be placed, then we can show the following:

Observer	XX	XX	XX	Participant

As Gold has argued, the intermediate roles all have aspects of both extremes, it is simply the emphasis that varies. Nearest the end of the continuum we have called the "complete observer" is located that field role which emphasizes the observational but which has some aspects of the participant: the observer-as-participant. It is this role that we will be concerned with in this chapter. Toward the other end of the continuum is located that field role that is primarily oriented toward the participation of the researcher in the activity being observed but which retains aspects of the observer (a role we will be concerned with in Chapter 5).

Logically, the center of the continuum would represent that field role that is an exact balance between the two extremes, the "participant-observer." Because it would be difficult to keep an exact balance between the two extremes, we will not deal with the "participant-observer" but, rather, with the other two intermediate observational roles.

While many persons may feel that the observation of human behavior at all levels actually does little more than report information on "trivial" aspects of human behavior, such is not the case. As an example of the utility of observation in the study of human behavior, we can note the study by Mann of "queue culture" (1969). In this study, the researchers both asked questions and observed the behavior of persons waiting in line to purchase football (soccer) tickets outside the Melbourne Australia Football Stadium. The researchers felt (Mann, 1969: 340) that a long overnight queue could be

> ... seen as a miniature social system faced with the problems of every social system, formulating its own set of informal rules to govern acts of pushing in and place keeping, leaves of absence, and the application of sanctions.

While one might assume that the pushing in would be found at the front of the line, such was not the case. The most extreme examples of pushing in were found at the middle and the end of the queue. The

---

another type of participant observation. Since one is gathering data here (and is not simply a member of the group), the scientific objectivity remains and one is acting both as a participant and also as an observer.

researchers report (Mann, 1969:347), when discussing pushing in, that:

> . . . people in the middle of the queue worked together to erect barri-cades from material left in the park. Keeping close interperson dis-tance also serves to maintain the "territory" in the face of would-be intruders.

The authors also observed a herd-like movement on the part of the per-sons involved in the queue. Just as among certain animals, the persons in the queue (Mann, 1969:347), when confronting danger

> . . . and in the hour before the ticket windows opened [demonstrated] a visible bunching together, or shrinkage, in the physical length of the queue, literally a closing of the ranks. The exercise of effective social constraints depends on the capacity for cohesive action on the part of the queuers.

Here, then, we find the observation of what might seem to be a trivial kind of human behavior—standing in line—that leads to some impor-tant conclusions about human behavior. As the authors summarize their findings (Mann, 1969:354), attempts at behavioral control

> . . . in the queue are informal, they are clearly identifiable, and it is appropriate to regard them as constituting a kind of culture. The queue, which possesses the characteristics of a social system, attempts to solve the set of functional problems confronted by every social system.

The queue is shown to be a social system, sharing with every other identifiable social system a set of functional problems that must be solved if it is to survive. Observing such behavior gives the sociologist hints about conclusions that could be drawn about other "more com-plex" types of behavior.

There are other examples of the observation of human behavior that have led to some important conclusions concerning "social" and "cul-tural" human beings. Edward Hall (1966) has suggested that people of different cultures require different amounts of space when in the presence of others. The personal bubble around the American will dif-fer from that around the German, the Englishman, or the Arab. Not only do the people of different cultures require different amounts of space around themselves but this space will increase and decrease de-pending on what the person is doing at the time. Space at a cocktail party will be smaller than will the space taken by a person when en-gaged in a conversation with a colleague. Roger Brown (1965:80–81), a well-known social psychologist, summarized his discovery of the ve-racity of Hall's observations:

> I am a little skeptical of this thesis [the idea that there are spatial boundaries between persons in interaction] and once had the oppor-tunity to express the skepticism to Dr. Hall in a face-to-face conversa-tion. While we talked, having the sort of interpersonal professional discussion that is supposed to go on at a "neutral" distance of four or five feet, Dr. Hall occasionally moved his chair forward. Whenever he

did so, I moved mine back. He somewhat shook my skepticism when, as we concluded our discussion, he pointed out that he had moved me a considerable distance across the room by repeatedly crossing a zone boundary.

Once again, a simple observation of social behavior leads Brown to begin to see the relevance of space and spatial patterning of social behavior. How trivial is the observation that Brown and Hall make? Is the idea that persons space themselves in conversation a trivial one? How do Brown and Hall come to the conclusion that such patterning is happening? They frame hypotheses, observe behavior, and draw conclusions from their observations.

As a first step in developing skills in observing, look around you. What do you see? Now look again, do you see any more? Can you identify all the items in your immediate environment? What, as a small example, is on the wall in front of you? Your first reaction may well be that this is a rather ridiculous question because a wall is only a wall. Is this a correct reaction? Obviously not, because there is, no doubt, a color on the wall, there may be wallpaper on the wall, there may even be pictures on the wall. Now look again, do you see everything on the wall this time? How about that small crack down at the bottom by the door? How about that pencil mark just above the floor in the middle of the room?

The point of the above is simply that there will be limits as to how much you will be able to see in any observation. You will have to define for yourself just how much you will look for in your observation. You will have to decide whether you will examine action or social action, or possibly both. There is clearly a difference between action that is social in nature and action that is not. Social action requires an actor and another person (or object) toward whom that behavior is directed. There must be action and reaction, and so on. The action that is basically nonsocial, is that behavior that is done with no external social object in mind, such as breathing, and drinking.

One of the most important assets of doing observation in research is that you can record the behavior as it occurs. You do not have to rely on what may turn out to be selective memory of the people in your study, because you are not asking what they think about something. Rather, you are simply watching what they are doing and the vagaries of the subjects' memory should not trouble you in your research.

At the same time that recording of behavior as it occurs is an asset, it is also a hindrance to research. You are not able *in a completely observational project* to ask persons to interpret for you what they are doing and thinking as they are behaving. Consequently, you must interpret their behavior yourself without benefit of being able to ask whether or not you are correct. As in the case with most research you must balance off the benefits with the disadvantages.

For this particular research approach, you should be prepared to take account of the following:[4]

1. The Setting

What is the physical setting in which this action is taking place? Not only what is the setting but what does it look like? What are its peculiar characteristics? How are the characteristics of this setting similar to characteristics of other settings in which similar behaviors take place? In addition to the physical setting in which the action takes place, you may want to identify the general social setting. What sorts of interaction would you expect in this type of setting? What sorts of persons might one expect to find in this sort of setting? For example, one might expect that there will be a different type of clientele in a Salvation Army kitchen at Christmastime than would be found at the Stork Club on the same day. In addition, it is not unreasonable to expect that while the interactions between the persons who are clients and the persons who are serving the meals would be similar on a general level, the interactions would vary greatly on a more specific level. Thus, both types of customers might order wine with their meals but only one type of customer is likely to get it from the servers.

2. The Actors

Who are the persons in this particular situation? What do the participants look like? Particularly, what does the main participant look like in physical appearance? If you have chosen to concentrate on a particular ticket taker or seller in a movie theater, for example, one of the first descriptions that would be necessary would be that of this central character in your scenario. Once you have described the main character you can then describe all other persons the main actor interacts with in the course of your observation. You want to be certain that you present all relevant socioeconomic characteristics of the persons involved in the interactions: sex, approximate age, approximate socioeconomic status, and so on. Obviously you will not be able to determine any of these characteristics (including sex) for certain but you can make approximations.

3. The Behaviors

What is it that the people you are watching (observing) do in the course of their interactions? Is there a standard pattern of behavior that each one presents as they interact with each other? For example, does the ticket taker in the movie theater always say thank you when returning the ticket stubs to the patrons or does he or she say nothing?

---

[4] See also on this subject, Selltiz et al. (1976:272 ff).

Is the behavior that you are observing primarily social or is it primarily nonsocial? Is the behavior that you are observing all of the same type or are there different types of behaviors depending on what the client requests? For example, does a waitress always put a glass of water down in front of a customer before he or she orders or does the presence of a glass of water depend on the size of the order? Does the waitress follow a different route around the restaurant if the customer orders coffee and a roll than if the customer orders a full meal?

4. Length, Amount, and Frequency

Are all the cycles of behavior that you observed of the same length? Are certain cycles longer or shorter than others, and if they are, why do you suppose they might be? For the ticket taker in the movie theater, the cycles will probably be about the same length for each customer. The only variation ought to occur when the person requesting the tickets (or presenting the tickets at the door) has more than one or two tickets to give. In this case, it may take longer to separate the tickets into halves. (There will also be longer interactions with people who have questions than with people who do not.) For the waitress or waiter, on the other hand, the duration of the cycle of behavior will vary depending on what the customer orders—from a mere cup of coffee to a full-course meal.

On the subject of time and duration of the behavior in question, you will be well advised to define for yourself and for your readers what you mean by "cycles of behavior." When we speak of cycles we normally mean a sequence of behavioral patterns that goes from a beginning to a middle to an end and then begins again. Thus, the days of the week occur in cycles; that is, they have a beginning (midnight) a middle (noon) and an end (midnight) with another day following. A behavioral cycle might be a waitress first asking a customer what he or she would like, through the getting of the utensils and the water, calling the order to the kitchen, bringing the order to the table, and finally presenting the check to the customer. The next cycle begins with the asking of the next customer what he or she would like. In such a situation, of course, there is a strong likelihood that the cycles will overlap so that the researcher must observe carefully in order to be able to separate the various cycles and their patterns. However you define "cycle," you must remain consistent throughout the research project.

5. Reason for Existence

While not absolutely necessary to include, it may be that you will want to note the reason for the existence of this particular type of interaction and spell out clearly why it exists. There may be a difference between the reason why people interact in a theater and why people interact in a bus terminal. While the actions of the two ticket sellers may appear *on the surface* to be completely similar, there may, because of the different requirements of the jobs, be some deeper differences that need to be explained. For example, it may perhaps be that the interaction of the persons with the ticket seller at the bus terminal may be more personal since there are decisions that have to be made in consultation with the seller, such as what to do with the luggage, what is the best route to take, and what overnight accommodations there might be. With the ticket seller in the theater, on the other hand, the only decision that might conceivably be made is whether your date will pay his or her own way or whether you will "pick up the tab."

While you note the reason for the existence of the interactions between the participants you may also want to make some guesses about the course of these interactions. How might interactions between particular participants occur; that is, will interactions between persons of varying social statuses differ from interactions between persons of the same social status? Such guesses about the direction and the nature of the participations in the interactions are actually your research hypotheses that will guide you in your research.[5]

In a slightly different context, Lofland (1971:40 ff) presents a series of suggestions for the researcher interested in cycles of interaction. In his discussions of the qualitative analysis of situations, Lofland presents a series of ideas that a researcher would do well to keep in mind. Lofland indicates that an "observer-analyst" should be aware of the following questions:

1. What member-developed and designated static patterns of participation are found in this social setting?
2. What static patterns of participation may I, as observer, reasonably articulate or construct on the basis of member activities I observe?
3. What phases or stages of participation are either already designated by participants here or might I as observer articulate and construct?
4. What cycles of participation might exist among the participants of this setting?
5. What types of standing . . . relationships exist among participants of this setting?
6. What phases do various kinds of relationships go through among participants in this setting?
7. What kinds of cycles do the relationships in this setting display?
8. Of what more general conception might this setting be an example? What type of setting is this?
9. If more than one setting is under observation, or the setting contains subsettings, what varying patterns do these settings display?
10. Through what stages, phases, or periods has this setting passed?
11. Through what cycles might this setting itself be passing?

---

[5] We will have more to say on this subject below.

By examining participants, relationships and settings, Lofland ends up at a point similar to ours. He is concerned with examining the total relationship in this particular setting and at this particular point in time. In addition, Lofland is dealing with the possibility that this set of cycles that he is observing may be part of a larger set of cycles and thus worthy of observation for that reason alone.

As a general rule, we might suggest that you design your field notes so that they can be as inconspicuous as possible (the reason for this will be made apparent in a moment). If you take a small pad of paper and divide it down the middle, you can separate the verbal transactions of the participants more easily. For example, if you are observing a ticket seller at a movie theater and a young person buying tickets for him and his date, your notes might look like the following:

Ticket Seller	*Customers*
	Couple (man and woman) approach ticket seller. Man dressed in sport coat and tie, mid-length hair, clean-shaven, between 16–20 years of age. Woman dressed in pants suit, long, straight hair, no apparent makeup, between 16–20 years in age.
"How many please?"	
	"Two please."
"That will be $4.50." Seller pushes buttons which eject tickets.	
	Man hands ticket seller $5 as he takes tickets from counter.
"Your change is $0.50."	
	"Thank you. Can you tell me when the next show starts?"
"It starts in 15 minutes."	
	"Thank you." Couple departs and enters theater.

Had you taken your notes on a large yellow pad or with a clipboard, the participants in the interaction would (might?) have noticed you and consequently changed their behavior. If they see someone observing them, it is not unusual for human beings to alter normal behavior patterns. For example, in an examination, students normally exaggerate their attempts to appear as if they are not looking on another student's papers. Even when they are not trying to glean information from another's paper, students exaggerate their appearances by looking up at the ceiling rather than looking around. When students know the instructor is watching them, they alter their behavior. The same is generally true of people being watched in other circumstances also.

Because watching people may cause them to alter their behaviors, it is important that you make a decision before you go out to observe. The decision is basic to any observational research and the main question is: Do you tell the persons you are observing them or do you remain an unknown observer? The way you answer the question has numerous implications for your research. As suggested above, whether you are open or concealed may make a difference in how your subjects act in your presence. The problem is more acute if you are an unknown observer, however. For example, suppose that you are watching a waitress in a restaurant and you see a busboy taking a tip meant for the waitress. What do you do? Another example would be observing a ticket taker in a movie theater allowing more than one person to enter the theater on a single ticket. Such behavior on the part of the ticket taker is clearly in violation of the organizational rules and regulations (as well as possibly being in violation of a law), so what would you as an observer do?

There are no easy and straightforward answers to the question just posed. What you do about violations of the law in your presence is clearly up to you. While it might be your legal duty to report violations of the law, it is possible that you have been discovered as an observer and you are being tested to see who (and what) you really are. For example, when I was conducting a study of truck drivers (Runcie, 1971), it became clear to me that I was not immediately accepted by the drivers. I always introduced myself as someone who was writing a book about truck drivers and also showed the drivers letters from company and union officials. While I thought that such credentials would be sufficient to get me accepted, such was not always the case. In fact, I was tested to see if I was a spy for the company or for the union. In one case I was told some information by a driver I was riding with that, if it had been true, could have gotten him a suspension. As we were approaching the terminal, the driver pointed to a bent signpost that he said he had hit with his mirror one night. He said that he had simply come too close to the side of the road and "clipped" the sign with his right-side mirror. He also said that he had told no one about his accident because he would have been suspended for a few days for a "chargeable accident." I commented about reporting accidents to the company and he said it was common not to report small accidents. It was not until later that I realized that I had been tested by the driver (and no doubt by his friends also). I doubt now that there ever was an accident involving that driver at that spot. If I had reported the accident to the company they would have checked and found nothing and the drivers would have been convinced I was a company spy. As it was, I said nothing and soon found the drivers extremely open and friendly toward me.

Here we have an example of a researcher "biting his tongue" and looking the other way at what are essentially violations of company rules and state laws. At the same time, the violations may or may not have happened. Had anything been done, had the story of the violation been repeated, the research would have been finished (in more ways than one). Researchers at all times must be concerned with the situation in which they find themselves and at the same time note the consequences of all their actions. The revelation of your presence in a situation has, then, many possible consequences not all of which involve your ability to gather data. Some of the consequences require the researcher to make what amount to ethical or moral judgments about the behavior of the persons being observed. As mentioned above, no one can make the decisions about the severity of the violations except the observer on the spot. While the decision about the legality of a type of behavior does not necessarily have to be made on the spot "in the heat of battle," it will have to be made at some time. It is better to think about what you might do ahead of time than to do something foolish in the heat of the moment.

Let us for the moment assume that you have made your decision about how to be seen as you do your observation. We want to return to the transcript of the observation that we presented above. What can you tell from the proceedings? Think about the material presented and see what you can tell about the participants. Can you tell if the participants are white or black? Can you tell anything about the gestures or the facial expressions of the persons involved? What physical interaction is there between ticket seller and customer and between customer and date? The verbal interaction is well recorded (at least, we can assume that it is), but what about the other interaction?

What we are suggesting here is that the interaction between ticket seller and customer is incompletely recorded. The researcher in this particular situation took a great deal of the interaction for granted. When you are engaged in a research project that is based completely on unstructured observation it is essential that all *relevant* behavior be recorded and, in this case, it is clear that some behavior was omitted. What, for example, was the facial expression of the customer when he learned that the price for the two tickets was more than he expected? What did the ticket seller do when he had to correct the combination he pushed on his machine when he mistakenly was about to sell two half-price tickets? What was the reaction of the customer when he realized that the ticket seller was a man rather than a woman as is more normally the case?[6]

---

[6] What is your reaction to finding out that the ticket seller was a man rather than a woman? Did you question the sex of the ticket seller when you read the transcript of the interaction? If not, why not?

The suggestion that one attempt to be like a camera and record all that occurs is important to understand but difficult to accomplish in reality. What we have in mind here is that you must define for yourself before you go to do your observations what it is that you will look for and then to record as much of that behavior as possible. Such a suggestion is another way of saying that one ought to have a series of hypotheses about the behavior that he or she is going to observe. If you define for yourself a series of research questions that you feel ought to be answered by your research, you will be in a better position to observe since you will be able to exclude information that is not relevant to your hypotheses. As in any research situation, one can only hope that the hypotheses chosen for examination will actually do what you want them to and that they will alert you to the behavior that you want to observe. The definition of the hypotheses is, as we have mentioned a number of times, a significant aspect of any and all research projects and something without which no research project can either proceed or succeed. The decision as to what is relevant is based on the hypothesized relationships you feel will occur in the "real world."

Before going out to do your own unstructured observation, it might be useful to go through the following transcript of an observation and see if you can criticize it. In your review of the following, be careful to note where the observer has taken too much for granted. Note also where material that is crucial for understanding has been left out. When you observe, plan to include all relevant material (as we suggest you should) and then you will have to think of yourself as a camera and record uncritically all that you see. For the present examine the following record of an observation and criticize what another observer has done. The interaction to be described in this observation dealt with the ticket taker at the Acme movie theater in New York on April 1, 1978, from 2:00 P.M. until 2:20 P.M. and again from 7:45 P.M. until 8:00 P.M. In both cases the ticket taker was the same individual.

Ticket Taker	*Customers*
The ticket taker is an older man who appears to be in his late 50s or 60s. The man is white, is about 5 feet 2 inches tall and seems not to weigh a great deal. His hair is white (gray) and was not combed down during the period of observation. The man is dressed in what appears to be a uniform of the theater: trousers that are shiny and a blazer that is ill fitting on him.	

Ticket Taker	*Customers*

The jacket has a crest on the breast pocket with the man's name sewn above it.

The area in which the ticket taker works is small in that his movements appear to be clearly regulated. He must take tickets of the customers as they come into the theater area from the lobby area, he must deposit one half of the ticket in a large receptacle and return the other half to the customer. In addition it would appear that the ticket taker has additional duties which remove him from the ticket receptacle on occasion.

Observation at afternoon performance: 2:00 P.M. until 2:20 P.M.

	A young man about 15 years old, white with rather long and unkempt hair dressed in blue jeans, sneakers, and an army fatigue jacket. Walks to the ticket taker and hands his ticket to him.
Ticket taker takes ticket, tears it in half and returns half to the young man. Ticket taker shows no emotion during the exchange. Looks at young man and says nothing to him.	
	Two young girls, one white, the other black. White girl, about 14 years, dressed in summer dress, has long hair neatly combed. Black girl, long "Afro" hair, also in summer dress, about the same age as the first. White girl hands ticket to ticket taker. "Has the movie started yet?"
Ticket taker takes ticket, tears it in half and not looking at the girl "No, it starts in two minutes." Hands half of the ticket to customer. As girl walks away he deposits half of the ticket in the receptacle.	
	White girl: "Thank you." Black girl hands ticket to ticket taker.
Ticket taker not looking at the girl tears ticket in half and deposits	

Ticket Taker

Customers

one half, giving the other to the girl. No words are exchanged.

Three men all white and of the age of about 14–16 years. All are dressed in identical fashion: dirty blue jeans, old sneakers, and high school jackets. All have long hair that is uncombed. All have let their facial hair grow so that they appear unshaven rather than hirsute. First young man hands ticket to the ticket taker. "Has the show started yet?"

Ticket taker without looking at the youth tears ticket in half and deposits one half in the receptacle. "No."

Second man, hands ticket to the ticket taker. "Will the movie start soon?"

Ticket taker looks at youth, frowns in disgust, tears ticket in half, drops half in the receptacle, hands other half to the youth. "Yes."

Third youth, hands ticket to ticket taker. "How long before the show starts?"

Ticket taker takes ticket, tears it in half angrily, hands half to the youth and jams other half in receptacle. "I just told the others it will start in about two minutes. Can't you listen?"

Two young women, well dressed and clean. Both have skirts and sweaters under open jackets. Both are white and are about 15 years old. First girl reaches for her friend's ticket and hands both to the ticket taker.

Ticket taker takes tickets, tears them in half and hands the two stubs to the first girl. As the girls walk into the theater the ticket taker turns and stares after them, whistles, nods approvingly, and turns back toward front of theater.

Two black youths, both males, about 15–16 years old. Both are well dressed, both have long "Afros" under hats. Both are laugh-

Ticket Taker	*Customers*
	ing and talking loudly. First youth hands ticket to ticket taker.
Ticket taker looking at both young men takes ticket and tears it in half, deposits half in receptacle and hands other half to youth. No verbal exchange.	
	Second youth hands ticket to ticket taker. Looks at other male and laughs.
Ticket taker takes ticket, tears in half and deposits half in receptacle. "You have to be quiet in there. No talking or laughing during the movie."	
	Both youths look at each other and laugh. Second youth: "Right."

Observation at Evening Performance: 7:45 P.M. until 8:00 P.M.

The ticket taker appears to be in the same clothes that were worn during the afternoon. His hair has not yet been combed, nor is his appearance altered in any observable way.	
	Couple, man and woman, black, well-dressed, in their early 20s. Man hands ticket to ticket taker.
Ticket taker takes ticket, tears in half, deposits half in receptacle and returns half to customer. No verbal exchange; no nonverbal exchange.	
	Woman hands ticket to ticket taker. "Has the show started yet?"
Ticket taker tears ticket in half, drops half in the receptacle and returns other half to customer. "Yes, about one-half hour ago."	
	Woman: "The main show started a half hour ago?"
Ticket taker: "Yes." Turns to stare at couple as they walk into theater. Shakes head in a negative manner as he turns back toward front of theater.	
	Three women, white, in their early twenties or late teens. Sloppily dressed in blue jeans and army fa-

Ticket Taker	*Customers*
	tigue jackets. Hair on all is long and unkempt. First girl takes tickets from others and hands them to ticket taker. Girls continue walking.
Ticket taker takes tickets, tears them in half and drops half in the receptacle. Turns as girls walk past him. "Hey, you have to keep these with you," as he gestures with ticket stubs.	
	Third girl, turns and walks back, takes stubs: "Well, all right." Turns and walks back toward friends. Turns toward ticket taker again. "Has the movie started?"
Ticket taker: "Yes, a half hour ago."	
	Second girl: "Rats." All three then continue on into theater.
	Couple, man and woman, early twenties, white, poorly dressed. Both have long hair that is unkempt. Neither is wearing a coat, they have matching sweatshirts. Man hands ticket to ticket taker.
Ticket taker takes tickets, tears them in half, drops half in the receptacle and hands other half to the man. No verbal or nonverbal exchange.	
	Couple continues on into the theater. Couple, man and woman, late thirties or early forties, medium-well dressed. Both are well manicured and have hair in place. Man hands tickets to ticket taker. "Has the show started yet?"
Ticket taker takes tickets, tears them in half and drops one half in the receptacle. As he returns the other halves to the man, "Yes the show started about a half an hour ago, sir."	
	Woman: "I told you we had to hurry but you wouldn't listen. We're late for something again." Couple walk off unhappily into the

Ticket Taker   *Customers*

                                                        theater. Couple, man and woman,
                                                        early twenties, well dressed, well
                                                        groomed. Man hands tickets to
                                                        ticket taker.

Ticket taker takes tickets, tears
them in half and drops one half
into the receptacle. Hands the other
half to the man. No verbal exchange. No nonverbal exchange.

                                                        Couple walks on into the theater.

Observation ended at 8:00 P.M.

What can you criticize about the report of the observation that you
have just read? Is there anything that you can find that was done incorrectly? If you find nothing wrong, we suggest you read the report
again. In the report there are a number of value judgments made by
the observer that do not belong in any scientific report. There are
phrases such as "neatly combed," "dirty blue jeans," "frowns in dis-
·gust," "well-dressed," included when they should not be. Such value
judgments should not be present because they are essentially unveri-
fiable by another observer even if that observer was there at the same
time. What is "well dressed" or "neatly combed" to one observer may
not be so to another. One can, as an observer, describe the situation
and then draw conclusions but it is not legitimate to draw the conclusions without including the supporting evidence.

If the observer had described the clothing that the person was
wearing and then had drawn the conclusion that the person was well
dressed that would have been acceptable. It is an acceptable technique
because then a person reading the report could either agree or dis-
agree with the findings. In other words, if we read that a person was
wearing a double-breasted suit with a hole in one elbow, a hand-
painted tie, pants with cuffs, length of pants such that the pants
dragged on the floor, shoes that had holes in the soles, and so on, and
then read that the person was "well dressed" we might be able to dis-
agree. If all we had was the description that the person was well
dressed, we would be misled if, in fact, the clothing was as just
described.

The same sort of misleading information is involved when we read
that the ticket taker "jams other half of ticket into receptacle." While
the ticket taker may be angry it may also be that the slot at the top of
the receptable is crammed full of other ticket stubs and the only way
to get the ticket stub into it is to jam it or push it as hard as possible.

Presenting a conclusion without appropriate supporting evidence is not legitimate in an observation.[7]

As mentioned earlier, while you are doing an observation of social behavior (and before you move to an analysis of the behavior) you should be as unemotional as a camera. It is important not to intrude any of your value judgments into the record of what you see.

When you move to the analysis of the situation you observed it is then, and only then, legitimate to draw conclusions about what you saw. It is legitimate because you can then look over the record and see if you are drawing conclusions that are based on the data or whether you are drawing conclusions based on your own predispositions. In addition, drawing conclusions after you have removed yourself from the source of your observations allows you time to think about what you have done and are doing. Finally, if you include the transcript of your observations in your report, you allow your reader to draw the same conclusions and to follow your logic. In fact, you allow your reader to disagree with your conclusions if the reader feels that disagreement is warranted. What you do not do is to leave yourself open to criticisms about value judgments.

THE ANALYSIS

While we have to this point not indicated that you would be doing any analysis of the data you are collecting, we feel that you should get some idea of what you can do with data once it is collected. For this particular exercise we did not ask you to gather data with any specific research objective in mind. However, it is possible to go back over the data you have gathered and bring some meaning out of the (essentially) unordered observations.

First, you may want to distinguish between that which is purely social in your observations and that which is not. As we mentioned above, you will want to watch for both social and nonsocial behavior. Was the behavior of the ticket taker primarily social or nonsocial (note we did not say antisocial)? Was the behavior social even when the ticket taker failed to look at or otherwise interact with the customers? It is possible, depending on how you answer the two questions, to begin to categorize the behavior of the ticket taker: you can count the number of times the ticket taker acted in a social manner and the number of times the ticket taker acted in a nonsocial manner.

The observational record also carefully indicates the number of times that the ticket taker refused to engage in verbal interaction with

---

[7] Go back through the record of the observation and find all the examples of value judgments made by the observer. Are there other errors in the record?

the customers. What types of customers did the ticket taker verbally interact with? What types of customers did he not verbally interact with? Were there any interaction patterns that clearly emerged from the transcript? Were there any patterns that seemed to be emerging from the data?

What about the behavior of the ticket taker when taken in isolation (assuming that we can do this analytically)? What types of accommodations has the ticket taker made in his routine? Is there a routine that the ticket taker follows for all customers? For most customers? On what aspects of the routine can there be found variation? To what influences do you attribute the variations?

What should be obvious to this point is that we are asking that you begin to categorize and summarize what you have observed. As you work through the exercise for this chapter, begin to think in terms of how you might put the data you are gathering into some form for analysis after you have finished. It is always a good idea to be thinking of the analysis stage as you are gathering the data.

Observation of
Social Behavior
in a Large Area

THE PROBLEM

Observe a relatively large area in which various types of social behavior are occurring simultaneously. The "large area" could be an area such as a shopping center. The time period for the observation should be of such duration that you can see regularities in behavior patterns. Record all that you see. Include in the report of your research, your field notes, analyses, and conclusions.

THE APPROACH

In the last chapter your assignment was to begin to sharpen your observational skills by looking at what was essentially a single person's behavior with the behavior of others impinging on it. Thus, your observation of a ticket taker in a theater examined a role player as the incumbent of that role interacted with other persons. In that particular situation we were mostly concerned with small-scale behavior patterns. By small scale, we meant small both in terms of the number of participants and also in the amount of physical space involved.

In the problem for this chapter, we want you to be concerned with social behavior patterns that occur in a large physical area and which potentially involve multitudes of people. One of the differences between this problem and the previous one is that in this particular setting you will be one of the interactants. Rather than being able to define yourself as part of the background as you did when examining the short cycles of interaction, in this approach, you will be both observing behavior and also, no doubt, causing some of this behavior simply by your presence in the scene.

In the problem for this chapter, a certain amount of interaction will be inevitable between the researcher and the subjects. It would be almost impossible to meander through a shopping mall without coming in contact (both figuratively and literally) with other persons. In addition, should the researcher decide to do a few small "experiments," it would be impossible for interaction not to take place. Consequently, the observer-as-participant will interact with the others in the social situation but will not have interaction as the main aspect of the research. It is not the participation but, rather, the observation that should be uppermost in the mind of the researcher at this point. In other words, while you will, no doubt, be interacting with other persons in the social situation, your primary occupation should be that of the trained observer who happens to be present during the behaviors in question.

The observer-as-participant must always keep in mind that his or her main task is the observation of the social behavior in the social situation and that a secondary task is to interact with the persons in the situation. While it is relatively easy to conceptualize such a distinction, in the real world of research the distinction is hard to render a workable one. As an observer-as-participant we do not feel that you should remove yourself totally from the interaction with the participants in the field situation although the observational aspects of the role are the most important. On the other hand, you also do not want to involve yourself to the extent that a complete participant would. The researcher in the observer-as-participant role has a fine line of distinction to draw: How much, and how little, interaction to allow between the researcher and the informants?

As in the problem that required you to be primarily an observer in a field situation, in this one also we want you to try to categorize the behavior that you observe. One of the first questions that comes to mind is: What possible kinds of social behavior might be seen in a shopping mall or other large area in which people are found? Our initial reply, that is at once too inclusive and also too general, is that most of the behavior of the persons you will see is social behavior.

What, for example, is not social behavior that is being done in the shopping mall? Is walking around the mall with the family a social behavior? Is sitting on benches and observing the other shoppers social behavior? Is staring in windows at displays social behavior? What about all those aspects of behavior that we normally think of as social: shopping, bargaining, courting, meeting old friends, and so on? While the latter group of behaviors is more clearly *social* behavior, it should be obvious that all the behavior described may be, and probably is, *social* behavior.

For example, when a person moves about in a crowd, he or she will normally maintain a physical area about his or her person into which other persons are not allowed to intrude. In our society, we normally keep approximately a three-foot diameter circle around us within which we feel secure and into which we let only our closest friends and acquaintances. What occurs as you watch people walking through the mall? Do the people try to maintain the personal bubble of space (see Hall, 1966:112) or do they decrease the size of the bubble knowing they are in crowded conditions? How hard do people work to keep others from infringing on the areas mapped out as their own? It would appear that since the areas people mark out as their own move with them as they move, so, the little bubble moves with them as they traverse the mall. (On this subject see also the relevant material in Chapter 3.)

The subject of the personal bubble of space has triggered a number of studies in recent years. One study, particularly relevant to the present problem, examined the spacing of persons in large areas. Edney and Jordan-Edney (1974:92) had as their main concerns in the research "to see how naturally occurring groups of different size and composition claimed territory and shared this type of unstructured space with others." Although the authors were dealing with the behavior of persons on a large public beach, the claims to personal territory in any large area are similar. The findings from the study indicate that women tend to claim smaller territories than men and that as the group grew in size, it did not necessarily increase the size of the territory in which it was found but rather increased the density among the members; that is, more members were packed into the same area. In terms of the study of the shopping mall, one could check to see if women claim smaller territories than men. In addition, one could see if groups increase the size of their territories as members are added or if they increase the density of the members. We know what happens on a public beach. Does the same type of behavior occur in other large, public areas? Would such behavior be found in other societies as it is found in ours?

As the students of proxemics[1] (see Hall, 1959, 1966; Sommer, 1969, 1974) argue, our conception of the personal bubble of space and the entire manner in which we deal with the concept of space are built into us by our cultures during the socialization period. In other words, we

---

[1] The subject area is also referred to as "kinesics" by some analysts. On this subject; see Birdwhistle (1970).

have little or no option in deciding how to structure the bubble or area that surrounds us. The area that surrounds us is there because the culture (as personified by our socializers) demands that we have one. Because the bubble around us is the result of the influence of our culture (as is the entire manner way in which we treat space) it must, by definition, be social.

One of the best summaries of the various studies of social space that have been done is Ball's (1973) work on microecology. In addition to presenting an extensive bibliography of studies utilizing the microecological approach, Ball also subdivides the field into three areas. The first he labels the *microgeographical* which is composed of (1973:3) ". . . distributional studies and prototheoretical statements of Robert Sommer and his colleagues." The second area Ball (1973:3) refers to as *proxemics*, which is composed of the "space-as-communication orientation of Edward T. Hall." Finally, Ball (1973:3) points to the tradition of *kinesics*, which is the ". . . movement-of-the-body-as-communication tradition. . . ." Whatever else the three areas deal with, according to Ball (1973:3) they all deal with ". . . *the spacing and positioning of persons qua physical bodies as well as social actors.* . . ." (emphasis in the original). Ball's work is especially interesting because it classifies the various studies into subject matter areas demonstrating the very similar nature of the approaches even when the studies seem to differ so greatly on the surface. One of the most interesting aspects of the field is that it is developing at such a rapid rate. New books on the subject of social space are being published at a fantastic pace. Altman (1975) examines the areas of privacy, personal space, territory and crowding in an attempt to present an overview of the environment and behavior field of study. Speier (1973) has presented a research text on the observation of face-to-face communication. We will return to the subject of space and human behavior throughout this book (see especially Chapters 3, 5, 10, and 11).

Because the culture determines what type and what size the bubble of space around us will be, it might also be of interest to examine the different ways in which people of apparently different ethnic or racial backgrounds treat this space. For example, can you, by observing the participants in the shopping mall, first, make a guess about their ethnic or racial backgrounds,[2] and second, suggest how different cultures or subcultures allow different distances between people? Do people of European descent allow people to come closer to them than do people of Middle Eastern descent? Do the Latin Americans move in closer to other people than the Germans? Do whites allow more space intrusion than nonwhites?

---

[2] You might, of course, first observe their treatment of space around themselves and then you might ask them a few questions, including a question designed to determine their ethnic backgrounds.

By adding the notion of race or ethnic background, we have simply added another variable to the list of those aspects of behavior being observed. In other words, we have subdivided the population of persons who frequent shopping malls by including another dimension of behavior. Rather than examining isolated instances of social behavior, by including additional variables we are cross-classifying the behavior and thus moving closer to an understanding of it. If those who are white maintain a larger bubble, this fact will also imply that they do not like others to approach them as closely as the nonwhites do. Thus, a certain amount of social distance would be maintained even in crowded situations. The next question, of course, is why they might attempt to keep this social distance about themselves at all times. Such questioning, while a part of any research enterprise, is somewhat beyond the scope of the problem as outlined here, although we will have more to say on the subject later.

A problem that surfaces at this point concerns the recording of the data that you are gathering on the behavior being observed. Your decision on the means for recording the data may possibly determine what data you will get. For example, a person who knows he or she is being observed may alter the normal behavior pattern (such as shoplifting) to appear to be something that he or she is not (law-abiding). If you are concerned with recording only the race and the size of the personal bubble of space, as in the example above, you may want to have only a checklist and put a check mark next to each category that you see. Thus, a white person with a small bubble of space will get a single check mark as will a black person with a large bubble of space. When your observation is over all that you will have to do is create a table and fill in the numbers. Should your observations be overt, some of those persons in the mall may change their behaviors; thus, you may want to do covert observations. If you choose to be a covert observer you will either have to find a means for recording the behavior on the spot that is not obvious, or you will have to find a means for leaving the scene to record the behavior. You might also choose to wait until you get home and then write down all that you can remember. As you will see, any decision that you make will affect both your data and your data gathering.

No matter what people in a shopping mall do to defend their personal spaces (and even if they do nothing), they are reacting socially to a situation. Because the people are reacting socially to the situation, their behavior becomes a subject for study by the social scientist. Because the behavior is social, it is behavior that you should be concerned with. Thus, even though aspects of behavior in the shopping mall seem less than social (for example, that of maintaining territorial integrity), they end up being, on closer observation, social and thus amenable to analysis.

While we are on the subject of the individual's use of space and the protection of the space around that person, it might be useful to extrapolate to the traffic patterns that might be observed. Imagine that you have observed behavior in a mall that is designed as shown in the schematic diagram in Figure 4–1.

As you may realize, there will be definite traffic patterns that will show up as you observe behavior in a mall. In fact, there will probably be a pattern that approximates that which Americans show when they are driving their cars. That is, shoppers generally will move from east to west along the northern corridor (in Figure 4–1) and will move from west to east along the southern corridor. As shoppers enter the mall through the main entrance, they will tend to walk along the west wall as they come in. At the same time, however, there will also be a number of people who will not follow the general pattern. There will, in other words, be deviants who do not follow the (unwritten) rules about the behaviors of the walkers. To take the title of a book by Kaufman (1964) and apply it here, there will always be persons who walk "up the down staircase." Now look again at Figure 4–1. The straight dashed lines indicate the more "normal" patterns of walking in a mall, while the others show what might be called a "deviant" pattern. Having someone "cut across" your line of walking may be a normal occurrence, but can it be considered "normal"?

The question of interest for us here might be, what do the persons who are walking in the "correct" manner do when they confront someone who is not doing things according to the rules? Are sanctions applied to those persons considered "deviant" by other shoppers? Who is it that defines what is or is not "deviant"? Is the "deviant" guilty of invading another's bubble of space and/or is the "deviant" guilty of breaking the traffic laws? As you hopefully realize, all the questions just asked relate to social situations and thus are situations that you, as an observer, should be interested in.

You might want to try some "experiments" or tests to see if you can discover what the unwritten rules are about traffic patterns in the mall. While you are observing, you might, for example, first locate and identify the accepted traffic patterns in the mall. Second, you could draw a diagram of the mall and indicate the accepted traffic patterns. Third, you could also examine what happens to deviants in this mall. Is there a secondary pattern of acceptable traffic patterns in the mall which while somewhat deviant is not sanctioned? What happens to the people who are "caught" walking in these secondary patterns? What happens to those persons who are so deviant that they are not accepted at all? What happens when, for example, people walk against the traffic ignoring those persons about them? Are they bumped and shoved? Are the deviants "cussed at" by those persons who meet them?

FIGURE 4–1
Diagram of Shopping Mall

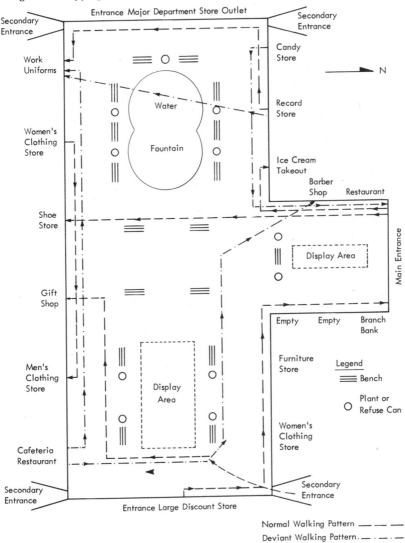

Normal Walking Pattern _ _ _ _
Deviant Walking Pattern _ . _ . _

acceptable crossing? What about the person who, in the mall diagrammed in Figure 4–1, walks from the record store directly across the mall to the store where work uniforms are sold (through the fountain)?

The final points to be made in a discussion of the approach to the research problem deal with the extent to which the observer in the social situation can be allowed to intervene or interact with participants in the situation. Remember that this problem is designed to deal with your role as observer-as-participant. We noted at the outset that you should attempt to remain outside the action as much as possible, maintaining the objectivity of the scientific observer. At the same time, since you are obviously a participant in the situation, you will, of necessity, be part of that social situation. Because of the dual nature of the role, there will be a certain amount of interaction between yourself as observer and the people you encounter in the situation. As mentioned above, it may be necessary for you to ask questions of the participants in the situation if you are to get a clear picture of what is going on. You might, as noted earlier, need to know the ethnic status of participants in the situation in order to determine why the people do what they do. However, as a social scientist you are not limited to asking only questions about the socioeconomic background of the participants. You might want more information from some of the people you see in the shopping center so that you would have an even more extensive picture of the reasons behind their behavior. You might want information on all aspects of their backgrounds such as race, age, sex, and religion. In addition, you might want information on why they came to this particular mall to shop, what they thought about this particular mall, what they liked or disliked about the design of this mall, and so on. You might also want to ask them general questions dealing with attitudes toward, for example, the concept of decentralized shopping areas and the impact on shopping habits of the creation of many multipurpose or single-purpose shopping malls.

As a final step you might want to see if you could change the behavior of persons in the mall by creating an altered situation of your own. While it might not be prudent for you to copy a true experimental design, you might want to see if there were actions that you could take that would change the patterns. There are many possible situations that you could devise to examine the social interactions of the participants in the mall situation.

One test, for example, would be to see if people in dyads (two persons together) would attempt to protect an area that encompasses both or if they each would attempt to protect their own areas.[3] If two people were walking toward you, would they split up as you attempted to go between them or would they both move to one side or the other? Could you subdivide the dyad by encroaching on their space or would they stay together?

Another way of testing social behavior would be to "cut across" the traditional paths of human travel within the mall. After determining

---

[3] On this subject, see Knowles (1972). The journal in which this article is printed, *Environment and Behavior*, publishes numerous articles which deal with the question of personal space and subsequent behavior. The journal is well-worth looking through for ideas for this project.

the "normal" paths taken by shoppers, one could see what happens when these traditional paths are ignored. If all travel is on the right side of the corridor in one direction and on the left side of the corridor in the other, simply cut in front of people to see what their reactions are. Do people ignore you? Do they suggest that you are in error? Do they tell you what they believe the norms to be in this particular subject area? What do they do?

The choice of the types of mini-experimentation or testing to do in this particular problem is totally up to you. You might choose to do no testing at all and simply be a member of the statistical group labeled "shoppers" and observe what the others in this statistical category also do. On the other hand, you may choose to orient your entire research project to testing one, two, or many hypotheses through the use of experiments. Whatever you decide to do, your choice should be carefully tied in with the discussion in the following section of this chapter, that of the analysis.

While some might argue that the inclusion of "experimentation" into an observational research project is out of place, we do not feel that it is. We feel that the experimentation can be an extremely useful tool for the student in learning what sort of behavior there is in any social situation that might normally be taken for granted. While the experimentation takes the research away from the more purely observational, and while the questioning of participants takes the research away from the more clearly observational, we see it as useful in that these are means for sensitizing the novice researcher to subtle situations that he or she might normally take for granted. In a different context (doctoral research, for example), such alterations in "normal" research behavior might be considered out of place and demand extensive explanation in the report stage. In the problem for this chapter, however, the experimentation and the questioning are used (hopefully) as a means for showing what is happening in the situation being observed.

THE ANALYSIS

In Chapter 3, we indicated that our primary goal for you in your observation of behavior was simply to get a feel for what the observer does and what it "feels like" to be an observer. In the present situation, we want you to become a bit more sophisticated and begin not only to categorize the behavior under observation but also to begin to quantify the behavior in the various categories that you set up.

In order to quantify the behavior that you observe, it is necessary that you design some categories for that behavior before you ever begin to do your observation. In other words, you will need to design some categories into which you can put your observational data *before you ever enter the shopping mall to do your observations.* Before you actually observe behavior you will need to make some educated guesses about what you think you will see.

Whether you begin your study with some grand theoretical scheme or whether you simply have some educated hunches about behavior in shopping centers, you will be able to guess what you will see once you get there. By utilizing educated guesses about outcomes in planning your research you are doing two things to your results: (1) you are making it easier once you begin to observe by already having the categories into which you will place the data as you gather it, and (2) you are predetermining your results, although not their magnitude.

In the first instance, by presetting your categories, you are saying that you do not wish to do a post facto analysis. That is, you want to be prepared to categorize data while you are in the field rather than having to do it when you have finished the field phase of your research project. In addition, by predetermining your categories, you are also calculating what effects which variables will have on which other variables. You are, in other words, creating hypotheses that you will be able to test. For example, if you are of the opinion that ethnicity will make a difference in how persons will react to invasions of personal space, you are suggesting a causal relationship (ethnicity leads to differential reactions to space invasion) between the two while at the same time suggesting two areas in which you will need to gather data.

In terms of the second influence on your research mentioned above —that of predetermining your results—by setting your categories ahead of time you are limiting the types of data that you will gather. Once your categories are finalized, the data that you will gather is also finalized and made finite. Thus, if you go into the field to gather data with 10 categories or areas that you feel you will be able to put data into, you will not be able (unless you are extremely lucky) to get back to the office or department and find 15 categories that you can use. You will be limited in what you can say about the shopping center data because you have limited the data that you gathered by predetermining the categories you are interested in.[4]

While it is not impossible to add categories to your data once you are doing the research, such additions can get somewhat "messy." For example, if once you arrive at the shopping center you realize that you left out some important categories, it may be possible to add them at that point without biasing the project. However, if you have already gathered data on a number of persons before you realize your omis-

---

[4] We will have more to say on this subject in Chapter 6.

sion, you will have to either deal with the first data as cases in which this particular information was not available (an assumption that may not be true), or you will have to go back to the persons and ask them new questions, or you will have to throw out the responses of the earliest subjects and seek more persons using all the questions. Consequently, should you happen to forget some important aspects of data (and we all do that once in a while) that you need to gather, all is not necessarily lost for you. The extent of your problem will be directly related to the severity of the omission.

A relatively easy means for categorizing behavior in a shopping center would be to count the number of persons in various racial categories, as was suggested earlier. Once the persons were categorized according to race they could then be categorized according to the size of the personal bubble of space they maintained during the traverse of the mall. The analysis of such data could proceed relatively easily by then constructing a table into which the information could be put. You could, for example, design a table such as the following:

	Bubble Size	
	---	---
Race	*Large Bubble**	*Small Bubble**
White†		
Nonwhite†		

* The terms large and small bubble may be defined in any way that seems reasonable either on the basis of your own knowledge or on the basis of some study or theory that you have read.
† The terms white and nonwhite will also have to be defined before they can be made meaningful for the analysis.

Assuming that you had counted people as they walked through the mall, and that you had some hypothesis about the relationship between the variables, you could now put the numbers into the appropriate spots (cells) in the table and then show how the data either conform to your hypothesis or they do not. A short textual commentary combined with the presentation of the results in the table should be sufficient.

Another possible means for dealing with the shopping center data would be to count the number of persons in various (general) age categories. If you were to design categories that were sufficiently wide, or general, so that you could with some ease place persons in them without questioning, you could test the hypothesis that different age groups will frequent shopping malls at different hours of the day. You might argue that such an hypothesis is simply stating the obvious, but is it really? Are the aged ever the predominant numbers in the population of shopping centers? If you say yes, when is this a true statement; that is, at what hours are the aged in the majority in terms of numbers? Are teen-agers (however, you might define such a category) ever in the majority? At what hours are teen-agers in the majority should your research discover that they are?

Given the hypothesis just mentioned (age groups will differ in the hours they frequent a shopping mall), it will be relatively simple to examine this assertion. First, it is necessary to design a set of general age categories to take account of all persons who frequent the mall. Such a categorization might be: Children (ages 0–12); teenagers (ages 13–20); young adults (21–40); older adults (41–65); elderly (65 and over). Such a series of age categories, while sufficiently general, may still give a few problems to the researcher. A precocious 12-year-old may be misplaced into the teen-age category and a particularly young-looking 70-year-old may be placed in the older adult category but generally there will be consensus on the categories into which subjects should be put. On the other side of our data, it is relatively easy to determine what time of the day (or night) it is. We might subdivide the day as: morning (before 12:00 A.M.); early afternoon (12:00–4:00 P.M.); evening (4:00–7:00 P.M.); night (after 7:00 P.M.). Once we have decided on the categories, we could go to a mall probably more than once and probably on different days (weekdays and weekends) and count the people who were in the mall at the different hours.

As a means for analyzing the data we could build a classification scheme and code our observations into it. We could use either actual numbers of people or we could take all those persons we counted, as a base, and then show our data in percentages. We could set up a table in the analysis which might show, for one day's observations, the following:

		Hours		
Age Groups	Morning	Early Afternoon	Evening	Night
Children	15%	15%	5%	22%
Teen-agers	10	20	40	18
Young adults	35	15	30	25
Older adults	25	15	15	20
Elderly	15	35	10	15
Total*	100	100	100	100

* Total of persons in each group equals 100 due to sample design. The sample was designed so that the first 100 persons walking past the observer stationed at a central point in the mall, would be counted. The times used were at approximately the middle of the appropriate time intervals. Findings are hypothetical.

The data in the table for this particular day show the elderly clearly predominate at the mall during the early afternoon hours. During the evening hours, on the other hand, the teen-agers are clearly the largest subpopulation represented among the frequenters of the mall. In the morning, it is the young adults with their children who are seen to be the most represented. Finally, we note that at night the groups are almost equally divided in terms of their proportion in the population who visit the mall.

Assuming that our data was reconfirmed in later (additional) visits to the mall, we might conclude that young adults bring their children when they do their shopping and that generally they do their shopping in the early hours of the day. In the afternoon, the younger people are replaced by the elderly who come to the mall because it provides an ambient atmosphere all year around, and they are able to sit on benches without being forced to fight the elements. In the early evening the population again changes: this time the teen-agers who have gotten out of school come to use the mall as an indoor courting arena where they can see and be seen. Finally, we might suggest that at night the mix becomes a more general one as persons set out to look through the various stores and to do some "serious" shopping.[5]

Clearly, a number of different types of research are possible on a large area such as a shopping mall. The research reported here is only one of the many ways in which sociologists can bring their approaches to a study of what others take for granted—behavior in public places.[6] We suggest that in your preparation for doing the research project for this chapter, you not only prepare yourself to go to the mall for the observation, but that you also set up some hypotheses to test and to see if you can set up categories into which you can classify the behavior that you see.

---

[5] While we do not suggest that this model necessarily represents what would be found at all shopping centers, it has been a consistent finding in and around the Flint, Michigan, area. It would be interesting to have other researchers examine shopping centers in other areas of the country to see if the pattern is repeated.

[6] See on this subject, Goffman's book by the same name (1963).

5

Participant Observation of a Small Group

THE PROBLEM

Conduct a participant observation of some group of which you are a member. The group to be observed should be one in which you interact frequently and in which you are a "member in good standing." Try to observe in such a manner that you cover the entire period of one of the group's meetings (preferably of one to two hours' duration). In your report include your analysis of the group situation as well as any field notes that you may have made.

THE APPROACH

Chapters 3 and 4 were designed to introduce you to the concept of observation. In Chapter 3, we suggested that you observe without any interaction. In Chapter 4, we asked you to observe with some interaction but as little as possible. In this chapter we want you to observe a group that is in action *and* in which your input is important. Rather than being a bystander, we want you to be a member of the group under observation and to report what happens as you both observe *and* interact with the participants.

For the moment, let us return to Chapter 3 and review the material we dealt with in discussing the various roles that a social observer might play in a social situation. The role we are most concerned with here is that labeled "participant-as-observer." As mentioned, in this particular observational posture, a most important aspect is the participation of the observer in the actions of the group. While we do not want you to lose your observer's status in the group, at the same time you will be part of the group, indulging in its actions and possibly even causing some of the actions of the group you are studying.

One of the first decisions you will have to make when you begin this project (and, in fact, any participant-observation project) is to decide whether you will reveal who you are and what you are doing. Earlier, in Chapter 3, we indicated the importance of such a decision for the purely observational research project. In a participant-observation study, however, the decision as to whether or not to reveal the nature of the research (or the fact that research is going on at all) is even more crucial. The primary reason for the increased number of questions associated with the hidden, or concealed, participant-observer occurs because the observer can alter the situation by his or her actions. The situation is similar to what has been called "entrapment" by the legal authorities. In a situation where there is entrapment, a law officer or other person leads another person to commit a crime or other deviant act, and then proceeds to arrest the person for committing the act. It is possible that the vice squads of our police departments entrap persons into the commission of the "crimes without victims" that we hear so much about such as homosexuality, prostitution, and the like.

The problem is not so much whether or not a "deviant act" has occurred but whether the observer caused an act which would not have happened otherwise. In a large midwestern city not long ago, a number of persons were arrested and charged with breaking into a national guard armory and making off with a number of military weapons. The local prosecutor was prepared to bring the case to trial, when it was surprisingly dropped. It soon became known that of the four men arrested, at least two and possibly three were agents of the police and there were (apparently) substantial questions of the entrapping of the fourth man involved. Again, the question is: Would the deviance have been committed had the law enforcement officers not aided, abetted, and led the others to the deviant act?

The participant-as-observer has the same problem as the law enforcement people in the above examples, especially, if the identity of the researcher is not known to the subjects. A number of years ago, I was working in a chemical plant in the period between college and graduate school. Because I was a college graduate and because I seemed able to handle the work, I was placed in charge of the supply room for the plant while the regular storeroom supervisor was on vacation. The stock room, or storeroom, was centrally located both physically and psychologically. Most of the employees made it a point to come to the stock room at least once during the course of the day to say hello and to talk about what was happening in other areas of the plant. In addition to being responsible for the stock room, I was also informally responsible for the dissemination of news about the plant. During my tenure in the stock room, the company was bargaining with the union of which I was a member. Each afternoon, the bargaining committee of the union would stop by after the bargaining session to talk about what had gone on. The members of the committee knew that I was a college graduate (probably the only one among the 300 or so union members in the plant at the time) and it appeared that they wanted my opinion about what they were doing. I was asked, among other questions, if I thought there should be a strike over the issues as they stood.

It is at this point that the more mature social scientist must enter and mention that here again is the core of the ethical question. Should I tell the other workers that I was observing what was going on and thus should not be included in the deliberations? Should I have offered the opinion that the workers should go out on strike so that I could watch what happened in a strike? What should the participant observer do in a situation such as the one just described? What I finally decided to do (and it may not have been the best decision under the circumstances) was to offer my advice in terms of what was being bargained for, what they might want to bargain for, and so on. What I did not do was attempt any social experiments such as finding out how workers react to strike situations. What I also did not do was tell the men I was working with that I was observing them.

The last decision was made (and it was this decision whose logic I questioned) in this way because it was not my primary purpose to be an observer in this particular situation. I was working at this plant mainly for the money and secondarily for any sociological information I might gather. I felt that revealing my alter ego would forestall any further real participation with my fellow workers and consequently I would have had an extremely boring and tenuous existence. I was, in other words, a worker first and a sociologist second. Had the important roles been reversed, however, I probably would have indicated who and what I was.

In any participant-observation research, the scientist has the opportunity to manipulate the behavior in the situation to fit whatever ends the scientist might have in mind. A word here or a gesture in another spot in the conversation can alter the direction the group might take. Whether the scientist alters the group on purpose or by accident, the change still occurs. In the case of the chemical factory, the possibility of major alterations in the existing situation in the plant was enormous.[1] To what extent can we, as social scientists, involve ourselves in research projects and then influence their results? Obviously, we should not attempt to alter the results but we should "flow" with events and follow what happens. But, what happens when we are asked our opinions of the "flow" of events? What does one do then? Hopefully, the objective social scientist will intrude his or her opinions as little as possble into the group's deliberations. Experimentation on or alteration of the processes taking place in the group being observed in order to cause the desired changes is (at least in our opinion) somewhat less than wholly ethical.

The long digression has been included not to show that sociologists can get out and work for a living, but rather to indicate some of the ethical dilemmas that one can get into when doing participant observation. In general, it would seem best to indicate who you are and what you are doing in that particular setting, rather than trying to hide and pretend to be something you are not. While some people may be upset with your presence in the situation, it is also the case that most people will soon forget that you are there and very shortly begin to act "naturally." By telling them that you are observing them in order to (a) write a book about them, (b) write an article about them, or (c) write a term paper about them, you will put them at ease and usually they will let you both participate and observe. On the other hand, if you do not tell them and they find out, your research, as well as yourself, may be finished. Consider the plight of an anthropologist who was secretly tape recording conversations during his field research. The people knew he was doing research but they did not know that he was recording every word on tape. That is, they did not know until the day the tape recorder reached the end of the reel and made a number of very loud, strange sounds. When the subjects found out about the duplicity, the anthropologist's research was almost destroyed because the people no longer trusted him. It was only by proving to the subjects that he would not do such a thing again that they let him back into the society. I might point out that our researcher was lucky here in at least two ways: (1) because his doctorate depended on this particular piece of research, he was fortunate that the subjects relented; (2) people often react strongly about being lied to and he was lucky he did not end up with a beating (at the least). Another author, Hunter Thompson, was not nearly as lucky with his subjects. Thomp-

---

[1] In this vein, the reader is invited to consider the problems of Project Camelot. Project Camelot was a study conducted by social scientists on the problems of revolution and counterinsurgency in Latin America. The project was stopped when it was found that some of the participants were helping the revolution along since it did not seem to be happening by itself. On this subject, see Sjoberg (1967: 141–161).

son (1967:277–278) was severely beaten and kicked by the Hell's Angels motorcycle gang when he displeased them while he was acting as a participant observer among them.

Before leaving the question of whether or not to reveal the purpose of your presence in the group, we should examine one additional study. The classic study of the Hawthorne plant of the Western Electric Company allows us to look into another aspect of the problems of the participant-as-observer. In the "bank wiring observation room" phase of the Hawthorne studies, Roethlisberger and Dixon (1939) describe how 14 workers were moved into a separate area of the plant so that they could be more easily observed. The men, who were employed to assemble banks of telephone equipment, soon developed an elaborate social structure among themselves. It is interesting to note here, that during the entire time of the development of this elaborate group structure, there was an observer stationed in the room. The observer stationed in the room was clearly labeled an observer from the very first moment. There was no attempt to supply a hidden observer: the men knew they were in a room to be observed and they knew which of those persons present in the room was the observer. As most students of sociology know, the workers in the bank wiring observation room, developed a group culture which, among other things, included restriction of output of finished equipment, trading jobs with others, helping other workers do their jobs, leaving the job to buy ice cream or candy, gambling, and so on. All of this behavior was clearly in violation of company rules. When the workers found that the observer would not report their deviant behavior, they began to include the observer in some of their deviances. When the workers sent out for candy or ice cream they would often ask the observer what he wanted from the store. When the men decided to bet on a horse race or other event, the observer often was asked if he wanted to put down a bet. The point, here, is that it does not take people long to forget or ignore that an observer is in the situation with them. In addition, it does not take long for the members of a group to begin to include an active participant observer in the doings of the group. Being identified as an observer in a situation is not necessarily bad.

We mentioned in Chapter 3 that one of the problems faced by the participant-as-observer was that of "going native." In the Hawthorne studies, the observer entered into some of the activities of the group and refused to enter into others. While he did nothing to stop the deviance in the bank wiring observation room, neither did the observer enter into the more blatant aspects of it. One can easily be "suckered" into becoming "one of the boys" in an interactive situation in which the participant observer finds himself or herself. One must always be careful not to become too much a member of the group being observed. As mentioned earlier, the loss of both objectivity and mobility result from going over to "the other side." When you become a member of the group you are no longer free to come and go as you please but are restricted to doing what the group says you may do. By being restricted you will or may lose the chance to see important aspects of behavior. If you are a member of the group but are not one of those normally permitted to see the "inner secrets," you will be, in fact, forbidden from seeing them. As an observer, however, you may be admitted to the inner sanctum to see these secret treasures (whatever they might be) because you are an observer and you have no emotional stake in the outcome of the rituals.

In one study I recently conducted, I chose to be an unknown participant observer, and this decision created a number of problems for the research. I was interested in learning firsthand about the workers on an automobile assembly line and, after discussing the project with the head of the plant, others from management, and the head of the local union, I was "hired" into the plant as another worker "on the line." I assumed that I could blend into the plant just as any other worker might, but I had not counted on Murphy's first law. On one of the first days I was in the plant, one of my former students recognized me, and I was forced to make up a story to tell him. I did not want to reveal who I was to him or to other workers because this might bring me "special" treatment from both workers and management and I wanted to find out what it was like to be a worker just like all the other workers. Whether the "special" treatment might have been positive or negative, I knew that I did not want it. At another point in the study, I was transferred into a new department on another part of the assembly line, and a rumor was started (by whom I am not certain although I have been told that it was the foreman) that I was from the local police narcotics squad, put in the plant to spy on the workers. When no one was arrested for using drugs, I think the other workers believed I was just another member of the work force. At another point, a foreman came up to me and asked who and what I was, saying that I did not act like the other workers and thus, I had to be someone from outside. As in the previous situation, I made up a story that seemed to satisfy him. Throughout the course of the time I spent in the plant, I constantly worried that someone would find out who and what I was and give the research away. No one did find out (that I am aware of), but I think many suspected. I should point out that, at the end of the study, I made it a point to go around to the persons I had worked with and explain what I was and the reason why I had been working in the plant. Most of the workers could not believe that I actually wanted to come to work in the plant, simply to find out what life on the assembly line was like. My experiences in the automobile plant highlight again the problems researchers have in trying to determine the type of research they will conduct. Whom do you tell you are a participant observer, and if you decide to tell someone, how much do you tell him or her?

In addition to making decisions about whether to reveal the true nature of the research and whether to be more a participant than a participant-as-observer, there are a number of practical problems to be dealt with. These problems include: How to record the data that one is getting from the other members of the scene; how to identify one or another key persons in the situation; how to transcribe field notes to be more complete after the conclusion of an observation session. All of these problems must be dealt with by the particpant-as-observer at some point. Rather than simply recounting details of what has been said in a number of other texts on research, we would like to take some time and present what happened in the study of truck drivers that has been mentioned as an example in Chapter 3. The example is somewhat extended and is included to suggest some of the preparations and techniques necessary in order to do participant-observation research. Each project will be different so the techniques discussed here may have to be adjusted to fit unique situations. We are not suggesting here *the* way to conduct participant-observation research but simply *one* way to conduct this type of research.

Because we knew it would be impossible to gather all the data on truck drivers and their occupational social relationships through the use of a questionnaire or interview, it was decided to observe actions firsthand. The participation-observation phase of the research was actually conducted in two different stages. In the first, a great deal of time was spent "hanging around" truck stops and repair garages. In the second stage, the author rode with truck drivers on trips both locally and long distance.[2]

In the first phase of the research—the "hanging around" phase—I was attempting to sharpen my initial perceptions of the occupation, its language, and its culture. In this phase, it was easiest to take the stance of the naïve observer, since that is, in truth, what I was. I was normally identified to the members of the occupation (and also to non-member intimates of those in the occupation) as a person who was writing a book about truck drivers and I told them that I wanted to learn as much about them as I could. The mechanics at one truck garage, in particular, always patiently answered my questions and let me follow them around as they repaired the trucks. In addition, these men introduced me to the drivers of the trucks and these introductions occasionally led to long and involved (although unstructured) inter-

---

[2] Although no actual count of mileage or time was made, it is estimated that about 500 hours were spent on the trips with about 3,000 miles traveled.

views often lasting several hours. At the restaurants frequented by truck drivers I was also led by the hand (often literally) to drivers and their conversations. I would be introduced by a waitress to a few drivers sitting at a table and from then on I could interview them as long as they remained at the diner. In addition, it was not unusual for me to see the same drivers again at a future time should I happen to stop in the diner at the "regular" time. The drivers already spoken to might then introduce me to other drivers and, consequently, I was able to meet a number of drivers that I might not have met otherwise. It is obvious to me, that the role of the naïve observer was the best role to have taken in this particular situation for at least two reasons: (1) it made the drivers feel important to be able to introduce me to other drivers and also to be able to tell me things I did not know, and (2) I could not have successfully "pulled off" any other role at that stage of the research. I was gathering my first impression of the occupation and I was not then knowledgeable enough to play the role of a group member (i.e., a truck driver.)[3] In the first half of the project I was more clearly an observer-as-participant since I was still naïve about many aspects of the occupation.

Once I began to ride in the trucks, I found that much of the material on participant observation from the sociological courses in research methods was not particularly applicable to the present research task. As Selltiz et al. (1959:210) point out, "The best time for recording is undoubtedly on the spot and during the event. This results in a minimum of selective bias and distortion through memory." Although such is probably the case, in the present research this method was not feasible. At the same time, it was almost impossible to memorize all that had happened and then to transcribe it later.

The suggestion of Selltiz, et al. (1959:211) on the subject of jotting down ideas is a good one. According to the authors, when it is impossible to take notes on the spot, trying to remember all the details for later transcription may cause important details to be lost:

> For such situations, it is well to acquire the habit of jotting down significant key words in an almost imperceptible manner, using a small sheet of paper, the back of an envelope, or other inconspicuous material.

Because the sharpness of both memory and details fades rapidly over time, the authors suggest (1959:211) that

> However the observer records his immediate impressions, he should write up, as soon as possible after a period of observation, a complete account of everything in the situation that he wishes to remember.

---

[3] Occasionally, however, I let the drivers define who I was for themselves, with no verbal cues from me. In these cases I was variously identified as a neophyte truck driver, an employee of the restaurant or garage, or a company spy. Before their imaginations ran too wild, however, I usually redefined myself as a writer.

The ideal method, then, is to jot down notes on a piece of paper and then at some later time transcribe them.[4] In the present situation, this time-tested method of taking notes was not totally practical. It was not practical for the simple reason that it is almost impossible to take notes in the cab of a wildly bouncing truck moving at 50 miles an hour along an old, two-lane highway. Not only is it nearly impossible to jot down the notes, but it is even more difficult to do this inconspicuously. Each time the truck would bounce, I would attempt to make my body rigid so that it would absorb the road shocks and not transfer the shocks to the pad of paper. Unfortunately, this only made matters worse. Eventually, I reached the point where I was unable to read the notes, much less read them well enough so that I could transcribe them at a later time.

I found that the only viable alternative was to accept the fact that the notes were going to be scribbled and that they might be very difficult to read at some future time. Consequently, each time something happened that I felt I wanted to remember, I made a very strong mental note of it and also made a note of it on my pad. When we eventually arrived at a place to stop, I made it a point to correct the atrocious handwriting in the note pad. In this phase of the research, it made little difference that I was taking notes: from the letter written by the president of the local union, I had already been defined as someone who was "writing a book about truck drivers." Consequently, the drivers did not seem surprised at my attempting to write while the truck was moving nor at the thought of my cutting short a coffee break so that I could get back in the truck to write notes, although the drivers did seem somewhat amused by my actions.

Originally, I had thought of using a tape recorder to record the material I thought important, both in the form of responses to my questions and also my observations of what was going on around me. I soon found that the noise of the truck was so loud that it made recording a voice, while the truck was in motion, an impossibility.[5] I did find, however, that it was worthwhile taking my tape recorder along with me on the trips. At the end of 10 to 14 hours on the road, it was much easier to record my observations into the tape recorder than it would have been to transcribe them onto paper at that hour.[6]

The method I finally evolved for this phase of the participant observation was as follows: while riding, I made rough notes and transcribed

[4] See also the discussion in the third edition. Selltiz, et al. (1976:269 ff).

[5] The noise also made conversation very difficult—with shouts, repetitions, and gestures; however, this difficulty was overcome.

[6] The tape recorder was also useful during the "hanging around" phase: I used it after leaving a restaurant to add to my brief notes. I also used it for dictation in the car on the way home after leaving the restaurant so that my note-taking would be at a minimum and would not "scare away" possible subjects.

them into readable notes at every opportunity; I attempted to remember the particularly important details so that when I transcribed the notes at the end of each day's trip, I would be able to include them; I dictated my notes into a tape recorder at the end of each day; and, finally, when I returned home, I transcribed the contents of the tape onto paper, adding details that I might have overlooked while on the road. The method seemed to have worked well, although I still wish that I had been able to develop some better means for taking notes in the truck's cab while the events were occurring.

One final note is important. When riding with the drivers I always identified myself to them. However, when we stopped at truck stops, loading docks and so on, I was often not identified as someone writing a book about the drivers; for all intents and purposes I was a truck driver and I was accepted by drivers as another truck driver. At this point my method changed from that of observer-as-participant to participant-as-observer for the duration of that occurrence. It was interesting to note the reactions of others to me (and my role) since I was not allowed to engage in any work: I sat and watched while the "real" driver loaded or unloaded the truck. My actions often brought comments about me from the other drivers which were not always favorable to me or my family. The comments usually dealt with why my "partner" had to work while I just sat, or who did I know that I did not have to work. (At this point my real identity was usually revealed.) In addition, when we stopped at truck stops I was often not identified except by name, and since I was now able to "play the game according to the rules" I was accepted as a driver. I was included in the conversations as if I was a driver, I was accepted as a driver by waitresses and other nongroup members, and so on. In this way I was able to gather information from the point of view of the drivers: what they were seeing and experiencing, I was seeing and experiencing.[7]

During the period when my true identity was not revealed, my research techniques were obviously altered somewhat. It was necessary to change my method since any note-taking would have instantly given me away. In these circumstances, I simply attempted to remember everything that was of importance and when I excused myself (for whatever reason) I would then go to the truck's cab or some other inconspicuous place, and jot down my notes. At the loading docks this often brought some comments akin to those mentioned above, but when I did this at the truck stops, according to the drivers when they came back to the truck, little comment was made. It would appear that the drivers who did not know my real purpose thought I had to go back

[7] By this time I had become acquainted with most of the jargon of the occupation, I had driven a tractor-trailer rig, and I had been around trucks a good deal, so that I knew what the drivers were talking about most of the time.

to the truck to enter my times in my logbook.[8] Thus, while playing the
role of participant-as-observer, I did not actively or openly take notes.
I waited until a more opportune moment to do so. Interestingly enough,
these moments came with some regularity so that I did not lose any
significant amounts of information, at least I do not think I did.[9]

Our study of the truck drivers should suggest to you some of the
problems faced by the participant-as-observer. In addition, it is important to realize that had we not used the participation-as-observation
approach, much important information would have been lost to us.
For example, we found that truck drivers tended not to discriminate
between types of drivers on a structured questionnaire. Such a finding
was contrary to our original hypothesis which suggested a clear hier-
archy among truck drivers—a social ranking system that we thought
was operative among all truck drivers. Had we not been observing in
the field we might well have let this finding go as being merely another
instance of an hypothesis not being proved. However, we found (Runcie, 1973) through observing drivers, that the real or important distinction was made between truck drivers and nontruck drivers (i.e.,
between truck drivers and everyone else) and it was this social ranking
that was important. Consequently, in this particular research problem, rather than go out to do our observation with some specific hypotheses in mind, we were, rather, looking to see if we could verify
what we had found using a structured questionnaire. It is obvious that
we could just as well have gone out with the idea that we would be
testing hypotheses and then use the questionnaire to verify our field
or observational research.

There is one side to participant-observation research that I suppose
most of us never come to accept and that is the great amount of time
it takes to gather what may turn out to be a small amount of usable
information. The participation in the realm of the truck driver extended over about two years with the majority concentrated in the first
six months of the project. There were times when days would go by
with little useful information being gathered, when the project seemed
to be totally meaningless and monotonous. On other occasions I could
not keep up with the information that was "coming in" to me. Or consider the research project on the assembly line. I spent five months as
a worker on the assembly line, trying to concentrate on writing up my
observations each day after spending eight (or more) hours building

---

[8] In the logbook are pages for each day (i.e., each 24-hour period) on which
must be recorded how a driver spends each hour of that day. The time is divided
into: off duty time; sleeper berth time; driving time; and on duty but not driving
time.

[9] I do not think there was ever an occasion when one of the truck drivers was
not eventually told who I was. My real identity was always revealed at some point.

cars. In addition, I spent two to three months interviewing the workers and in administering a questionnaire to them after I had revealed my purpose to them. In this project one must also include those days that were extremely monotonous as well as the days when I could not keep up with the flow of data that was coming in.

One must realize that the time problem in any research project using participant observation (not just the few outlined here) is (at least) twofold. First, one must invest a tremendous amount of time before any valuable information is gathered, and second, one must invest time if one wants information that cannot be gathered any other way. However, simply because you become a participant observer in some group, by itself, does not guarantee that you will find out any sociologically important information about groups and their behaviors. The investment of your time and energy ensures only that you *may* locate valuable information, not that you *will* locate valuable information.

While we have described one approach to participant-observation research, realize that many of your problems have yet to be solved. In the study of the truck drivers, we solved the problem of taking notes by indicating that a study was being done. You still have to decide if you will be a hidden or obvious observer. If you decide to be the hidden observer, how will you go about taking notes on what is happening? While it may sound facetious to suggest, you can always find reasons for short absences from the group and spend the time writing down as many notes as possible on what is happening. In addition, you still have to decide what you are looking for in this particular group that you are studying. What sort of legitimation will you use to justify your studying that particular group when you write up your field notes? All questions such as these should be answered before you ever set out to attend the meeting of the group that you will observe.

For the present research problem, we want you to do the research as if you were verifying data already gathered from other sources. While you may be testing hypotheses in this problem, that should not be uppermost in your mind. We want you to play a mental game in this problem; that is, you are to examine a group for aspects of behavior that you see as important and at the same time assume that the things you want to look at already have been measured to some extent. You will be assuming that you have already gathered certain kinds of data and that you are now in the process of verifying that data.

THE ANALYSIS

Because we are asking that you will assume that you have already collected a certain amount of data, we do not think you will need to go to a great deal of trouble describing your hypotheses. In this regard, we will suggest certain ideas that you may want to examine as you do your participant-observation. The following list includes ideas that you may assume have already been discovered about social groups and their members.[10]

1. In semiformal proceedings, the leader of a group will receive al-most as many communications as he or she will send out.
2. In any group, not all communication will be relevant to the task of the group or even be relevant to the topic that is being discussed.
3. Unless the opposition is well organized, the leader will control the actions of even the most democratic group. This finding will be true on even the most trivial of issues.

While there are, no doubt, other aspects of group behavior that you might want to examine (and you may add ideas if you wish), these should suffice for this particular problem.

While you have specified the relationships that you may want to examine in your research, you have, to this point, done nothing to indicate how you might measure what the relationships are. You have not yet shown how you will know when, for example, the leader of a group has received as many communications as sent out. How will you measure such information? One way to answer the question is to de-fine what you mean by the concepts in the hypotheses that you set out to study. In order to define the concepts, you can operationalize them. By operationalization, we mean that you will suggest some empirical measurement that can be taken as an indicator of the concept in your hypothesis. As Babbie (1973:134) shows:

> *Operationalization* is the process whereby the researcher specifies em-pirical observations that may be taken as indicators of the attributes contained within a given concept. . . . Typically, the researcher will specify several such indicators and combine those during the analysis of data to provide a composite measure (index or scale) representing the concept.

We might take agreement to a statement on the supremacy of the white race as being indicative of racism on the part of the respondent. We would be using the empirical indicator (agreement to a statement) as a representative for the concept (racism). In the same way, in par-ticipant-observation research, it is important to specify what you will be looking for in the way of empirical indicators. If you can specify with some precision, you will be ahead in the long run because you will not have to refine the measures during the course of the research.

Suppose we are interested in examining the hypothesis concerning the fact that not all communication will be relevant to the task of the group. How might we operationalize this concept? One way would be

---

[10] See Chapter 6 for additional possible relationships to be tested.

to suggest that an obscene joke told during the group session would be sufficient. Is one joke enough to show that not all communication is relevant to the task? What happens if no jokes are told but one person asks another for a date for that evening? Obviously, here is an indication of some communication not relevant to the group task. The researcher must attempt to outline all the possible empirically observable instances that will confirm or deny the truth of the research hypotheses. By specifying all possibilities the researcher will be stacking the cards somewhat in his or her favor. The listing of possibilities will give the researcher alternative means for showing how the data relate to the hypotheses. Thus, if jokes are the only nontask relevant material specified, then asking for a date is not a usable datum (except for those involved, of course). The approach to take ought to be that you as the researcher specify all possible items of information that will be relevant to your hypothesis testing and then choose only those that seem the best on the basis of your theory, and maybe also on the basis of some educated guesswork. If your observations, which you have determined are representative of the concepts in the hypotheses, occur as you predict, then you will have confirmed your hypotheses. If the observations do not occur as you predict, your hypotheses are not confirmed and you must then attempt to explain why.

In your observation see if you can find qualitative evidence that will support the above "hypotheses." Can you show how the above concepts do or do not apply in the group that you are observing? Can you record quotations from the participants that uphold (or refuse to confirm) the hypothesis presented above? The following are additional items that should be included in the field notes of the participant-as-observer.[11]

Total Description. Depending on your ability to recall events (assuming that you are not able to record on the spot), you will have to decide how complete a description of the events in the setting you want to include. Most social scientists will indicate that your records should be as complete as possible but there will be differences as to what this statement means. Completeness may be 5 pages of notes, or it may be 50 pages, on a three-hour meeting. Try not to summarize the events, try to recall and include as verbatim a transcript of what occurred as you can possibly remember. Can you remember exact quotes by the participants? If so be certain that you include them. If not, summarize them as well as you can. If ideas occur to you that are relevant to the examination of the "hypotheses" mentioned above, put them in also but be certain that you label them clearly for yourself so that you will know to what they refer when you come to analyze the notes of your observation. A member's sentence or other random comments without

---

[11] On this subject, see also Lofland (1971), chapter 5; McCall and Simmons (1969), chapter 3; Denzin (1978), chapter 25; Filstead (1970), parts 3–4.

any accompanying identifying material may well become so much meaningless gibberish after two to three days away from the meeting. Included in what we can call the "total description" of the observed scene might be all those aspects that we could call "scientific" observations. Here we include all those aspects of the context which are "documentable" in one sense or another; for example, all those parts of the scene that are relevant to the testing and examination of your hypotheses.

Personal Opinions. To be included in a description of an observed scene, descriptions do not always have to be what might be called "scientific observations." It is legitimate to include your opinions and impressions of the participants in the scene you are observing. If, for example, you have the feeling that a member of the group is bullying the other members but you have no actual proof to support your contention, you might well want to include your guess in your field notes to be looked at later in the context of the notes from the entire meeting. A feeling that you might have early in the meeting may well be supported later. Simply because something you might include in your notes does not fit the canons of scientific methods does not mean that it should not be included. What is required of the observer is that he or she label what is being included as opinion. If the material to be included is not labeled as opinion, it may well be given the strength of a fact when examined at some later date.

Side Conditions. It may also be relevant to include material that is not strictly part of the scene being observed if it seems that such material might be important. What, for example, is going on in the larger world of which this group is a part, that is influencing the deliberations of the group? What decisions made by the World Council of Churches at its most recent meeting might influence the church group meeting being observed? What happened at the club's last meeting that is influencing what is happening at this meeting? In other words, material that is not part of the present happenings of the group being observed may be more important to the current scene than that which is occurring at the time. We feel that you should be concerned with both the history of the group and also the current events that surround it in the larger society.

What the above comments should indicate to you is that the good participant-as-observer is a good listener. You should be alert to the many different currents that are eddying through the social context of the meeting. As an observer you may want to pursue these various undercurrents with questions that allow you some insight into them. On the other hand, of course, if you have chosen to be a hidden observer you may not want to push the questions and questioning too hard for fear of giving yourself away.

6

Systematic
Observation

THE PROBLEM

Construct a sociogram and sociomatrix using preference choices made by persons living in a coed dormitory section at a large midwestern university (the data are included at the end of the chapter). In addition to the construction of a sociogram and sociomatrix, describe and analyze the patterns shown in the choices made by the students.

THE APPROACH

To this point, we have been asking you to do observations that were unstructured. By unstructured we do not mean that they were unscientific. On the contrary, the observations that you have done were done strictly according to the norms and precepts of the scientific method. The observations were not, however, done in any sort of systematic fashion. For example, we asked that you go to a shopping center and see what sorts of social relationships you could discover. We asked that you observe a group of which you were already a member and show what social relationships existed in that particular group.

What we did not do was to ask that you completely structure the situation before you went into it. We did not ask that you specify the number of persons you would observe. We did not ask that you specify the exact form of the social relationships that you would watch for in advance. We did not indicate that you should set up unvarying categories of behavior that you would look for in your observations. In summary, we did not ask that you set up your observation as one might construct an experiment before you went to do it.

In this chapter, we want you to do a systematic observation of a group, utilizing categories of behavior that are set up beforehand. You might, for example, observe a group and its interactions using only categories of behavior that you had determined ahead of time. You might also ask people questions about interaction and then map the structure of the group on the basis of these responses. While there are numerous possible ways to approach the systematic observation of human behavior, in this chapter we will deal with two: interaction process analysis and sociometry.

An example of a technique for observation is "interaction process analysis." According to Robert Bales (the inventor of the technique), interaction process analysis can be used on small groups to identify uniformities of interaction and communication that occur in all groups under all manner of varying conditions. As Bales (1952:146–147) indicates:

> One of our basic assumptions is that there are certain conditions which are present to an important degree not only in special kinds of groups doing special kinds of problems, but which are more or less inherent in the nature of the process of interaction or communication itself, whenever or wherever it takes place.

Through the use of experiments in interaction and communication, Bales indicates that the uniformities of behavior can be isolated.

The setting for the experiment using the Bales approach is a small room that is designed to facilitate the recording of the subjects' behaviors. There is a one-way mirror behind which the experimenters sit to record, manually and/or mechanically, the interactions of the subjects. The subjects themselves are chosen from a subject pool and (hopefully) do not know each other beforehand. The subjects are asked to deal with a "human relations case" as if they were members of a company actually considering such a case. Once the subjects are situated in the test room, they are

> . . . given separate identical copies of the case [to be discussed] to be read ahead of time and were told that, although each was given accurate information, we intended to leave them uncertain as to whether they each had exactly the same range of facts. The cases were collected after they had been read by the members individually, to prevent direct comparison of typed copies, although members were allowed to take notes. The task defined for each group was to assemble the information, to discuss why the people involved were behaving as they did, and decide what was to be recommended as action for the solution to the problem presented. The groups were asked to time themselves for 40 minutes and to dictate the group solution for the

sound record in the final one or two minutes of the meeting (Bales, 1958:437–438).

The situation then is an artificial one in which the groups are given tasks to solve in a specified amount of time. As mentioned, it is from the experimental groups and their deliberations that the uniformities of behavior have been discovered.

Bales and his colleagues have devised a series of 12 logically exhaustive categories into which they feel all communicative behavior can be placed. Every act that occurs in a group experimental situation can be coded into a category, there are no residual categories. The 12 categories are shown in Figure 6–1.

FIGURE 6–1
Categories Used in Observations of Interaction Processes

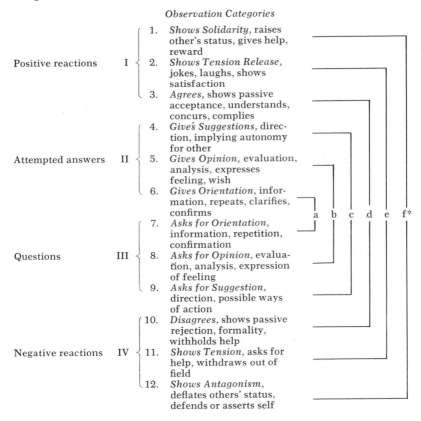

* Categories are paired giving positive and negative emotions.
Source: Adapted from Bales (1952:149).

As indicated by Bales, the categories are exhaustive and cover the range of possible types of interactions available to a common member of some group. In order to measure the interactions and to record them, Bales stations observers behind the one-way mirror who simply check off the interactions as they occur on a sheet of paper. In some of the experiments, the check sheets were on a moving piece of paper so that changes over time could be shown. The paper moved at a known rate so that when analyzing the data all interactions from the first minute to the last minute could be shown. The process involved assigning a code number to each of the people in the group and assigning another number to the group as a whole. Once the participants are identified in this way it is a simple matter to record each interaction. For example, one could put a question addressed to the leader by the number three participant as 3→1 under the category labeled "Asks for Orientation." All other interactions could be dealt with in a similar way.

Using the 12 categories (and all the possible combinations, some of which are shown in Figure 6–1), Bales (1952:147) points to the abstract qualities of all groups and their interaction patterns. Thus, according to Bales, there are a number of problems that must be dealt with sequentially by a task-oriented group. These problems occur with regard to:

a. Aspects of Orientation. All members of the group feel that they should share a common definition of the situation and will try to build this commonality through interaction.
b. Aspects of Evaluation. All members of the group will come into the situation with differing value systems and these systems must be merged if the problem is to be solved.
c. Aspects of Control. All members will try to control the outcome of the decision-making process because the problem relies on an eventual group decision.

One criticism of the method which might be made at this point (and which Bales anticipates, 1952:147) is that this method is best suited to a particular type of group rather than any and all groups. Bales agrees and suggests this method is best for the newly formed, initially leaderless small group engaged in a task solution. While one might be tempted to suggest a lack of generalizability from these studies, Bales (1965:446) adds that the ". . . patterns described and illustrated can be understood to refer to approximate or average uniformities in aggregates of large numbers of group meetings under randomly varying external conditions . . ." although they will be more likely to hold true under conditions similar to those in the experiment.

Not only can the uniformities in the communication within the group be identified, but so can a series of uniformities of interaction. The uniformities identified are those of (Bales, 1952:151 ff):

a. Profile. Where different sorts of acts (qualitatively different sorts of acts) tend to balance each other out in the course of the group's discussions. Here Bales expresses the total number of acts among the 12 categories as a percentage of the total. Different types of groups will produce different types of profiles. Thus, a group in which a democratic leader emerges will show a different proportion of acts in each category than will a group where an authoritarian leader emerges.

b. Matrix. Where different members of the group tend to reach a balance in the types of acts they initiate and receive. In addition to the types of acts received, the qualities of these acts also tend to balance. For example, groups without designated leaders tend to be more equal in their distribution of acts than are other groups. Even accepting differences such as these, certain uniformities emerge. People in all groups tend to receive about one-half as many communications as they send out. While it may appear impossible to receive back only half as many communications as one sends out, such is not the case. As Bales demonstrates, one can communicate with other members of the group and with the group as a whole. When all communicative acts are counted up (both to individuals and to the group), one can then compare an individual's total input of communications with all communications in the group. What the comparison will show is that each individual in the group sends out communications to the group *and* to individuals while that person only receives communications from persons. In other words, while a person can communicate with the group, the group (as an entity) cannot communicate with a person. One-half as many communications coming in as are going out is not as impossible as the statement would seem at first. Another uniformity that Bales has discovered is that higher ranking members of the group tend to be initiators of communicative acts while the lower ranking members tend to be reactors to those messages.

c. Phase Movement. Shows the changes in the quality of the group's activity over time. Thus, where the group feels the need for orientation during one part of the session, the group and its members will later have to move into socioemotional activities. Thus, questions early in the session will result in both positive and negative reactions later. Or, as Bales indicates (1952:158): "we note joking and laughter so frequently at the end of meetings that they might almost be taken as a signal that the group has completed what it considers to be a task effort, and is ready for disbanding or a new effort."

Given all that has just been indicated about the Bales system of interaction process analysis, what might we as researchers conclude?[1] First, the approach relies almost entirely on pure observation of the most systematic sort. There is little interaction of the observer and the observed so that interactional biases may be eliminated as far as possible. In another attempt to eliminate bias, there is systematic control exerted over the action in the group: members are carefully selected, goals of interaction are selected, and the environment in which the group interacts (the laboratory) is carefully selected. In addition, systematic control is also exerted by specifying in advance the categories of data that are to be gathered; the data are precoded; and the observers are highly trained so that high correlations between observers can be achieved (observers will come very close to agreement on how they see the same interaction and interpret it). While there are many advantages to this method (systematization and generalizability, for example), there are also problems associated with its use. Particularly important are problems in terms of its being restricted to relatively small groups and the elimination from concern of all that is happening outside the experimental room. When used correctly, however, the method is extremely useful (and reliable).

Another interesting approach to the systematic observation of data is that employed by the sociometrists. In the sociometric approach, the researcher specifies the type of data that is acceptable and then proceeds to build a map of group interaction from the data. As in the problem given at the beginning of the chapter, a sociometrist would examine a series of choices made by persons in a group, and on the basis of these choices would construct a picture of the group at that point in time. The sociometrist could also use this method to examine changes in the group's structure over time. Thus, examining friendship choices at two points in time will show who no longer likes whom and who is now close friends with whom. Before examining the means for analyzing sociometric data, let us look into the background of this approach in the same manner we did for the Bales approach.

One question that comes to mind, is what is it that the sociometrists actually study when they do all this mapping of interaction? According to Moreno (1947:288), the "father" of sociometry, the field studies "sociomicroscopic" configurations of people which are assumed to be the ". . . preliminary and indispensible groundwork to most macro-

---

[1] You could adapt the Bales technique for use in your participant observation of a small group. You could count the various types of communicative acts between members of the group during the time of your observation. You could also use the Bales technique to show how the profile of acts changes over time moving from orientation toward the group's task to a phase of "fun and games"

sociological investigations." The "sociomicroscopic" configurations of people who are studied by this method (Moreno, 1947:288) are not only

> . . . the informal small groups, but the dynamic social units of which they are comprised, the pattern variants of social atoms, the clustering of social atoms into larger associations invisible to the eye of the human observer (social molecules), psychosocial networks, the clustering of such networks into more comprehensive formations. . . .

Finally, Moreno indicates that the informal groups that are studied, range in size from the dyad (two persons) all the way up to chains of persons (Moreno, 1947:288). According to the proponents of this approach, then, the description of the interactive chains of behavior are the building blocks on which the rest of the study is built. Consequently, if we are able to discern the patterns at the micro level, we should be able to describe the patterns at the larger or macro level since the two pattern structures are approximately the same.[2]

One problem that confronts the student of research the first time he or she encounters the field of sociometry is the question: What is being measured in this study? In other words, what is it that sociometrists measure? Do they measure group properties? Do they measure individual attractions and dislikes? According to Northway (1967:49),

> . . . sociometry does not measure, it *discovers*. It is essentially a technique for locating the relationships which are formed between individuals. Sociometric scores, of course, do measure; they measure the number of relationships of which the individual is a part, but not the intensity of these.

Because the sociometric scores do not measure intensity, Northway (1967:49) argues that they measure the width of a person's social value but not the depth: how many persons does one know rather than how well one knows them. Sociometry, then, discovers the attractions and the repulsions felt by members of groups. How strongly does a person contribute to the well-being of the other members of the group? How strong is the attraction for a particular individual held by the other members of the group? How strongly do the members of a group dislike certain other members? All of these are questions that potentially can be answered using the sociometric approach.

---

by the time the meeting ends (if that is what happens). You could also work in teams: one person dealing with the more qualitative data of the group and the other person(s) keeping track of the types of comments made over time. For another example of the uses to which this method can be put, see Parsons and Bales, 1955.

[2] See also: Moreno (1953); Jennings (1950, 1965); and Bjerstedt (1956).

In addition, the sociometric approach can be used to (1) isolate those persons in the group who are leaders, (2) isolate those who are central persons without being leaders, and (3) show who are isolated from other members of the group, and so on. By examining the choices of members of the group, it is possible to show roles played by persons in the group and what appears to be the consensus of the group toward all other members.

Rather than spend a great deal of time outlining the sociometric approach, we will, instead, go through a small problem utilizing sociometric data. First, however, we will note some of the criticisms of sociometry and also look at some of the changes that have taken place in the use of the sociometric approach recently.

One major criticism of sociometry (as well as of "interaction process analysis") is that the observer is isolated from the subjects of the observation. Systematic observation means also that systematic control over the situation will be held by the observer. Thus, questions are specified in advance, techniques for the analysis are specified in advance, and the number of choices a person can make is specified in advance. There are also similar problems in the two approaches. While theoretically there is no limit to the size of the group that could be mapped using the sociometric approach, reality suggests there will be a finite upper limit, although, it will be somewhat larger than that for the interaction process approach. The sociometric approach is also static in that: (1) it does not allow for changes (except by repeated administrations of the questions), and (2) it does not allow for happenings outside the immediate group (i.e., it fails to take account of happenings in the "big world").

In recent years the approach we have called "systematic observation" has undergone a number of changes. One of the more interesting developments in sociometry has been the application of the major concepts and approaches to nonhuman networks. Levine (1972) utilizes sociometry in his study of the interlocking directorates of banks and corporations. Levine, in describing his approach, states (1972:14).

> As a sociologist I approach this network as a problem in sociometry. My problem is to "understand" a large network in the crude, almost a-theoretical sense of being able to represent it, to discern its major outlines, and to distinguish important links from those which are not.

Levine summarizes his findings (1972:26) by indicating that "the banks and industrials have been mapped into a joint space in which distance corresponds to interlock: the industrials most strongly linked to a bank are near it in the space." As Levine and others have shown (see especially Allen, 1974) the mapping of social relationships can be done for human as well as extrahuman groupings. In this type of research (as in most others we have discussed) students (really all researchers) are limited only by their creativity and imagination.

Bales and his colleagues have also revised and expanded the techniques of systematic observation. The most recent iteration of Bales' method (see Bales, 1979; and Bales, Cohen, and Williamson, 1979) is the SYMLOG Approach.[3] SYMLOG, an acronym which stands for the SYstematic Multiple Level Observation of Groups, allows group members to evaluate their own and others' performances in a small-group situation. Rather than provide a two-dimensional level of analysis as the interaction process analysis tended to do, SYMLOG allows the observer (in this case a member of the group) to create a three-dimensional picture of the group's interactions as the group members worked together to solve a group problem. In a manner reminiscent of the interaction process analysis approach, small groups are given a task to solve. However, rather than rely on trained observers sitting behind a mirror to record behavior, the SYMLOG approach requires the group members to retrospectively analyze their own—and other group members'—behavior during the session. The use of the retrospective approach gives each group member the opportunity to show what he or she thought the group looked like (or should look like) and acted like during the course of its deliberations. As Bales (1979: ms page 13) suggests:

> In the SYMLOG Group Self Study each individual not only provides observations of his own and others' behavior, but also adds up the scores, constructs a diagram summarizing the results, and thinks about the implications of the diagram in preparation for the discussion session.

As noted above, the two-dimensional system of the earlier work has been replaced by a three dimensional space in the SYMLOG approach (see Figure 6–2).

For each combination of dimensions in the SYMLOG three-dimensional space (UNB, UN, FPD, and so on) there are both values and behaviors that can be identified. By scoring individual group members and the group as a whole on these values or behaviors, a profile of the group can be assembled. As Bales (1979: ms page 17) suggests:

> we can locate the way an observer feels about the behavioral qualities shown by a person in a given period in a given dimension by adding together the scores the observer has given the person on the nine items which tap one direction of the dimension (say the Upward direction) and subtracting from this total the scores of the nine items

---

[3] I am grateful to Professor Bales and his publisher, The Free Press, for giving me access to these materials while the materials were still in manuscript form.

FIGURE 6–2
The SYMLOG Three-Dimensional Space

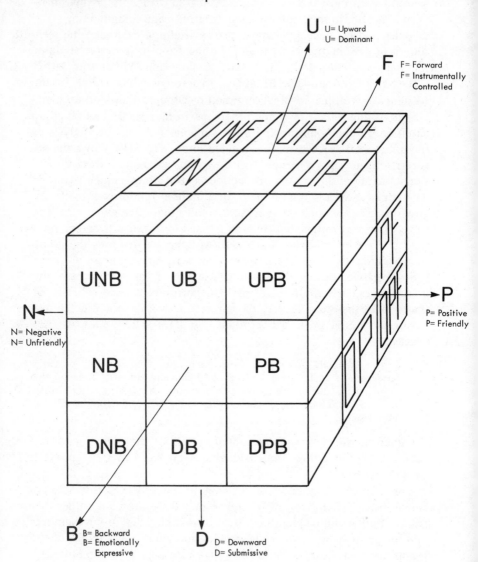

The SYMLOG Three-Dimensional Space, showing classes of directions, or locations, defined by logical combinations of the six named reference directions. (The cube is seen from an outside point. The directions are named from a reference point at the intersection of the three dimensions, looking forward.) From Bales, 1979: ms. page 14.

which tap the opposite direction (the total of items measuring the Downward direction). This can be done for each of the three dimensions, U-D, P-N, and F-B. . . .

By adding and subtracting scores on the various dimensions, and using some of the materials included with the "Kit," a number of questions relating to group and individual behavior can then be examined: To what extent does the group tend ". . . to hang together as a unified whole or to break down into polarized sub-groups" (Bales, 1979: ms page 25)? To what degree is the group ". . . being dominated by one or a few members" (Bales, 1979: ms page 33)? To what degree are ". . . members or important values 'dropping out of sight' and being rejected because of the constellations of dominant images" (Bales, 1979: ms page 33)? To what extent are some members isolated or in danger of being isolated from the group (Bales, 1979: ms page 34 ff)? and so on.

The approach developed by Bales and his colleagues is an extremely interesting means for showing group members—in retrospect—what they have just gone through in the group experience and why.[4] The techniques noted here also point out the fact that the methods of research do change over time to fit changing situations. When we develop a technique, we want to improve it over time so that it will better explain human behavior.

At this point we want to take you through a small problem using the systematic observation approach, a problem in sociometric analysis. In this way we will be able to demonstrate the utility of the systematic observational approach while at the same time showing how the approach is accomplished. Before we examine the approach, however, realize that the approach of the sociometrist is similar to that of the researcher using interaction process analysis or SYMLOG. In all cases the observer is isolated from the subjects of observation and is able to systematically control the material that will be included in the analysis (albeit for SYMLOG the isolation is one of time rather than of space).

THE ANALYSIS

We can begin a discussion of the techniques of analysis of sociometric data by making a few assumptions. First, we can assume that you have somehow obtained the information on which you will build your analysis. Second, the techniques that will work for the data in a small example will work as well for larger groups of persons.

---

[4] An exercise using the SYMLOG approach might be a useful means for extending the understanding of the systematic observation approach for a class— or parts of a class.

For our purposes, we can begin by looking at a six-member group. In this hypothetical group, each member was asked to pick two persons in the group with whom he or she wished to be friends.[5] The results were:

Student	Choice
A	B
	E
B	A
	C
C	B
	X*
D	X*
	X*
E	A
	B
F	B
	A

* Indicates a choice went outside the group. Thus, student D made no choices of friends from within the boundaries of the group.

Realize that the relationships demonstrated by asking for the friendship choices of the students will be drastically different than relationships which can be shown when we ask for choices based on dislike. We could, using the sociometric approach, map different types of choices and rejections to see how the structure of the group changes depending on the circumstances. We could ask the respondents to tell us their three friendship choices, to show us their three most antagonistic choices, to show us those with whom they have the most conflict, to show us those persons to whom they go for information (of whatever type), and so on. Each sociogram produced by mapping these responses will be different, as we will demonstrate below.

What do we know about the six-person group that will help us understand the dynamics of the relationships among the members? In this particular instance, by giving us the friendship choices we know more than we did before we asked. One of the things we could do to aid our understanding of the group processes at work in this particular group would be to draw a sociogram of the relationships reported above. In a sociogram, we would connect people to one another by the use of arrows. A one-directional arrow would indicate that a person chose another but was not chosen in return. A two-directional arrow would indicate mutual choices: each person chose the other as a friend. From our example above, we would construct a sociogram as shown in Figure 6–3:

[5] We have chosen letters to represent names here. The order of persons in the group has nothing to do with their names. The fact that they are in alphabetical order is purely chance.

FIGURE 6–3
Sociogram Showing Friendship Choices
Made by Members of a Six-Person Group

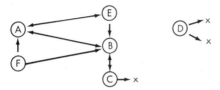

The sociogram is relatively easy to draw when there are only a few people in the group. As you will note in your assignment, when there are a great many people to be dealt with, there are other means that can be used first before the drawing of the sociogram.

What can we say about the relationships demonstrated in the above sociogram? First of all, it is obvious that D is an isolate—D is chosen by no members of the group and also does not choose into the group. B is chosen by more persons in the group (4) than is anyone else and so might be considered the informal leader of the group. At the same time, close behind is A who is chosen by three persons. E and C are each chosen once and they are chosen by the two most chosen members of the group. Finally, there is F who chooses into the group but is not chosen by any members of the group. F is only slightly less of an isolate than is D—F is a member of the group by his or her own choice, not by the choice of the group's members.

Before going on, we want to go back and show how asking the initial question differently will lead to a different picture of the group. Had we asked our hypothetical respondents to tell us those persons to whom they go for information, the sociogram would show a different pattern. If our group members picked as follows:

Student	Choice
A	C
	D
B	F
	X
C	D
	E
D	X
	X
E	D
F	D
	X

then the group relationship that can be depicted will be greatly different than that shown in Figure 6–3 above. The sociogram of those persons and their sources of information would be (Figure 6–4):

FIGURE 6–4
Sociogram Showing Information Sources of Members
of a Six-Person Group

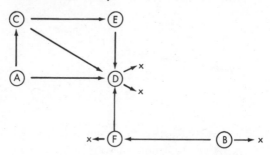

As suggested, the second sociogram shows a clear change from the first. In the first sociogram, D was clearly shown to be an isolate and B was seen as the center of attention. In the second sociogram, the picture is reversed and D has become the center of attention with B now on the outside. In addition, while many people in the group now choose D, he still chooses no one in the group. An explanation for the picture presented in the second sociogram might be that B, while an extremely popular and handsome athlete is not considered to be a good source of information by the other members of the group. The individual D, on the other hand, while generally "average" in most physiological areas, happens to be a straight-A student who is also a student employee of the Dean's office. What may seem like minor differences in choices can lead to striking patterns in both large and small groups.

As is obvious in the above examples, the description of the interrelationships is relatively easy to accomplish in a small group. What might happen if the group was three to four times as large? How should we then go about the description? The easiest manner in which to begin is to draw a sociomatrix first. The sociomatrix is simply a cross-tabulation of all the choices that are made from one individual in the group to another. In the matrix to be drawn, we can put a one (1) in the cell in the table that represents a choice from one person to another. Where there is a no choice from one person to another we will put a zero (0). For the matrix, we can put the persons who are choosing others down the side of the table (in the vertical axis) and the persons being chosen across the top of the table (the horizontal dimension). From our example above, such a sociomatrix would be illustrated as in Figure 6–5. In the sociomatrix, we put a dash on the diagonal line through the matrix since there are few of us who would choose ourselves if given the opportunity (not that we might want to but that it simply is not done). Realize here that whatever order you have for

FIGURE 6–5
Blank Sociomatrix Showing Chosen and Chooser in a Group of Six Persons

Chooser \ Chosen	a	b	c	d	e	f
A	—					
B		—				
C			—			
D				—		
E					—	
F						—

the chooser, that same order must be used for the chosen. Thus, if choosers are A-B-C-D-E-F, chosen must also be a-b-c-d-e-f.

Beginning with the first person in the list of choosers from the first example, we would then go to the matrix and fill in the blank spots. For subject A, there are two choices made within the group, to B and to E. Thus, across from person A, we would put a 1 under both the letters b and e. We use small letters in one direction to differentiate the chooser from the chosen since the same person can be both. In the same way, we can show that for person B, there are also two choices within the group, those to a and to c. Returning to the matrix for chooser B, we can add a 1 for a and c in the chosen dimension. The remainder of the matrix can then be filled in, as shown in Figure 6–6:

FIGURE 6–6
First Approximation of a Sociomatrix Drawn for Friendship Choices Made by Members of a Six-Person Group*

Chooser \ Chosen	a	b	c	d	e	f
A	—	1	0	0	1	0
B	1	—	1	0	0	0
C	0	1	—	0	0	0
D	0	0	0	—	0	0
E	1	1	0	0	—	0
F	1	1	0	0	0	—

* At this point the ordering of persons in the matrix is purely for the sake of simplicity and implies no other reasons.

By scanning the matrix, it is possible to note that exactly the same information is included in it as in both the initial list of the choices
made by persons in the group and also in the sociogram drawn earlier.
Once again we return to the problem of what might happen if we had
a greater number of persons in the group than the six we have shown
here.

Now you may be asking yourselves why bother to draw a sociomatrix
when the information can be presented just as clearly (and possibly
even more clearly) using the sociogram alone? The answer to this
question is simply that as one gets into more and more advanced kinds
of relationships between people the matrix can more clearly show the
relationships than can the sociogram. Through the use of matrix alge-
bra, one can transform the matrix as shown in these examples to show
the indirect choices made between members of the group. We could,
using the matrix method, show how A chooses C by way of B. There
is an indirect choice made which is obvious for the smaller group but
would be more difficult to see if the group was much larger. At the
same time, the matrix may lead you to see some relationships that you
would not see otherwise even in the smaller group. The use of the
sociomatrix to present your data can do you no harm and, in the long
run, may actually help you to better present the relationships between
the group members.

As the matrix is drawn in Figure 6–6, it is not really very efficient.
In the present case, we can refer back to the sociogram and see that,
for example, A and E are really quite close together: they have mutual
choices for each other and they have a mutual friend in B. Thus, to
show A and E at opposite ends of a matrix does not really do justice to
the relationship they have. The relationship can be much more clearly
demonstrated if we could make the matrix more efficient. We could
make it more efficient by bringing those persons with close ties more
closely together in the matrix itself. Once we could show the closeness
of the relationship in the matrix, we then could draw the sociogram
and show the closeness in the "map" of the group. For larger groups,
in other words, it is more efficient to draw the sociomatrix before we
draw the sociogram.

In order to draw an efficient matrix, two general principles are involved: (1) you should try to get all the mutual choices near the top
left-hand corner of the matrix (that is, you should deal with mutual
choices first), and (2) the deviations from the diagonal should be at
a minimum. Most students at this point say something under their
breaths which sounds suspiciously like, "yea, right." Let us take the
rules one step at a time.

By trying to get the mutual choices near the top left of the matrix,
you are getting them out of the way early and you are clustering them

together. Thus, you are explaining the closest mutual choices at the earliest possible time in your matrix (the first positions in the matrix). We can vary the positions of the members of the group in our matrix since we have assigned letters instead of names for simplicity's sake and for no assumption of ordering. Because we are concerned first with the mutual choices, let us see who was chosen mutually. For present purposes we can go back to the sociogram and show that the mutual choices were:

$$A \longleftrightarrow B$$
$$B \longleftrightarrow C$$
$$A \longleftrightarrow E$$

We might note that the same information could be retrieved from the sociomatrix drawn above. In the sociomatrix we would simply go across a row and see what choices were made. Then we would look to the persons chosen and see if there was a 1 in that box also. If a 1 existed in both boxes, a mutual choice would be recorded.

The three sets of mutual choices that we noted would then be placed in the first four spots in the redrawn matrix, because four persons are involved (see Figure 6–7):

FIGURE 6–7
Partial Sociomatrix Showing Only Mutual Friendship
Choices by Members of a Six-Person Group

Chooser \ Chosen	a	b	e	c
A	—	1	1	—
B	1	—	0	1
E	1	0	—	0
C	0	1	0	—

In the same way we would then move to include the one-way choices next since these also represent a type of groupness on the part of the choosers. The next information to be included would be the persons toward whom no choice was made but who did choose into the group. These persons are the "semi-isolates" who are the least tied into the group of all those who can be called group members. The one-way choices to be included are:

$$F \longrightarrow A$$
$$F \longrightarrow B$$
$$E \longrightarrow B$$

Finally, the choices made by the isolate would be included; that is, D who made no choices into the group. Completing the redrawn matrix, we would show (Figure 6–8):

FIGURE 6–8
Second Approximation to Efficient Matrix Drawn for Friendship Choices
Made by Members of a Six-Person Group

Chooser \ Chosen	a	b	e	c	f	d
A	—	1	1	0	0	0
B	1	—	0	1	0	0
E	1	1	—	0	0	0
C	0	1	0	—	0	0
F	1	1	0	0	—	0
D	0	0	0	0	0	—

We have, in this redrawn matrix tried to group the mutual choices nearer the top left of the matrix and then added the less efficient choices downward and away from this corner so that the farthest person away from the top left corner is the isolate, D. To improve the efficiency of the matrix in other words, we put in first, those who show mutual choices with others. Second, we show those persons who are tied to the groups through both one- and two-way chains. Third, we include those people who choose in but are not chosen. Finally, we include in the sociomatrix those who neither choose in nor are chosen by group members.

Now we can move to the second rule mentioned and see if the matrix shown in Figure 6–8 is, in fact, the most efficient matrix we could have drawn under the circumstances. As we suggested above, the most efficient matrix is one that minimizes the absolute deviations away from the diagonal (that is, the deviations in either direction from the diagonal). We can then count and see how far each number 1, each score, is away from the diagonal in the above matrix. In other words, each step the number 1 is away from the diagonal is counted as a deviation. The deviations for each number are then summed and that is the total of the deviations from the diagonal. We can show the deviations by redrawing the above matrix (see Figure 6–8) with a slightly different purpose in mind, as shown in Figure 6–9. For example, to count the deviations in the first row, we count over from the diagonal until we reach the first 1 and that gives us one space; that is, there is one unit between the diagonal and the first 1. We then retrace our steps to the diagonal and begin again, counting until we reach the next 1. In this case there are two units between the diagonal and the second 1. We then enter, since this is all the 1s there are in the first row, the sum of 1 and 2 deviations at

FIGURE 6–9
Second Approximation to Efficient Matrix Drawn for Friendship Choices Made by
Members of a Six-Person Group with Deviations from Diagonal Included

Chooser \ Chosen	a	b	e	c	f	d	Deviations
A	—	1	1	0	0	0	1 + 2
B	1	—	0	1	0	0	1 + 2
E	1	1	—	0	0	0	1 + 2
C	0	1	0	—	0	0	2
F	1	1	0	0	—	0	3 + 4
D	0	0	0	0	0	—	0
						Total	18

the right-hand side of the table. In the second row, we go through the
same procedure, counting the number of units between the diagonal
and the number 1 (representing a choice between members of the
group). In the second row, we find that there is 1 deviation to the left
of the diagonal and there are 2 deviations to the right of the diagonal.
In the fifth row, there are 3 deviations to the left of the diagonal plus
4 deviations to the left of the diagonal, for a total of 7 deviations in
the fifth row. (The row that represents choices by F.) You should
satisfy yourself that the other totals for the various rows are accurate.
For the total matrix as shown in Figure 6–9, there are 18 deviations
from the diagonal. Is this an efficient matrix? Unfortunately there is
only one way to know this for certain and that is to try to draw a
more efficient matrix. In order to try again, simply reorder the en-
tries in the columns and the rows (that is, put the choosers in a different order) and see if you can reduce the number of deviations
from the diagonal. Once you have tried this a few times, you will find
that there is some minimum that can be determined.[6]

As we have indicated, both approaches to the systematic gathering
of observational data have positive and negative aspects, and it might
be useful to once more remind you of them. The systematic observation of data will allow you to observe without, at the same time, interacting with the participants in the social situation. At the same time,
the systematic observational techniques discussed here will let you go
to your research with the categories of data already specified so that

---

[6] The matrix that is drawn in Figure 6–9 is not the most efficient that can be
drawn. There is at least one more efficient way in which to draw this particular
representation. As a hint, put C first.

you will know what you are looking for before you ever begin. In addition, the data are pre-coded and thus you are able to examine the relationships without at the same time having to determine the categories in the field. Further, the data are in such a state that you will be better able to quantify the results than you might be with other observational data (witness the ease with which you can show mutual choices in the sociomatrix).

On the negative side, of course, is the fact that you are restricted to relatively small groups in which you can do your systematic observations. You will also be limited in that you are not able to interact with the participants in the situation—interaction with participants often gives a greater depth of information than can be achieved with the structured or systematic approach. Finally, by specifying the categories beforehand, you are limited in the amount of innovation that you can do "in the field." Whether you use this approach or not in an actual research situation, however, it is important that you know what it is and that you are aware of how to use it. The systematic observation of interaction may be useful in a triangulated research program (Denzin, 1978:28–29). It is useful as an adjunct to other approaches and may support data gathered in other ways.

THE PROBLEM

The following are the responses given by the members of a coed dormitory section at a large midwestern university in response to a question asking who they would prefer to study with before a major final examination. Whenever you see an X it represents a choice that is made outside the dormitory section. Include in your analysis all choices made by all persons in the section.

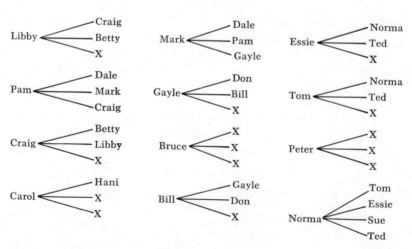

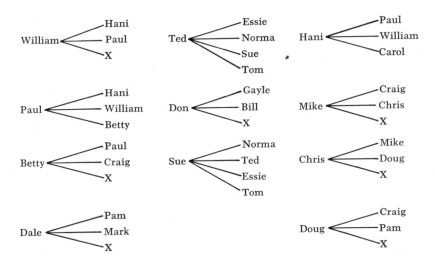

7

Survey Sampling

THE PROBLEM

Draw a 10 percent random sample of your social research class. Ask your subjects their ages and any other information you choose to gather. Based on your sample, compute the subjects' average age. Using the data from each student's sample, compare the data from the samples taken with the real population value. How right (or wrong) were you? Why?

THE APPROACH

Often when one decides to do research, it is neither possible nor feasible to question the entire population about the information one is seeking. When one conducts a systematic observation, as was the case in the last chapter, it is necessary (and usually possible) to question all the persons about their preferences concerning dormitory roommates. However, suppose that you wished to question persons living in a large city concerning their feelings about the establishment of a pornographic theater in their neighborhoods, or suppose you were interested in the employment patterns of working persons in your state, or suppose you were interested in the percentages of males and females in the United States, or suppose you were interested in learning what were the television-viewing habits of the people living in the United States? In order to do these research projects, it would be possible to conduct surveys asking all the people what they thought or did. The cost of such surveys, however, would be astronomical. The alternative to conducting such a total survey of the population (often called a census) would be to question only some of the people and then use the information gathered from those persons to make predictions about what the total population would do or say. When you question only some of the people out of a total population, we say that you are taking a sample of the population or conducting a survey.

A sample, then, is some part of a population that is selected in any one of a number of ways. Data based on a sample of the larger population are called statistics (the same information for the total population would be called parameters). As mentioned, there are many ways in which to draw samples of the population, some of them a great deal more rigorous than others. The more rigorous the sample selection techniques, usually, the more the researcher can say about the sample and the information contained in the questionnaires from the sample (at least from the point of view of the generalizations that can be made to the larger population). For example, if we know that a sample is chosen randomly, then we also know the degree to which each case in our sample (each element in the sample) represents some number of cases in the larger population.

By way of example, suppose that we are interested in asking a sample of persons in college whether they have ever taken a nude sunbath. The answers to a question of this nature are going to be either yes or no. Since the answers are dichotomous, we can look at what is called a binomial distribution (one that has either of two possible answers, yes or no, and that can be looked at in terms of the percentage of the sample that answers either yes or no). It is possible that our sample will respond either 100 percent yes or 100 percent no, or some combination in between. In other words, we can look at the percentage of our sample (and by inference, the whole population) that will say they have engaged in nude sunbathing. Suppose we decide to draw a random sample of the population of your college and that we will ask them, among other questions, whether they have ever done any nude sunbathing. We decide that we will draw a sample randomly of 100 students who are currently enrolled at the college. Finally, suppose we take our sample and ask our questions and find that 60 percent of the students in the sample from your college have engaged in nude sunbathing. What do we now know about the total population of students at your college? Can we say that 60 percent of the students at your college are also nude sunbathers? Maybe.

Before examining the problem of sampling in more detail, let us outline the procedure that might be followed in selecting our sample of college students for this study. In order to accomplish our sampling of the college population, we could write each student's name on a piece of paper. If we then put all the pieces of paper with the names into a hat and thoroughly mixed up the pieces so there was *no* order to them, we could then pick out the first 100 slips of paper and we would have our simple random sample of the college. Or would we?

A mathematician would point out that, while the probability of choosing the first person's name is one out of some number x, the probability of choosing the next piece of paper with a name on it is 1 out of $x-1$, the probability of choosing the next piece of paper is 1 out of $x-2$, and so on. As you continue to remove the pieces of paper from the hat, the probabilities for choosing the next piece of paper also change. The more pieces of paper you remove, the better the odds that one of the remaining pieces of paper will be included in the sample. Take the most obvious case. Suppose, for example, you were interested in a sample of 25 students out of 26. Once you were down to the last two scraps of paper, each one of them would have a 50 percent chance of being included in the sample. Would you still have a simple random sample?

Before we move to an examination of the means for determining how close the sample data are to the data for the college population as a whole, it is important that we describe in some detail what we mean by the concept of a *simple random sample*. Realize, first, that when we use the expression *random* we do not mean iffy or slipshod. The term has quite specific meanings when applied to the selection of a group from a larger population. When we say that we plan to choose our subgroup from the larger population through the use of a simple random sample, we mean that each and every person in that larger population has an equal chance of being included in our sample and that all combinations of a given size are equally probable. We cannot, for example, exclude one person because he or she is a color we do not like, or exclude a person because his or her grade is too high (or too low). Nor can we exclude people because we become too tired to continue after numbering only some of the population, and so on. For a sample to be a simple random sample, each and every element must have an equal chance of being included. As Blalock (1972:510) says, "If, on any given draw, the probabilities of all remaining individuals being selected are equal regardless of the individuals previously selected, then we have a simple random sample." The problem remains, what about changing probabilities?

One of the techniques for eliminating the problem of changing probabilities is to replace the pieces of paper in the hat after you have copied off the relevant information. This approach, as you may have guessed, is called sampling with replacement. The other technique, mentioned above, is called sampling without replacement.

When sampling from an extremely large population, it is often permissible to sample without replacement since the probabilities for each element chosen change very little with the removal of each other element. For example, if you are taking a sample of 100 persons from a population of 1 million, the probability of the first person's being chosen in your sample is 1 out of 1 million. The probability of the next person's being chosen is 1 out of 999,999. Numerically, this means that the probability of the first being chosen is 0.000001, while that of the second person is also, according to my calculator, 0.000001. Once you have removed the first 500,000 persons from your population, the probability of choosing a person increases to 0.000002. Consequently, in large populations you do not really have to worry about replacing persons into the group from which your sample is being chosen. In a smaller sample, such as the example we are working on here, replacing persons in the population is a good idea.[1]

For the instances of sampling with and without replacement we will follow Kish (1965:38), who suggests ". . . we shall refer to *simple random sampling* (srs) when sampling without replacement; and to *unrestricted sampling* when sampling with replacement." In this same section, Kish proceeds to an important point (1965:38):

> In practical survey sampling we seldom actually use an srs design. Why, then, does srs loom so large in sampling theory? First, because of its mathematical properties, most statistical theories and techniques assume simple random selection of elements, though usually from an infinite population or with unrestricted selection. Second, all probability selections may be viewed as restrictions on simple random selection, which suppress some combinations of population elements, whereas srs permits all possible combinations. Third, the relatively simple srs computations are often used on data obtained by more complex selections. This procedure leads to good approximations in situations where the distribution of the variable in the population is effectively random. But this assumption of random distribution is often wrong and leads to gross mistakes. Fourth, srs computations can often be used as a convenient base, then adjusted for the design effect of the sample design actually used.

Kish is suggesting that, while most researchers discuss their techniques as if they were done using the simple random sample method, such is not always the case and ought not to be the case.[2] There are many times in research when one wants to use a method other than that of the simple random sample. While statistical techniques are usually based on simple random sample selection of elements, other

---

[1] Statisticians have formulae to correct for nonreplacement. See Blalock, 1972.

[2] Kish's book, *Survey Sampling*, is often considered the "bible" for those persons engaged in survey research. While often difficult for the beginner, the book should be on the bookshelf of anyone who plans to be involved in survey research.

methods are often no worse than simple random sampling and often may be a good bit better.

Someone about now is probably saying to himself or herself, "But is it not possible when replacing persons in the population to pick a sample that is composed of the same person every time?" The answer is that it is possible that such a sample would result but highly unlikely.

We can now return to the example begun earlier. If we take a single sample of the student population, even if it is a large sample, larger than our sample size of 100 students, it is only an estimator of the actual number of students in the population who have sunbathed in the nude. In our example, we found that the students indicated they had engaged in nude sunbathing about 60 percent of the time (another way to look at that is to say that 60 percent of the sample said they had sunbathed in the nude). If we show all the possible answers to our question, in terms of percentages, we show a straight line with a beginning at 0 percent (none of the sample said they had sunbathed in the nude) to 100 percent (all the persons in the sample said they had done so). Our sample would fall somewhere between the two extremes.

Once we had drawn our sample, we might well feel a bit of disquiet as to whether or not it really represented the percentage in the population. If we proceeded to draw samples (let us say five more), we would find that samples tended to cluster around some value that we call the population value.[3] If the five additional samples had values of:

Sample	Value
Original	60%
1st	35%
2d	55%
3d	49%
4th	75%
5th	58%

we could then plot them on a graph and show how they distribute themselves around the population value.[4] A graph of these six sample values would be as shown in Figure 7–1.

Suppose that we decided not to accept a few samples as the final answer but continued to draw samples from the population for an infinite number of samples of 100 students each. If we were then to graph the results, we would see an interesting phenomenon. With a greater and

---

[3] Even though we do not know what that value really is.

[4] Realize that, in reality, it is rare for the researcher to know what the population value actually is. We can do so in our problem since we have a fictional example.

FIGURE 7–1
Distribution of Six Samples of Students Showing Percentages Who Said
They Sunbathed Nude

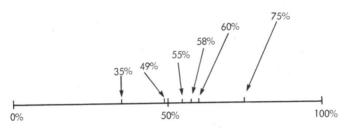

greater number of samples, our sample percentages would tend to distribute themselves around some midpoint. For the purposes of our example, we can assume that the real percentage in the total population
who had sunbathed in the nude was 50 percent. The sample distribution around the real population percentage would be as shown in Figure 7–2.

FIGURE 7–2
Sampling Distribution for Percentage of Students Who Indicate
Nude Sunbathing

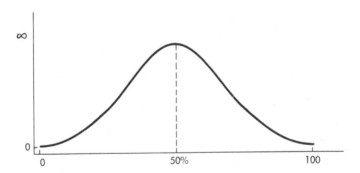

As you can see, the samples tend to form a curve that centers around
the value that we have said is the population "score" or percentage.
This curve, which has the appearance of a bell, is what is called an
approximation to the normal curve (or a bell-shaped curve). As you
can also see, some of the values in the samples would come closer to
approximating the real value of the population than would others.
Some of the samples would find percentages that exactly matched
the percentage in the population, while others would diverge greatly
from it.[5]

---

[5] The distribution shown by the curve is a distribution of the values from the
sample as they cluster around the true population value. Consequently, this is why
this distribution is called a sampling distribution.

What is important from our point of view is that, if the sample we have chosen is random, then we can calculate how close to (or how far from) the population percentage our sample is (or should be). That is, we can say, with some degree of certainty (which we are able to specify) that the percentage we found in our sample differs from the percentage in the population by only a specific amount and that we are 95 percent (or some other number) certain that we are correct when we say that. We can say all these things about our findings because there are a number of interesting properties of this thing we have called a normal curve.

As a beginning, we can redraw the curve to show some of its properties. We will have a similar curve, but this time, rather than the percentage of the students who have sunbathed in the nude, we will replace the population figure with a zero (denoting a central point).

FIGURE 7–3
Normal Curve Approximation

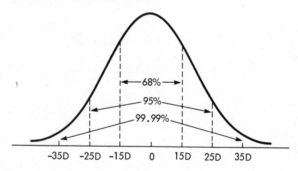

Once we have specified the center of the distribution, and when we know that it is a normal distribution, we know a number of additional facts.[6] Once we have placed a zero point at the center of the distribution, we have standardized the distribution so that we can show any variable that is distributed normally if we can convert the value to some standardized score. By standardizing the values, we can show how far (in standard terms) any sample value deviates from the population average. One measure of deviance is called the *standard deviation*. Generally, we speak in terms of one, two, or three standard deviations away from the average of the population in either direction. We do this because we know how many of our samples are likely to

---

[6] You can see that the curve never touches the horizontal axis but simply approaches closer and closer to it. This is to suggest that, if you have a large population and take an infinite number of samples, some of those samples will be extremely far from approximating the average for the population.

fall that far away from the average. If the curve is normal, then one standard deviation in either direction will contain about 68 percent of all the possible sample averages. Likewise, two standard deviations in either direction will contain about 95 percent of all the sample averages, and finally, three standard deviations in either direction will contain about 99.99 percent of all sample averages. In other words, sample averages will tend to cluster around the population average so that some of them tend to be reasonably good predictors of what the population value is. If you know how far away the sample average is from the center point, you have a pretty good guess as to how well it approximates the population average. The point here is that there are good reasons for making certain that the sample you have drawn is a random one, the major one being that you will then be able to make some statements about how good your data are in terms of their ability to say something relevant about the value of that item in the larger population. Thus, if you know about where the value of your sample for the students is in terms of the sampling distribution, you will know what the probability is that you are accurately predicting the actual percentage of nude sunbathers with this particular sample value.[7]

It is possible now to look back at our sample and, based on some statistical manipulations, we can decide whether or not we are willing to accept our sample percentage as representative of the true percentage. In order to do this, we need to know the standard error of our sample value and the number of people in the sample. Because we are using the mean of our sample to estimate the mean (or average) value of the population, we refer to its standard deviation as the standard error. We call it a standard error (rather than standard deviation) (1) to distinguish the two measures one from the other and (2) to alert the reader, again, to the fact that samples and measures computed on them are estimates and, as estimates, they may be in error. The formula we would use to calculate the standard deviation (remember estimating for the population as a whole) is:

$$\text{Standard deviation} = \sqrt{\frac{P\,Q}{N}}$$

Where:

P and Q are the binomial values the population would show were we able to find them out by asking all persons in the population how many sunbathed nude.[8]

N stands for the number of persons

---

[7] For more complete discussions of the statistical method used here, see: Blalock, 1972; Frank, 1974; Hays, 1963; and Kish, 1965, among others.

[8] $P = Q - 1$ and $Q = 1 - P$. Unfortunately, if your data are not in percentages, a different formula is called for. See below, note 9.

One tends to run into trouble if one does not know the actual value of the percentages in the population. However, since the largest value for P times Q is found when P and Q each are equal to 50 percent, we can use these values as our best-guess estimate of the population values. Substituting in our formula we have:

$$\text{Standard deviation} = \sqrt{\frac{(.50)\,(.50)}{200}}$$
$$\text{Standard deviation} = \sqrt{.00125}$$
$$\text{Standard deviation} = .035$$

Now that we have computed an estimate of the population standard deviation, we can use our result to help us construct a confidence interval around our estimate. The formula for computing the confidence interval is:

$$P_s \pm 1.96 \sqrt{\frac{(.50)\,(.50)}{200}}$$

Where:

P_s = the percentage of nude sunbathers we found in our sample of the population (60 percent, or .60 for the formula; the two numbers mean the same thing).

1.96 = the number of standard deviations away from our proposed population percentage that will give us a 95 percent confidence level for our estimate.

We use the value of 1.96 standard deviations from the mean because that allows us to work with 95 percent of the area under the normal curve. We use the figure for 95 percent of the area under the normal curve as a way of "hedging our bets." Those who work with statistics argue that they would like to be wrong only 5 times out of every 100 predictions they make about population values. If we work with 95 percent of the area under the normal curve, we are saying that we think that 95 percent of the time the value we discover will fall into this area. Why not some other area? Because social scientists have decided on this value.

If we now go back and substitute in the formula, we find:

$$.60 \pm 1.96 \sqrt{\frac{(.50)\,(.50)}{200}}$$
$$.60 \pm 1.96\,(.035)$$
$$.60 \pm .068$$

We can now look at the 60 percent figure (the .60 in the formula) and put our confidence limits around it. Using the 1.96 standard deviations, means that we think that 95 percent of the time the true value for the percentage of persons who have sunbathed nude would be 6.8 percent above or below the value we have found from our sample. Thus, we can say that 95 percent of the time, we think the true population percentage of those who have sunbathed nude would be between 53.2 percent and 66.8 percent.

Now that we have done all the statistical "game playing," what exactly do we know about our sample and how well it represents the percentage in the population? We know that we are confident that 95 percent of the time, the real population percentage of those who sunbathe in the nude will be between 53.2 percent and 66.8 percent. We feel pretty confident that our estimate adequately represents the population value. Realize, of course, that our estimate could represent the 5 percent of the time when we will be in error ($100\% - 95\% = 5\%$). We as researchers, however, are usually willing to be wrong 5 times out of every 100 times when we present confidence intervals that look like the ones above. Said another way, 5 times out of 100, a confidence interval as presented would *not* correctly represent the population percentage. We know all these facts because we began with a random sample of the population of students at the college. It is the reliance on random sampling that allows us to make statements about our findings.

While we have spent a great deal of time dealing with simple random samples, we have repeatedly stressed that they are not the only kind of samples that we will deal with. It is important, following Blalock (1972:509), to distinguish between probability and nonprobability samples. As Blalock suggests (1972:509), ". . . the distinguishing characteristic of a probability sample is that every individual must have a known probability of being included in the sample." In a nonprobability sample, it is not possible to know what the probabilities of selection of each element are (or will be). In this discussion, we will spend the greatest amount of our time discussing probability samples and how to draw them, and then we will briefly discuss the nonprobability samples.

As we have suggested throughout this chapter, the simple random sample is the most basic form of the probability sample. One of the techniques for selecting a random sample is that suggested above: We take all the scores and write them on separate pieces of paper, mix them up in a hat, and then select the ones we want included in our sample. Another technique, and one that is probably more widely used in practice, is to give each element in the population a number and then refer to a table of random numbers, taking the first x amount of the random numbers that will allow you to fill your total for the sample. In other words, if your sample size is 50, then you would enter the table of random numbers and take the first 50 random numbers that correspond to numbers of elements in your population. As you can see in Appendix A, random numbers have no ordering that is apparent and, consequently, they are supposed to give you an unbiased selection procedure for your sample. When one uses a table of random numbers, it makes no difference where you start in the table or whether you want to move down columns or across rows. All that you should do is (1) make your decisions before you begin and (2) remain consistent throughout the sampling procedures. Suppose we wished to choose a sample of 10 persons from a population of 1,000 persons, all of whom had been given numbers that were consecutive from 001 to 1,000. Each element must be determined to have a unique number assigned, one not duplicated by any other person in the population. If we then were to choose a sample, we could simply open the book to one of the pages of random numbers, let our finger hit the page, and then begin. For our purposes, we will go down the columns, picking either three- or four-digit numbers that correspond to numbered elements in the population, until we have chosen the ten persons we want. Using the random numbers in the Table 7–1, we begin where the arrow is and choose.

TABLE 7–1
Random Numbers

80149	54187	32644	00232	81067	57848	79389	82826	06426	84746
35199	16009	69814	60275	10908	52193	16002	12014	27608	57613
06888	77507	14802	29621	32274	40015	56728	12687	48951	59662
56493	51337	99588	22502	72306	37880	99346	77619	63034	09342
83581	99353	94901	06872	32339	95240	11542	51796	25861	77485
47556	43388	68872	57938	41865	60560	38774	09447	97019	77517
75123	85725	95533	21770	31215	37123	53873	09753	38104	34442
41454	98644	31366	92865	95690	24449	22680	46319	01078	11849
76358	61463	83596	11395	26703	89051	16667	42369	23497	48502
95294	40334	87223	65615	06592	85625	77340	24729	21342	64111
	START								
37004	97392	54517	96093	61969	15548	27777	85607	22501	92841
48593	00413	80814	89520	19498	21795	21426	46789	41950	43215
76317	63969	30354	57446	06656	85245	86715	66893	48876	68171
35458	44736	74185	25062	39358	96634	21854	74382	36058	39726
02340	09602	93024	60237	52050	18315	60075	75244	46991	78737
17315	70525	57884	86772	24035	09697	33803	99992	24529	26396
15973	29212	69833	27638	09388	29418	02872	85196	21381	38839
13657	44807	89449	28615	90867	11932	07120	59073	98040	75978
50980	78043	36212	85699	17275	47473	98954	56577	35232	20960
41717	25633	38792	51649	10653	88024	14628	50360	95161	55748
77638	92514	14073	63818	78394	41353	11863	21433	47409	33744
19274	58884	86895	46992	41353	90328	96211	32408	30022	85679
96990	15406	38232	62274	78496	82433	51260	89515	11742	78692
70562	73804	77738	30026	22116	67311	80734	36520	00742	08297
31605	29308	02748	62615	97160	03409	98644	03994	27176	89803

From: RAND Corporation, *A Million Random Digits with 100,000 Normal Deviates* (Glencoe, Ill.: Free Press, 1955), p. 161.

Once the starting place (point) has been chosen by chance, the rest is relatively straightforward as long as one is careful and systematic. We begin wherever our finger lands (in this case where the arrow is) and move down the column, checking the four leftmost digits in each sequence to see if it is representative of one of our sample identification numbers. Remember, any four-digit sequence from 0000 to 1000 can be chosen as it will represent one of the elements in the sample. Since we are only interested in the left four digits, the first sequence is not chosen (96093 does not fall into the acceptable range), neither is the next sequence (89520), nor the next (57446). It is not until we have progressed all the way down this column, moved to the top of the next column, and moved about halfway down it that we find the first sequence of digits that fits our requirements: 06656. Since the set of digits 0665 falls in the range for our sample of 0000 to 1000, we record this as the first of the identification numbers of our sample elements. Continuing down this column and on to the next columns we locate the identification numbers of the sample elements as:

1.	0659	6.	0287
2.	0665	7.	0712
3.	0938	8.	0944
4.	0969	9.	0975
5.	0340	10.	0399

We can now easily move from the identification numbers of the sample's elements to find the persons associated with the numbers and either ask them our questions, or do whatever it was we had in mind to do to them (assuming they would allow us to do it, of course).

A slight variation on the simple random sample is the systematic sample. When one draws a systematic sample, one simply moves down a list and takes very *j*th element beginning with the *k*th element. Both the starting point and the distance between elements chosen should be arrived at using a table of random digits. Once you have those values, however, you can simply go through the ordered arrangement choosing the sample elements. Suppose, for example, you wish to conduct a study of attitudes held by college sophomores at your university. It would be possible (probably) to get a list of all the sophomores, then give each person a number, then draw some specified number of elements from the table of random digits. A somewhat easier approach, however, would be to determine that there is no inherent biasing order to the list, choosing to start at the 49th name and then taking every 12th name until you have the desired sample size.

According to Blalock (1972:514), ". . . if the ordering used in compiling the list can be considered to be essentially random with respect to the variables being measured, a systematic sample will be equivalent to a simple random sample." In terms of the list, it is generally important to note that first, the list, if alphabetical, is not random. People's last names tend to cluster in ethnic groups: the Fitzpatricks, Fitzgeralds, and Fitzgibbons, for example. Such ordering may be to your advantage in that it provides you a more true "shape" of ethnic groups as formed by people's names. It is also important to realize that a list may have some type of trend in it and this will bias what you will have when you choose a sample. Thus, if your sophomore list was compiled with those persons registering first being at the top of the list and those registering last (or late) being at the bottom, it is possible to get all early registrants, and that, in itself, may bias your results. It is also possible that the number you have chosen to use as the range of your choice, every 15th, for example, may bias your results if every 15th sophomore you choose lives in a room next to the main stairs in the dormitory. Your sample would not, then, be one of all sophomores, but of sophomores who live nearest the main stairway. If it is true that persons who live near intersections are different from those who do not, you may well have a biased sample for your trouble. If you can be certain that the list has no inherent order that will bias results, then you might as well use systematic sampling, as it will certainly speed up the procedure for you.

Another modification on the principle of simple random sampling is the use of the stratified sample. When one uses a stratified sample, one divides the population into strata that one wants to make certain will be represented in the final sample and then randomly samples from the strata. It is possible, for example, to choose a random sample of the population and have it turn out to contain only males, or only females, or only persons of German descent, or only almost anything. In order to counteract this potential problem, one could stratify the sample into males and females and then sample from each group, thus making certain that the final sample includes representatives from both groups. When you select a stratified sample, it is important to consider whether you will sample proportionately to the size of the groups in the larger population, or whether you will try to simply set equal the numbers of persons chosen. If you sample the groups proportionate to their size in the population, you will have a better assurance that your final sample, at least on this characteristic, will look much the same as the larger population. For example, if you were to take a sample of the population of the United States that you had stratified in terms of sex and you were going to do it proportionately, out of a 1,000-person sample, about 485 would be male and about 515 would be female. While stratifying your sample does not guarantee any better findings, it may help your research to more adequately represent the population. In fact, stratifying your sample and then choosing from each stratum randomly can never be worse than a simple random sample and has the potential of being a great deal better.

The last type of probability sample we want to discuss is the cluster sample (also called the areal probability sample). If you use this type of sample, you do not sample the elements in the population directly but choose clusters of them and then deal with some number of the elements in each chosen cluster. For example, suppose you wanted to conduct a survey of attitudes among the population of a moderately large city. If the population of individuals was in the 50,000-to-100,000 range, it would be difficult (if not impossible) to give each person a number and then choose randomly the people to be included in the sample. A much easier approach is to take the city block as the cluster that will be sampled. If you number the city blocks and then draw a certain number of them randomly and, finally, interview all persons who live on those blocks, you have saved yourself a great deal of time and energy.

One of the most useful aspects of samples in research is to use your sample data to estimate various parameters in the population. For example, if you can measure the average number of persons who live on blocks in the city, you can get a rough approximation of the total population and its attitudes. Thus, if there are 1,000 blocks in the city and 50 people (on the average) living on each block, and you determine that you want to choose 10 blocks for your sample, then you will end up interviewing 500 persons rather than the 50,000 who would have been involved if you had tried to question them all. In this case also, you will know that each person you talk with will be the "spokesperson" for 100 people in the city.

Before leaving the discussion of cluster sampling, we might also note that this approach can be used in a more complex fashion if an extremely large area is to be covered using a rather small sample. In this case, what one might design would be a multistage cluster sample. Here you might begin, as done above, by sampling the 10 blocks from the city of 1,000 blocks. Instead of interviewing all people on those ten blocks, however, it would be possible to make a list of all dwelling units[9] and then sample some number of them in each block. If we found, for example, that our ten blocks each had exactly 50 families living in them, we could decide to sample 10 families from each block (chosen in any number of ways). Now we have a sample of 100

[9] Not just houses, since some people may live in apartments in those blocks.

families that represents the population of families in the city. If we happened to ask the person we interview in each of the dwelling units how many members of the family there are, we could then obtain an average and multiply that by the number of families in the city to get an estimate of the total population of the city. Thus, if we knew that the families averaged 6.72 persons per family, we could estimate the population of the city as 336,000 persons.

It is important to realize that there are some potential problems in using cluster samples. The most serious problem arises because, when you make your initial choice of certain blocks, that effectively eliminates all other blocks from being included in your sample. While such an occurrence is true for all random sampling techniques, in cluster sampling you have the potential of choosing blocks that are all similar. Thus, you might choose only blocks in the wealthiest, or poorest, sections of town. In addition, you may bias your results by having too great similarity within clusters. The sophisticated analyst notes this potential as results from the survey begin to come in.

An additional problem can occur in choosing your second level of clusters. Again, what happens if all happen to be corner houses or vacant lots? The most important problem, however, concerns the fact that, once you have chosen your initial clusters, only those persons living in those blocks have a chance of being in your sample. At that point, the chance of selecting people in any other part of the city drops to zero. Likewise, the only persons who now have a chance of being included in the sample are those in the chosen blocks, thus altering the probability of their inclusion.

It is on the samples that we have called the probability samples that statistical tests can reasonably be computed. The researcher uses nonprobability samples illegitimately when he or she conducts tests on them, since these samples violate one of the cardinal rules of statistical testing—that is, that the data the statistical tests are being conducted on were gathered randomly.

The nonprobability samples are just exactly that: Samples in which the probability of inclusion of any one element cannot be computed. Generally, the nonprobability samples rely on the interviewer to include or exclude persons from the group of persons being interviewed. Even the words used as names for these types of samples imply nonprobabilistic techniques for choosing, i.e., judgment samples, quota samples, and so on. In all of these techniques, the interviewer is given some general notion as to the types of persons who are to be included in the sample and then it is left up to the interviewer to include them. For example, the director of the research project might specify that an interviewer is to interview, out of every 100 persons, 52 females, 48 males, 10 blacks, 82 whites, 8 members of other races, 46 Protestants, 40 Catholics, and 14 Jews. How those particular proportions of persons are chosen is left to the interviewer. The problem is that the interviewer may choose only those persons he or she thinks are "good-looking," or only those persons who are taller than six feet, or only those persons who are "well dressed." By leaving the interviewer with such discretionary powers, we have eliminated the element of randomness from the sample selection process. We do not know how to calculate the probability of inclusion of any of the elements in this type of sample and therefore are unable to conduct any of the standard statistical tests on the data with any feeling of accuracy (we can always conduct the tests; we simply do not know what the results are telling us).

When we choose a sample, we generally want to know what the probability associated with the inclusion of any element will be. If we are concerned with pretesting a questionnaire, or if we are concerned with a "quick and dirty" survey of some attitudes, we might not use the probability samples, but the nonprobability sampling techniques. We would use these nonprobability sampling techniques because they are generally faster and cheaper than the other approaches. For a pretest, for example, we might want to know if the questions we have designed in our questionnaire are understandable by members of the population, if they are relevant to our hypotheses, and if the order of the questions is logical. In order to determine answers, we might not want to go through the bother of a probability sample; we might only want to go out and ask the first 25 persons who pass us on a street corner. Or if we were to be a bit more rigorous, we might want to pretest our questionnaire on a group of persons similar in many ways to those who will be in the final sample.

For the truck driver questionnaire, for example, I went out to a number of truck stops and asked drivers if they would fill out the questionnaire, knowing that they would not be the drivers who would be included in the final sample to be chosen later on. My concern was not the statistical results I might be able to compute for this group, but rather whether the questions I had worked so hard and so long on were relevant to people in truck driving. Was I asking questions that would give answers to the questions I thought I was asking? In other words, one can create a purposive sample in order to determine how the instrument will work later, rather than to test the hypotheses now.

THE ANALYSIS

As an example of the uses to which sampling might be put, let us assume that we are instructors in a class in social research at a university where instructors are expected to be active in many committees in addition to their assigned teaching. We can also assume that we are, as the class instructors, unable to get all statistics computed for an examination and have the test returned to the class as promised. What we can do, however, is to compute some sample statistics on the examination rather than actually doing all the computations. We can, in other words, let sample statistics stand for the population parameters we would have computed had we had the time (i.e., had the administration allowed us the time).

Suppose the following represents the grades for the midterm examination for our class in social research. The scores are on the basis of 0–100 points. The scores are shown in Table 7–2.

TABLE 7–2
Grades for Students Taking Midterm Examination

Student Number	Test Score	Student Number	Test Score
1	65	14	78
2	72	15	75
3	80	16	72
4	94	17	85
5	57	18	86
6	40	19	88
7	78	20	92
8	85	21	99
9	97	22	75
10	89	23	38
11	83	24	59
12	80	25	69
13	68	26	80

Because we are pressed for time, we can draw a sample of any number (how about either five or ten people?) and use this sample to estimate what the value is for the class. As we have mentioned, while the sample we draw may not exactly represent the average of the class as a whole, the information we get from the sample can tell us (1) what we think the average for the population is and (2) how close to being correct we think we are.

Before we move to computation of the sample data, we can look at some other measures of what the statisticians call the measures of central tendency. Measures of how much the data tend to be bunched together are measures of central tendency. The average score we will compute later is one of these measures. The two others that we will deal with are (1) the mode, and (2) the median. The mode is defined as the most often found category in a distribution. In the present case, we would locate the mode as that score that the most persons in the class had. In order to locate both the mode and the median, we can put

the scores in rank order, from the lowest to the highest, as shown in
Table 7–3.

TABLE 7–3
Rank Order of Student Scores on Midterm Examination

38
40
57
59
65
68
69
72—2
75—2
78—2
80—3
83
85—2
86
88
89
92
94
97
99

You can see that, while there are a number of scores that at least
two of the students attained, there is only one score that three of the
students attained, that of 80. Thus, the score of 80 is the modal score
for the midterm examination for this class.

The median is also a measure of the central tendency of the distribution but is defined as that score attained by the person at the exact
middle of the score distribution, in this case, the score for the 13th and
the 14th person (or person 13½, actually). What one does in this situation is to count 13 spaces into the distribution and see what the
score is for that person and then see what the next score is. Finally,
one takes the average of the two scores. The score for the 13th person
is 78, for the 14th person is 80. We add the two scores (78 + 80) and
divide the total in half to give us the median. The median score, then,
is 79.

Before leaving this subject, we could also locate at least one of the
measures of dispersion of the distribution—that is, How widely do the
scores separate themselves? For this measure, we can look at the range,
which is defined as the distance between the lowest and the highest
scores. In this case the range is 38–99 points.

We have now discussed how widely dispersed the distribution is,
computing the range, and also how much the distribution seems to
hold together, namely, the measures of central tendency. We can now
look at the last measure of central tendency that we have time to compute, the mean or average. For our purposes, the average will be the

sum total of all scores for those persons included in our sample, divided by the number of persons in the sample. Let us take a sample of five persons randomly from our class and compute the average of the sample. We can draw our sample with replacement using the tables of random numbers, and if we do, our sample is as follows:

Student Number	Test Score
20	92
7	78
16	72
13	68
22	75

When we calculate the average, we find:

$$\text{Sample average} = \frac{385}{5}$$
$$= 77.0$$

At the same time, we might also want to compute the standard deviation of the sample average, which turns out to be $S_x = 9.17$.[10]

Before we move to a determination of how close we are to being correct in our estimation of the true class average, let us also draw a sample of ten persons to see if the information we get is drastically different from what we have learned from our sample of five persons. If we draw a sample, again using the tables of random numbers, we find the results in Table 7–4.

TABLE 7–4
Comparison of Two Samples of Student Grades on Midterm Examination Showing a Sampling with and without Replacement

A. Without Replacement		B. With Replacement	
Student Number	Test Score	Student Number	Test Score
4	94	4	94
17	85	17	85
7	78	7	78
18	86	18	86
17	85	11	83
22	75	22	75
12	80	12	80
23	38	23	38
14	78	14	78
10	89	10	89

[10] The formula for standard deviation is $S = \sqrt{\frac{\Sigma x^2}{N} - \overline{X}^2}$. See Blalock, 1972:83.

Notice here that, if we sample with replacement, we will have two of our scores, and also two of our elements, the same; number 17 has been chosen twice. We might then choose to replace the second number 17 with another element, in our case the number 11, with a score of 83. If we compute the mean for the two samples, the one, a sample with replacement, and the other, a sample without replacement, we can see how much of a difference the choice of one method over another makes.

The average for the sample chosen with replacement is:

$$\text{Sample average}_{wr} = \frac{788}{10}$$
$$= 78.8$$

On the other hand, the sample without replacement has as its average:

$$\text{Sample average}_{w/o\,r} = \frac{788}{10}$$
$$= 78.6$$

The difference is .2 for the two samples, a figure that might be important with samples of only ten persons each, but that surely would not affect the outcome very much in larger samples. The standard deviations for the two samples are: $S_{wr} = 15.44$, $S_{w/o\,r} = 15.36$. As you can see, the difference in the standard deviations is only .08, again a somewhat insignificant amount.

We still do not know, of course, how well our sample data estimate the true values in the population. We could return to our technique of creating a confidence interval and suggest that we use the idea that our mean replace the percentage from the earlier formula, that the standard deviation be used as it was in the earlier formula, and that we again use the idea of a 95 percent level of confidence. If we did so, our formula would be:

$$\overline{X} \pm 1.96 \text{ (st. dev.)}$$

Unfortunately, if we did that we would not be calculating the figures correctly. In this case, we must replace the normal standard deviation with the standard error measurement which involves dividing the standard deviation by the square root of the sample size.[11] If we do that, the formula becomes:

$$\overline{X} \pm 1.96 \frac{\text{(st. dev.)}}{\sqrt{N}}$$

---

[11] See Kish, 1965:41, for a more complete explanation.

For the five-person sample drawn earlier, the formula would show that the values are:

$$77.0 \pm 1.96 \, \frac{(9.17)}{\sqrt{5}}$$

$$77.0 \pm 1.96 \, (4.03)$$

$$77.0 \pm 7.89$$

Thus, for the five-person sample we would say that we are 95 percent certain that the real population average lies between the values of 69.11 and 84.89. If we also then computed the values for the ten-person sample, the values would be:

$$78.8 \pm 1.96 \, \frac{(15.44)}{\sqrt{10}}$$

$$78.8 \pm 1.96 \, (4.88)$$

$$78.8 \pm 9.58$$

and for the sample taken without replacement:

$$78.6 \pm 1.96 \, \sqrt{1 - \frac{10}{26}} \left(\frac{15.36}{\sqrt{10}} \right)$$

$$78.6 \pm 1.96 \, (.784) \, (4.86)$$

$$78.6 \pm 7.46$$

These two formulas then give us values for the actual population average of 69.22 and 88.38 in the first case, and 71.1 and 86.1 for the second case. If you have been carefully following the computations, you will note that we sneaked an extra term into the last set of computations:

$$\sqrt{1 - \frac{10}{26}}$$

That term had to be added in this case because, when we sample without replacement, we are dealing with a finite population (eventually, we will reach the last element that we can remove from the population). In order to correct for the finite nature of the population we are dealing with, we must insert this term, which is called the finite population correction factor and which is defined as:

$$\sqrt{1 - \frac{\text{Number of persons in sample}}{\text{Number of persons in population}}}$$

Correcting in this way gives us a bit of an edge when calculating population averages based on formulas derived for infinite populations when using finite populations.

Now that we have done all the calculations for the samples, we can go back and do the same sorts of calculations for the population as a whole to see how far we are from being correct in our estimates. Assuming once again that we are the instructor and that the class hour is now over and we have sufficient time to sit down and do the calculations, we can now see how far our estimates differ from the real population values. The average for the population as a whole is:

$$\bar{X} = \frac{1985}{26}$$
$$= 76.31$$

The population value also has, by the way, a standard deviation of 15.34.

We can see that, while we did not exactly locate the average for the population as a whole using our sample data, we were not very far off the mark. In fact, we were farther from the true population value when we took the larger samples than when we were using estimates based on the smaller sample (the five-person sample). Most of the time in research we will not be this fortunate. Smaller samples generally show greater divergence of the standard deviation from the population standard deviation than do larger samples. While we will rarely be closer to the mark with smaller samples, it is nice that one does not always have to draw larger and larger samples to ensure precision of estimates.

SUMMARY

In this chapter, we have given you a very brief overview of the problems and procedures of sampling. In addition, we have tried to suggest some of the statistical techniques at your disposal for determining how well your sample approximates the population. For those persons interested in pursuing statistics, a standard textbook in statistics (better yet, a standard course) is highly recommended.

8

Survey of Attitudes Using a Questionnaire

THE PROBLEM

Using a questionnaire designed in class or using the questionnaire supplied in the text, question five people (students or others). The questions in the interview schedule should be primarily closed-ended (that is forced-choice alternatives) although they do not all have to be so. Submit the completed questionnaires and any comments you may have on the design or the responses. For example, what questions "worked" and which did not?

THE APPROACH

Up to now you have been primarily concerned with watching social behavior and with interpreting what you see. We now begin to further develop skills that are used in the asking of questions about behavior. There are a number of reasons for shifting to the questioning of persons about their behavior but one of the main reasons is that you cannot always see the behavior that you think is important.

In any effort to develop a comprehensive analysis, the question of how to study "private behavior" is a continuing problem for the conscientious observer of the social scene. There are always behaviors that people will not let you watch. Not only will people not let you watch them cast votes in elections, it is also illegal for you to watch (except in extraordinary circumstances). Likewise, it will be difficult for the sociologist of deviant behavior to watch the majority of deviant acts as they are being committed. In addition, what about actions that are not necessarily deviant but are considered private by the persons involved? Sexual activity between husband an wife, for example, often could be used as data for a research study but there are few couples who would allow the necessary observations to be made.

While many people will not let you watch certain aspects of their behavior, there are also certain things that you could not physically observe even if you wanted to. For example, how would you go about observing behavior that happened during a subject's teen-age years? How would you observe the actions of a person who was active in the 1937 General Motors Corporation sitdown strike? In addition, behavior that has yet to occur is also not amenable to observation. You cannot watch behavior that will happen when a person becomes a senior citizen (unless you as a social scientist wait until then, and watch what happens). If the person happens to be 24 years old now, that means a long wait for you. What you can do in all of these circumstances, however, is ask the persons involved what they think about what they are doing (or will do).

You can ask people what they will do when they become senior citizens—or what they think they will do when that happens. You can ask individuals to think back to when they were teen-agers and ask that they reconstruct for you what happened at the time—what the dating patterns were, what sorts of music were being listened to, and so on. You can ask participants what happened during the sitdown strike and what other people were doing during the conflict; what could a person on strike see from the roof of the building, did the wives bring in food to the strikers, and so on. You can also ask a person what sorts of sexual activities are engaged in within (and outside of) marriage (if you do not lead into such questions rather carefully, you may end up with no answer, or at least not the answer you expected).

You should be getting the idea at this point that researchers do not simply walk up to someone and begin to ask the first questions that come into their heads. The way you ask a question may well be as important as what it is that you are asking. In other words, the construction of the questions, while it is extremely important, is not the only thing that you, as a social researcher, have to worry about. The way you ask the questions, the way you are dressed, the image that the respondent has of you, all will influence the answers you get to the questions asked.

You could ask a person, "What is your marital status, are you single, are you married, are you widowed, are you divorced or separated?" You could ask the exact same question but a second time, ask it much louder—that is, raise your voice so that you are shouting at the respondent. You have not changed the content of the question, but you have certainly changed the type of response you are likely to get. If the person bothers to answer at all, the answer may be something (again) that you did not expect. Let us present some additional examples of problems involved in the design and construction of questions. Assume for the moment that our fictional social researcher does not vary the tone in his or her voice and that all that is being varied is the content of the questions. Suppose that your hypotheses deals with the question of the influence of a respondent's sex on the content of the attitude that respondent has toward minority group members. That is, suppose your hypothesis argued that males would be more likely to be anti-minority than would be females. In order to test your hypothesis, it will be necessary to ask questions designed to get at the respondent's attitudes toward the minority group in question and also, at the same time, to determine, on your questionnaire, what the sex of the respondent is. Because you need to know a person's sex, you will have to ask what the sex is. The problem arises when you try to decide how to ask the question. There are a number of ways to ask the question, some of them (unintentionally) designed to get you "funny" answers. For example, if you put together a questionnaire and somewhere in the section dealing with biographical data you included a question:

SEX: _____.

You might get answers such as the following:

SEX: Male_____. SEX: Female_____.
SEX: Enough_____.
SEX: Twice per week_____. SEX: Neither_____.
SEX: Yes_____. SEX: I thought you'd never ask me.

As you no doubt have already seen, such a question leaves the researcher open to all manner of problems. The researcher would have done much better to have asked the same question in a slightly different way, a way that hopefully would allow fewer strange (funny?) answers:

SEX: Male_____; Female_____.

If you design the question in this manner, you will have fewer problems in your analysis. By careful design you will minimize problems, although you will never eliminate them completely (remember Murphy's first law).

Let us present another example of question design that might give you trouble in an analysis. Suppose, as above, that you needed certain kinds of biographical information on your respondents because your hypotheses indicate certain causal relationships. You may need to know, for example, the relationship between religious experience and religious affiliation. Your hypothesis might be that those who believe in the more "fundamentalist" religions will show more personal religious experience than those not in "fundamentalist" type religions. In order to find out the information about the hypothesized relationship, you will have to ask your respondents about their religious affiliations. How you ask your respondents about their religions will determine what you will find out about them. Examine the following questions, all of which ask a respondent to identify his or her religion:

1. What is your religion? Catholic_____; Jewish_____; Protestant _____; Other (specify)_____.

2. What is your religion? Christian_____; Jewish_____; Muslim _____; Buddhist_____; Other (specify) _____.

3. What is your religion? Christian_____; Atheist_____; Agnostic _____; Satanist_____; Other (specify) _____.

All of these questions ask a person to indicate his or her religion but at the same time, all three are eliciting different types of information about the respondent's religious preferences. Because each elicits different information, your conclusions will vary depending on which question type you choose to use.

One final example of biased questions can be included at this point. This example is a classic although it is rarely found in this exact form in questionnaires. At the same time, however, questions just like it have been found in questionnaires designed by some of those persons who think they are fairly good research methodologists. Suppose that you are interested in husband-wife relationships and you suspect that persons in the lower socioeconomic classes are more likely to engage in physical acts of aggression against each other, while those in the higher socioeconomic classes will take out their aggressions against their mates in verbal assaults. You could ask a question dealing with the socioeconomic class position of the respondent and then ask additional questions about the supposed violence inflicted by one against the other. For example, you could ask the following question sequence:

1. What social class do you feel you are a member of? Upper_____; Middle_____; Working_____; Lower_____.
   IF upper or middle ask A.
   IF working or lower ask B.
   A. Do you and your spouse ever engage in verbal arguments? Yes_____; No_____.
   B. When did you last beat up your spouse? _____ _____.

In this situation, you make an assumption about the behavior of your respondents and then you bias your results by asking a biased question based on your assumption. There is no possible answer that will not potentially get the working or lower class respondent in trouble. What do we do for those persons who do not beat their spouses?[1]

Up to now, the discussion has revolved around the problems inherent in designing the questions that will be put into the questionnaire that is to be administered. We have not, however, dealt with any of the background problems that go along with the actual design of the instrument you will later be using. The major problem that must be dealt with (and it may sound somewhat simplistic to say so) is to determine the reason for the questionnaire's existence. Why are you going out and asking people questions, anyway? What is the purpose of your research? What empirical questions do you hope to answer by talking to a group of people?[2]

If you examine the questionnaire that is included at the end of the book, you will find that it is somewhat different from many questionnaires that are given to college students. Why might it be different? For one reason, it was developed for a specific reason and to fit a specific occasion. The administration of the school in which this questionnaire was used was concerned with the question of whether or not to construct new dormitory facilities, and, if the students felt that new dormitories should be built, the administration wanted an estimate of how large such structures might have to be. At the same time, other persons at the school were concerned with how large a geographical area was served by the school, the means of transportation to and from the school (should car pools be encouraged?), and so on. The school at which this questionnaire was used is primarily a commuter college and, at the time the instrument was designed, was the owner of a number of apartment buildings that were being used as dormitories. The questions faced by the university and the questions to which they needed answers were: Do students want the college to provide dormitory space; how many of the students would actually use the space if it were provided; and, by implication, should the college be in the dormitory business in the first place?

While information could have been gathered on only the dormitory preferences of the students, it seemed logical to also try to find out some socioeconomic information at the same time. The designers of the questionnaire felt they needed the demographic information for at least two reasons: (1) they wanted to get a picture of the student body and this was the only way to do so, and (2) the feelings about the

---

[1] An excellent description of the pitfalls of question writing as well as the means for avoiding many of the problems can be found in Selltiz et al. (1976), Appendix B.

[2] On this subject, also see Warwick and Lininger (1975).

desirability of the dormitory might well vary among social categories and groups. Further, the faculty was interested in securing a picture of the student body of the school because they did not feel at all certain that they actually knew what types of students were attending the school. Many faculty members had hunches about the students and their backgrounds, but none of the faculty were certain the hunches were correct. The faculty thought this survey would be an easy way to take a census[3] of the students and thus arrive at a composite picture of a "typical" student.

As we have been suggesting throughout this book, it is often important to know more than the fact that, say, 43 percent of all persons questioned on a particular topic are in favor of it. Suppose for a moment that we had found in our study of the students at the commuter college that 43 percent of the 2,000 students questioned were in favor of the school providing dormitory space for the students who wanted it. What does this fact tell us about which students want dormitories? Unfortunately, the fact tells us nothing about *which* students said that the college should provide "dorm" space. If, on the other hand, we had asked the students information about themselves at the same time that we were asking them questions about the dormitories, we could do our cross-tabulations and find out which groups want what. We might have found, for example, that of the 860 students indicating an interest in dormitory availability, 700 lived within five minutes of the campus and were also of upper middle-class parents. Were we to have found this, we might well have discounted, to a certain extent, the expressed "interest" in the provision of dormitory space, because the probability is quite low that any of the 700 students would have utilized the space if it were provided for them. On the other side, of course, is the fact that 160 other students also answered in the affirmative on the question of dormitories. Should they happen to be full scholarship students whose parents lived more than 200 miles from the campus, we could feel somewhat more comfortable about advocating the building of a limited number of rooms for housing a limited number of students. We must, in other words, not only include questions on the subject that is most important to us, we must also include questions that we can use as means by which we can subdivide our results to examine the differences between people.

While you may use the questionnaire provided at the end of the book, you are by no means limited to its use. The knowledge of the design and construction of an instrument is one of the basic tools of the social scientist. In a class I taught recently, the group was asked

---

[3] A census is a complete count of all the members of a population. One might refer to it as a 100 percent sample of the population.

to design a questionnaire on any subject in which they were interested.[4] In the city at that time, a mini-controversy was raging over the location of an "adult" movie theater in what was primarily a residential section of town. Because there had been a good bit of space in the local press devoted to the theater, the students decided to go to the neighborhood and question the residents to see, if in fact, there were strong local feelings about the location of the theater. The students were interested in determining whether all the residents felt threatened by the existence of the theater or whether those most threatened were but a small, vocal, minority. At the same time, the students included questions about the whole notion of censorship and its relation to "adult" or pornographic movies. Finally, the students asked the residents whether they would object to the existence of the theater if it was moved to another area of the town. Was the location of the theater, in other words, the thing that worried the residents or was it the content of the movies being shown? The class, when left to their own devices, devised a rather interesting research project that was based almost solely on the content of two or three newspaper articles as inspiration. While not all research projects are as easy to develop, there is no reason that the building of rationale for a research project, and the designing of a questionnaire, should be painful.

The choice of a research topic is totally up to the person (or persons) conducting the research. In addition, the means by which to examine the research questions can also come from anywhere. You can, if you give proper credit, use another's research questions if you want to see if they hold in many different cases. If you see questions in a sociological (or other) article you might want to include them in your questionnaire. If you happen to read a book or article about research in which a series of questions is reprinted you might want to include them in your questionnaire. You might even come across a book that is a collection of questions that have been used in previous research studies and which you could use in yours.[5]

We can for the moment, assume that you have designed your hypotheses and the questions that go along with them; that you have decided how you will analyze the data once you have questioned all the people you are planning to talk to; that you have designed the codes to be used for the data processing; and so on. You are now ready to go out and ask the questions. What do you do next? The first thing that you had better do is to decide who you are going to question. What is the population that you are going to question? For the questionnaire

---

[4] At the same time, the class knew they had a questionnaire to fall back on should they have needed it.

[5] On this subject, see Miller (1977); Robinson, Athanasiou, and Head (1969); and Southwick (1975).

included at the end of this book, the population would be the students at your school. For the questionnaire about the "adult" movie theater, the population might be the residents of the neighborhood that is near the theater. The problem with indicating that the residents of the neighborhood are the population for the questions is: What size is the neighborhood? Within how many blocks of the theater will the questions be asked? Will the questions be asked of all persons in the area? Will a sample be taken and the questions asked of only those who are in the sample? What type of sample will be drawn? The questions of the sample and how it is drawn may be as important as the design of the questionnaire itself.[6]

For the questionnaire dealing with student responses, it may be sufficient to ask all the students at the school the questions. This will cause trouble for the researcher if the school happens to have a student population of more than 2,500 students. It would be possible to take a random sample of all the students at the school and then ask those students the questions. The use of a random sample, as we noted in the last chapter, will then allow us to know how close we are to being correct when we begin to say things about the student population based on the small group of students actually questioned. Suppose that we have a student population of 10,000 students at our school. We could take a random sample consisting of 500 students.[7] In this case, we would have taken a 5 percent sample of the total student population. In order to take a sample of the students, we might employ a systematic sample taken from the student directory. We might also enlist the computer at the university to randomly generate a list of 500 students, taken from the enrollment list kept by the administration. We could also choose to take samples other than random ones, of course.

Assume for the moment that you have designed the questionnaire and have decided on the manner in which the sample will be drawn. The next question that you must decide is how will the questions be asked of the persons in the sample. Will you (as the interviewer) ask the questions or will you simply give the questionnaire to the respondent and ask him or her to fill in the answers? If the respondent does fill in the answers, you may find that there are many persons who do not understand the questions as they are asked. If you do not stay with the respondent as the questions are being answered, those questions that are unclear may be left blank. If you ask the questions, you may be in a better position to explain the question if there is some doubt. Assuming, of course, that you decide that explanations will be given if there is uncertainty. You may feel, as the researcher, that no

---

[6] Refer back to Chapter 7.

[7] Or, within certain rather flexible limits, almost any size sample.

explanation should be given as that will bias the questions (or the answers). If you ask the questions it might be best to give no help and simply tell the respondent that he or she is to make the best answer possible under the circumstances. In the case of this project, it may be best that you ask the questions so that you get practice in asking questions. Again, you will have to decide, as a class, how much explanation you will allow during the administration of the question-naire to the respondents.

Let us summarize to this point what you must, as survey research-ers, do in order to prepare for questioning people:

1. Decide *what* it is you are going to ask questions about. What is the focus of the survey to be? The implication here is that you will also be deciding *who* you will question at the same time.

2. Determine the specific research questions (the *hypotheses*) that will be asked of the persons in your study.

3. Decide *how* you will choose those persons who are to be included as the respondents in the study.

4. Decide who will write down the answers: you or the respondent.

5. Determine the wording of the *questions* that will be included in the study. This differs from (2) above because here you are de-ciding on the exact wording of the questions that will be asked of the respondents. Also you will be deciding on the ordering of the questions to be asked, what sorts of responses you will expect, which questions will be closed-ended, and which will be left open so that the respondents can elaborate answers, and so on.

6. Determine the codes to be used for the questions in your study so that you will be prepared to analyze the data as they come back to you. The Appendix at the end of the book presents what might be called a sample coding manual that accompanies the questionnaires also included at the end of the book. Developing codes for answers as you develop the questions will often allow you to eliminate problems at the design stage. You may, for ex-ample, find that what you have in mind cannot be coded easily from the questions you are trying to ask and you may want to redesign questions at this stage.

7. *Pretest* the questions before going to the actual group to ask them. Find out if the questions "work" and if so, do they get at information that you want. At this stage you should eliminate as many potential problems as possible.

8. *Redesign* the questionnaire to take account of all changes.

9. Pretest the redesigned questionnaire. Continue doing (7) and (8) until all the problems (or at least as many as you have found) have been eliminated from the questionnaire. You also will, at this time, be trying to eliminate as many problems as pos-sible from the administration of the instrument.

10. Once all (most?) problems have been eliminated, *administer* the questionnaire to those persons chosen for inclusion.

THE ANALYSIS

In the analysis of a questionnaire and its design, we are interested in having you go back over the design stage and look at what you did, to decide if there is anything you might have done differently or would do differently if given the opportunity. You and I know that neither of us makes errors, but it is often a good idea to check just in case.

As was noted in the flow chart in Chapter 1, a series of feedback loops has been built into the research design process. Most people have no idea how easy it is to design a research project that does none of the things its designer intended. Not only can one have trouble with the entire project, one can also have difficulty with questions and question wording. The way a question on religion was worded determined, we noted earlier, the kinds of information that could be gathered and also determined the types of results one could have.

Once you have begun the research design, you can continue to cycle through the feedback loops until you are satisfied that you have done all you can. Moving from the creation of the methods of research back through the hypotheses is not, as we have said, necessarily a onetime procedure. It may be that you should go back through the loop a second time (or more) to make certain that all changes have been made and that nothing has been left out. It is especially crucial to work back through the feedback loops whenever you change any items due to circumstances of pretests.

The pretest is the place where you test your instruments as well as your hypotheses to see whether in fact they will work for you when you set out to do the actual research project. In a pretest you may have to put your ego away for a while, as you find all your hard-won ideas shown to be worthless. It is possible, of course, that a pretest will show that all you have created is perfect and that you are ready to move to the actual research project. The probability that this will happen is approximately equal to the odds that the president of the United States, Miss Universe, and the Easter Bunny will together visit you and give you a check for $1 million.

The important point to remember as you conduct your pretests is that they are for your protection. If you set out to do a research project and you do no pretests, you may well find that nothing you hypothesized works out. Had you conducted some pretests, you would have already known this and would have altered your hypotheses to take account of this anomaly. It is during the pretest also that you can revise the questions that you are asking to take account of changing conditions. One other use of the pretest situation is important to mention at this point. You may well use the pre-test to determine the categories that you will use in the variables that you are interested in testing. For example, you might have developed a hypothesis that there was a relationship between a person's self-perceived social class position and the degree of job satisfaction that he or she felt. You might begin your pretest with a question dealing with social class, such as:

> What social class do you feel you are a member of?
> 1. Upper _____
> 2. Middle _____
> 3. Lower _____
> 4. Other (please be specific) _____

While most of us would imagine that a majority of our respondents would put themselves in the first three categories, it is possible that a number of persons would write in some other social class designation. In pretesting the questionnaire that was eventually used in the truck driver study described earlier, a number of the drivers wrote in that they were members of the "working class." Others indicated that they were members of the "middle-working class," and so on, suggesting that we should add a category dealing with the working class to the questionnaire in order to deal with this large number of people. By adding a category for the "working class" we were removing a group of people from the general category "other" and creating an additional category to be included in the analysis. If it turned out that the addition of the category did not make any difference in the results, we could always move the people in the group labeled "working class" back into the "other" category. However, if we did not have the category "working class" on our final questionnaire, we potentially would have lost a great deal of useful information. By rights, once you have altered your questionnaire in a pretest, you should go out and test the changes. If you make additional changes, you should go out and test those also. In practice, I suspect that few questionnaires go through more than two to three pretests, and most probably go through no more than one (if that).

Once you are satisfied that you have done all you can to make your questionnaire, your questions, and your educated guesses about the relationships between variables as good as possible, the next step is to go out and administer the questionnaire to your sample. Many times, the actual administration may seem anticlimactic to you. In a recent research project carried out in the Middle East, the questionnaire went through five revisions before we had it translated, then through two more revisions once it had been translated. By the time we transported the questionnaires to the country (and got them through the customs checks of two separate countries), mapped the areas to be studied, and hired the translator/interviewers, going out and asking the questions of our sample respondents was almost like taking a vacation. The only problem was that in this particular research project, Murphy's first law seemed to be in operation all the time. Imagine what it might be like to have to locate your respondents in a country where you do not speak the language, where residences do not have street numbers, and where many of the streets do not have names. Locating our preselected respondents involved following such directions as "drive past the airport, to the market on the corner of the intersection where five streets come together, turn onto the second street, continue past the school to the second market, turn left until you come to a statue, turn left and go to the third large house; the apartment is on the third floor." The problems here are, of course, to determine what a "market" is, and what is meant by the phrase "large house" (among other obvious problems with the directions).

As suggested above, the analysis of the process of questionnaire design is to make certain that you have done all you can before you move out into the field to ask your questions. Once you are convinced there is no more you can do to revise and refine the questionnaire, you ought to waste no more time. Too many research projects fail because their authors cannot bring themselves to finish the revisions and move to the data collection stage.

The following is a sample questionnaire such as the one you will be using for the class exercise. We have included a copy here so that you will have a permanent copy should you tear the others out of the book.

SOCIOLOGY QUESTIONNAIRE

My name is _____ . I am a member of the Sociology research class in the

department of Sociology. Because there is so little known about the students here at _____

University, we thought it important to design a questionnaire to get some information. The

Sociology Department and the research methods class are conducting the research and we would

appreciate it if we could ask you a few questions. The responses you give will be completely

anonymous and confidential. The responses will be used by the Sociology Department for

statistical purposes and will not be connected with the statements of any individual.

ID Number _____

1. What is your sex? Male _____ Female _____

2. What is your age (at your last birthday)? _____

3. You do not have to answer this, but what religion are you?
   Protestant _____ Catholic _____ Jewish _____ Other (please specify) _____

4. You do not have to answer this, but what race are you (please mark all that apply)?
   White _____
   Black _____
   Native American _____
   Mexican–American/Chicano _____
   Oriental _____
   Puerto Rican–American _____
   Other (please specify) _____

5. Are you: Married _____ Single _____ Widowed _____ Divorced _____

6. Are you: Freshman _____ Sophomore _____ Junior _____ Senior _____ Other
   (please specify) _____

7. Are you full–time student (12 credit or more hours)? _____
   Part–time student (less than 12 hours)? _____

8. What is your major (or what do you plan to major in)?
   Business Administration _____
   Education _____
   Humanities _____
   Physical Science/Math _____
   Social Sciences _____
   Other (please specify) _____

8(a). Do you have a specific plan for what you wish to do upon graduation?
   Yes _____ No _____

(b). If yes, what is your plan? _____

9(a). If you are working, what is your occupation (please be specific)? _____
   _____

(b). For what company do you work? _____

2

10. What is the amount of your father's education?

Grade School	High School	College	Graduate
1 2 3 4 5 6 7 8	9 10 11 12	13 14 15 16	17 18 19 20 more

11(a). What is your father's occupation (please be specific)? _____
_____

(b). For what company does your father work? _____

12. What is the amount of your mother's education?

Grade School	High School	College	Graduate
1 2 3 4 5 6 7 8	9 10 11 12	13 14 15 16	17 18 19 20 more

13(a). Does your mother have an occupation outside the home? Yes _____ No _____

(b). If yes, what is your mother's occupation (please be specific)? _____
_____

(c). For what company does your mother work? _____

14. If you are married, what is the level of your spouse's education?

Grade School	High School	College	Graduate
1 2 3 4 5 6 7 8	9 10 11 12	13 14 15 16	17 18 19 20 more

15(a). What is your spouse's occupation (please be specific)? _____
_____

(b). For what company does your spouse work? _____

16. Answer only if you are married: What is your approximate total family
income going to be for this year from all sources (parents, spouse's job, etc.)?

$0–$2,999 _____	$9,000–$10,999 _____
$3,000–$4,999 _____	$11,000–$12,999 _____
$5,000–$6,999 _____	$13,000–$14,999 _____
$7,000–$8,999 _____	$15,000 and over _____

17. Answer only if you are not married: What is your approximate total personal
income going to be for this year from all sources (parental, scholarship,
work–study, jobs, etc)?

$0–$2,999 _____	$9,000–$10,999 _____
$3,000–$4,999 _____	$11,000–$12,999 _____
$5,000–$6,999 _____	$13,000–$14,999 _____
$7,000–$8,999 _____	$15,000 and over _____

17(a). Do you get scholarship or work–study money? Yes _____ No _____

(b). If yes, how much per year do you receive? _____

18(a). Do you pay city income tax? Yes _____ No _____

(b). If yes, what rates do you pay? Resident _____ Nonresident _____

19(a). If married, does your spouse pay city income tax? Yes _____ No _____

(b). If yes, what rates does he/she pay? Resident _____ Nonresident _____

20(a). Do you own: Car _____ Truck _____ Motorcycle _____ Camper _____ Other _____

(b). Do you drive to school? Regularly _____ Occasionally _____ Split with others _____

21(a). What is the distance, in miles (one way), from your home to the university? _____

(b). How long does the trip take? Hours _____ Minutes _____

3

22. Where do your parents live?
   In this town _____
   In this county _____
   Outside of the county but within 50 miles of campus _____
   More than two hours from campus _____
   Other (please specify) _____

23(a). If married, do you have children?   Yes _____ No _____

(b). If yes, how many? _____

(c). How many are in public schools (grades Kindergarten – 12)? _____

(d). How many are in private schools (grades Kindergarten – 12)? _____

24. How many brothers and sisters do you have? _____

25(a). Where do you live?
   Own home _____
   Parents' home _____
   With relatives _____
   In apartment _____
   In college housing _____
   Other (please specify) _____

(b). Where would you prefer to live?
   Own home _____
   Parents' home _____
   With relatives _____
   In apartment _____
   In college housing _____
   Other (please specify) _____
   Why? _____

(c). Where would you prefer not to live?
   Own home _____
   Parents' home _____
   With relatives _____
   In apartment _____
   In college housing _____
   Other (please specify) _____
   Why? _____

26. How important were the following factors in the decision you made to attend this school?

	Very Important	Important	Unimportant	Very Unimportant	Undecided
The amount of money you have available					
Distance to class					
Distance to work					
Distance to movies and other entertainment					
Distance to go for dates					
Lack of campus social life					
Studying atmosphere					
Other (specify) _____					

4

27. Please put in order from 1 (like) to 8 (dislike) the following aspects of where you live _now_:

Studying atmosphere _____   Distance to work _____
Distance to school _____   The people _____
Cost _____   Distance to entertainment _____
Parents like it _____   Other (specify) _____

28. Who was most important in helping you make the decision to live where you now live?

Yourself _____   Relative _____
Friend _____   Other(specify) _____
Parents _____

29(a). What are your chances of living next year in the same place you now live?

Very good _____   Not good _____
Good _____   Very bad _____
50-50 _____   No chance _____

(b). If you expect to change, why do you think you will change? _____
_____

30. Did you:

Begin here as a freshman _____
Transfer from a junior college _____
Transfer from a public 4-year college _____
Transfer from a private 4-year college _____
Other (specify) _____

31. Why did you pick this college? _____

32. If you were to transfer from this college, where would you go?

State university _____
Another state college _____
Private college in this state _____
Other (specify) _____
Why? _____

33. What are the things you like about this college? _____
_____

34. What are the things you dislike about this college? _____
_____

35. If you had the power, what would you change about this college? _____
_____

Please use the remaining space to add any comments you might have.

9

Analysis of Data

THE PROBLEM

Analyze the data from the questionnaire designed in class or the questionnaire supplied in the text. In your analysis include your hypotheses as well as tables showing the relationships you tested and your conclusions concerning these relationships. If time does not permit a complete analysis, you should prepare the hypotheses to be tested as well as the rationale for the hypotheses. Further, you should submit dummy tables showing the variables you would use to test the relationships.

THE APPROACH

Once the data have all been collected—or at least when a good portion of the data have been collected—the researcher can move to an analysis of the data. Part of the problem with any research project, is that the relationships that are hypothesized between variables do not always show up in a visual inspection of the questionnaires when they are completed. Because the relationships are not always clear, it is often necessary to code the data into a machine readable form so that an electronic data processing machine can do the data manipulations for you. By "electronic data processing machine" we do not necessarily mean a computer. It is also possible to analyze data using an electronic card sorter: such a machine will divide your data cards into separate

160

piles (and often will count them at the same time) thus allowing you to make the cross-tabulations that will make your data meaningful. Since most colleges and universities today possess computers, however, the remainder of this chapter will be generally oriented to their use.[1]

If you have gathered information on a great number of people, the easiest means for analyzing the data is to transfer the information to data cards for use in machines. As a first step in this process, it is necessary to edit the questionnaires so that missing data can be dealt with. In the editing process, the researcher must examine all questionnaires to see that the majority of the information is present and that the answers are legitimate. The editor is responsible for eliminating the "funny answers" from the questionnaires (some students as well as other respondents like to supply "funny answers") and, in fact, is responsible for eliminating those questionnaires that are—for whatever reason—totally unusable or unacceptable. During the editing process is also the time when the identification number can be assigned to each questionnaire. As the questionnaires are logged into the office and edited, someone must have the responsibility for seeing that each instrument is assigned a unique identifying number. Each instrument is assigned a unique code number so that throughout the analysis (and even afterward) comparisons can be made between the questionnaire and the data cards. If errors are found on data cards, the only way to connect the cards to a unique questionnaire is through the use of the identifying number.

Once the questionnaires have been edited, the assigning of code numbers to responses can begin. In this phase of the research, the questionnaire is gone through, question by question, and a numerical code is assigned for each answer. The easiest way to do this, of course, is to precode the answers so that few questions have to be coded at this time. To precode a questionnaire, the researcher simply places a number next to each of the alternatives provided the respondent on the questionnaire. Thus, when we ask our respondents what class they were in college we might have constructed the question as:

Are you: Freshman (1)_____; Sophomore (2)_____; Junior (3)_____; Senior (4)_____; Other (5) (Specify)_____.

---

[1] A footnote regarding the use of computers is important at this point. Many persons when confronted with a computer have the tendency to be overwhelmed by it which often results in reluctance to utilize this electronic marvel. While computers are terribly fast means for analyzing data, it is important to remember two facts about them: (1) they do only what they are told, no more, no less; (2) they are nothing more than very sophisticated adding machines. Computers do not sit and think or scheme when no one is watching. They "think" only when told to do so by a programmer.

As we went through the questionnaire it would be easy to then transfer the appropriate codes to a data card. As you can see on the enclosed questionnaire, we did not precode the answers. We chose not to because the questionnaire would have been extremely "cluttered" with numbers and answers. While we did not precode the answers on the questionnaire, we did build a coding guide as we went along (which is almost as good).

The coding of the questionnaire can proceed using the coding manual (see Appendix B). As previously mentioned, the assignment of the numbers can be done on the questionnaire itself or it can be done on a separate code sheet. The code sheet that seems to work best for us is one which consists of a single 8½ by 11-inch piece of paper divided into 80 boxes. Each box represents one column on a standard data processing card and each sheet of paper represents a separate data card. Once the numbers are written into the code sheet, the key-puncher can then easily transfer the codes to the data card.[2]

Suppose that we had a series of questions from our student questionnaire that looked like the following:

ID Number <u>0001</u>

1.   What is your sex? Male <u>X</u> Female ____
2.   What is your age (at your last birthday)? <u>33</u>
3.   You do not have to answer this, but what religion are you? Protestant ____ Catholic ____ Jewish ____
        Other (please specify) <u>Agnostic</u>
4.   You do not have to answer this, but what race are you (please mark *all* that apply)?
        White <u>X</u>
        Black ____
        Native American ____
        Mexican-American/Chicano ____
        Oriental ____
        Puerto Rican-American ____
        Other (please specify) _____
5.   Are you: Married <u>X</u> Single ____ Widowed ____ Divorced ____
6.   Are you: Freshman ____ Sophomore ____ Junior ____
        Senior <u>X</u> Other (please specify) _____
7.   Are you full-time student (12 or more credit hours)? <u>X</u>
        part-time student (less than 12 hours)? ____
8.   What is your major (or what do you plan to major in)?
        Business Administration ____
        Education ____

---

[2] For another explanation of this process, see Moser (1967), chapters 13–14; and Dial (1968).

Humanities _____
Physical Science/Math _____
Social Sciences __X__
Other (please specify) _____

8(a). Do you have a specific plan for what you wish to do upon gradua-
       tion? Yes __X__ No _____

8(b). If *yes*, what is your plan? ___Graduate Study_____

9(a). If you are working, what is your occupation (please be specific)?
       Stock Clerk_____

9(b). For what company do you work? ___Acme Retail Auto Parts Company

Once we have determined that the data were reasonably correct (at
least insofar as this is possible by editing the instrument), we would
then use the code book and code the answers onto our 80-box sheet.[3]
We might do this as follows:

1	2	3	4	5	6	7	8
O	O	O	/	/	3	3	4
9	**10**	**11**	**12**	**13**	**14**	**15**	**16**
4	/	2	4	/	5	/	O
17	**18**	**19**	**20**	**21**	**22**	**23**	**24**
5	3	5	O	2	6	O	6
25	**26**	**27**	**28**	**29**	**30**	**31**	**32**
5							

In this manner, all the questionnaires could also be coded and eventually keypunched onto the data cards. You should work through
the example as just presented so that you can determine how the
coding is done. Can you find any errors in the above coding? If you
find none, we strongly urge you to go back through the example until
you do. There are two clear errors of interpretation in the above example, which you should find.

The first error is of a type that is normally attributed to sloppiness
on the part of the coder. The second error is one of interpretation. The
first error is found in the code assigned to the marital status of the
respondent. The respondent indicated that he was married, yet the
coder entered a 2 in column 11. As is obvious from the code manual,

_____
[3] Refer to Appendix B at end of this book for the codes being used for the
questions.

the number 2 stands for a person who is single. The second error deals with the industry in which the respondent works. On the questionnaire, the respondent indicated that he worked for a retail auto parts store but the code used for the industry shows a wholesale auto parts store. The correct code in this instance would have been a 656 and a 6 in the next column (columns 22–25) rather than the 606 and the 5 as is there at present. Now go back through the coding and see if there are any additional errors that are present. Now, if we both can say there are no more errors, we are in agreement.

From this point it is then possible to code all additional questionnaires that have been done. It is important to remember that questionnaires all be given an identifying number and that no two questionnaires be given the same number. One study we worked on, managed to give a great number of questionnaires duplicate numbers. The problem was of such magnitude that several of the assistant study directors had to leave their other jobs and spend two to three weeks straightening out the duplication of identifying numbers. The problems were multiplied in this particular study because the main office for the study was in one large city and the interviewing was being conducted in another. In order to get the correct number on the correct questionnaire, we had to spend a great deal of time on the phone with the on-site director who had to look up the code for each questionable instrument and then see if we had the correct one. When we found the instruments with incorrect identifying numbers each had to be given a new code number and the new number had to be transmitted to the field office where their records could also be changed. The problem may seem to have gotten out of hand, but realize that for this study we were gathering information on about 18,000 people and we had to know who was who in order that we could check back with them for any needed, missing, or additional information. Without the correct identifying number such rechecking would have been impossible. Now look at the questionnaires and code book for this problem again. The questionnaire identifying number is the first four columns in each of the two 80-column data processing cards required per questionnaire. In other words, by utilizing eight columns out of the 160 available to us, we have (hopefully) averted a problem before it ever started. While other errors will always crop up, it is important to keep errors of coding to a minimum.

Now we must add to the research checklist we began in the previous chapter. Once the data have been gathered, researchers must:

11.   *Edit* the questionnaires to locate missing or incorrect data. If necessary go back to the respondents in order to fill in missing data.

12. *Code* the data into a form that makes it more amenable to analysis.

13. *Check* the coding for all questions to minimize the number of errors that are carried through into the analysis of the data.

Once the coding of the data is completed, and once the data have been entered into a data-processing machine, you can begin the process of analyzing the results. At this point it is necessary to return to the discussion of the relationships you have hypothesized between the variables in your research. As was suggested earlier, the hypotheses you generate are educated guesses that you make about the relationships you think exist and that you are testing by the questions that you have asked.[4] As you begin the analysis of the data, there are a number of aspects of determining relationships between variables that you will want to take into account.

Possibly the most important feature is the establishing of a causal relationship between the variables in the research. While we can clearly show a relationship between the incidence of ice cream eating and the number of street robberies committed in a city, we cannot show anything approaching causation in the statement. Digging deeper we could show that the two items in the above example (the two variables) are related to another factor, a causative third factor: the heat, or temperature. In such a problem we are showing how two variables vary together rather than showing how one causes another. The problem of separating covariation from causation is always a tricky one and, as will be suggested below, one is never absolutely certain that true causation has been demonstrated. No matter what type of research project is being undertaken, there will always be the need to show the causal relationship between variables (or else why bother to do the research in the first place). The problem with asserting that a relationship is a causal one is that simply because an occurrence A is always followed by another occurrence B we cannot unambiguously say that A causes B. There may be other (hidden) factors at work causing both A and B as in the above sample. We are discussing a causal relationship when, following Simon (1978:485–487), we can indicate that the following statements are upheld by our data. First, the association between the two variables is strong enough so that the researcher believes he or she can predict one from the other, consistently. Second, for the relationship to be considered causal, there must not be too many "all other things being equal" statements made about it. Third, the relationship must be shown to be non-spurious;

---

[4] On this subject, see "The Research Process" in Chapter 1.

that is, not caused by some third factor. Fourth, "the more tightly a relationship is bound into (that is, deduced from, compatible with, and logically connected to) a general framework of theory, the stronger is its claim to be called 'causal'" (Simon, 1978:486–487).

The series of statements just made about causality suggests a number of related factors about research approaches that must also be dealt with, and, in fact, will be found in any search for causality. One important factor in determining the causal relationship between two variables is the time order of the relationship between them. If one variable is the supposed cause of a second, the causal variable may not follow the other in time. In other words, if X is the independent variable (the causal variable) and Y is the dependent variable (the caused variable), then X may not follow Y in time. At the same time that X may not follow Y in time, X and Y should also not appear at the same time. If both appear at the same time then it may be that some other variable is causing them both. In the relationship mentioned above, the ice cream eating and robberies, both events appear at about the same time and are shown to be caused by another variable operating prior to both of them in time. We must also be careful when asserting causality that we deal with one variable causing another and not with a sequence of causation where a variable X causes some other variable Z which, in turn, causes the dependent variable Y. In such a case the research has discovered an intervening variable and not a directly causal relationship.

One of the most difficult problems to overcome in any social science research project is that there is always the possibility of a rival interpretation for the relationship that you, as the researcher, have asserted as causal. For example, you may, on the basis of your research, be able to assert that a causal relationship exists between two variables. However, you may not be able to generalize the relationship to extend to people other than those you questioned while gathering your data. For example, in order to suggest that there is a relationship between attitude toward minorities and sex of the respondents among all persons, you will have to be able to demonstrate that your research included persons of all types and that none (or, at least not too many) of them expressed attitudes that differed from the majority. If it can be shown that your sample did not include persons of both sexes, you as the researcher will be hard pressed to substantiate your claim. If you have neglected to include both men and women in your sample, there is the chance that a rival interpretation of the findings may be legitimate in this case. In addition, no matter how generalizable you show your findings to be, there may still be a rival interpretation that can be used to explain the relationship. Because human beings are so inherently variable, it is possible that no matter how carefully you selected your sample and conducted your research, another variable may be the cause of what you have discovered.[5] As sociologists we might facetiously argue that while we may be incorrect we are never uncertain.

Another factor common to all research is that it is an attempt to describe a situation that the researcher believes to be true. While such a statement may sound trite, it warrants a short discussion. It is not always easy to design a research project that will show us when our assertions about the social world are either true or false. It is much easier to suggest assertions (hypotheses) that cannot be shown to be incorrect when tested in a research project. If, for example, we hypothesize that all persons possess something that might be called a culture, such an assertion is one that cannot be disproved. We could not disprove such a statement because we would be unable to question a person we suspected to be without a culture because part of the definition of culture is that it is composed partially of the language of the people being investigated. When a research project is in the design stage it is necessary to make the hypotheses testable in the sense that they can be shown to be false. Are you certain that you did that?

At the same time, of course, you will realize that, simply because the relationship you have hypothesized fits all the above criteria, there is no guarantee that the relationship will be causal. There is no substitute for common sense in assessing the degree of causality in the relationship. Even though a relationship fits all the criteria and even though it passes all the statistical tests you might want to conduct, the relationship might still be one of those freak situations where it is not causal but spurious. At this point, mature researchers will enter and say that, on the basis of their knowledge of other studies that have been conducted and on the basis of the other information gathered in this research project, this particular relationship is a spurious one, regardless of what might appear to be the case.[6]

We can assume that you have remembered all the warnings about spurious causation and that all the data are now ready to be analyzed. What do you do next? The first step is to construct some dummy tables so that you will have someplace to put your data after the computer generates cross-tabulations and statistics for you. The process is similar to that we discussed in Chapter 4, when we suggested you set up tables before going out to do your field observations in a shopping center. If we were analyzing the data from the student questionnaire, we

---

[5] While one might eliminate such a problem by testing all variables that might explain the relationship, the possible combinations are infinite and the research would never be concluded. All you can do is to test as many possible combinations as is feasible and then draw your conclusions based on your attempts.

[6] See on this subject Hyman, 1955.

might have hypothesized a relationship between the student's sex and his or her field of study. A dummy table is shown in Table 9–1.

TABLE 9–1
Dummy Table: Sex of Students by Major Field of Study

Field of Study	Male	Female
Business Administration		
Education		
Humanities		
Physical Sciences/Math		
Social Sciences	———	———
Total		
N		

The argument for such a relationship might be that the socialization of males traditionally has been in the direction of the "hard sciences" and business, while that of females has been in the direction of education, the humanities, and the social sciences. If we should find a predominant number of males in the sciences and business and a predominant number of females in education, social science, and humanities, we could argue that our hypothesis was not rejected.

The next step would be to have our electronic data-processing machine create the table for us. In this case, we would ask the computer to construct a table using the two variables, Student's Sex, and Student's Major Field of Study. An alternative method would be to take all the questionnaires and physically put them into ten separate piles, counting the results and entering the data into the dummy table. Thus, there would be one pile for Male BusAd majors, one for Female BusAd majors, one for Male Ed majors, and so on. One important aspect of the creation of the table that must not be omitted would be the direction of the percentaging.[7] It might even pay to ask the computer to percentage the table in a number of directions so that you can examine the output and see what direction makes the case the best for you. As you can see from the computer printout shown in Figure 9–1, it is possible to have the information percentaged in all directions, and then it is up to the researcher to sort out the relationships. In this case also, you can note that it is possible to have a number of statistical tests performed on the data as the computer prints it out for you.[8] This saves time and energy for the researcher. It is a good idea, however, to check the calculations, as occasionally the computer uses figures for its calculations that are not what you expect.

---

[7] See above, pages 47 to 53.

[8] A number of computer programs are available that will provide output such as shown here. SPSS (Statistical Package for the Social Sciences) is one of the more popular; see Nie et al., 1975.

FIGURE 9–1
Example of Computer Output for Variables Two (2) and Ten (10)

TWOWAY CROSS-TABULATION

10. VAR 10		2. VAR 2 MISS	(1)	(2)
N = TOTAL = TOT% ROW% COL%	1528 1627	3	742 48.6	786 51.4
MISS TOT% ROW% COL%	93	3	43	50
(1) TOT% ROW% COL%	251 16.4	0	208 13.6 82.9 28.0	43 2.8 17.1 5.5
(2) TOT% ROW% COL%	463 30.3	1	85 5.6 18.4 11.5	378 24.7 81.6 48.1
(3) TOT% ROW% COL%	130 8.5	0	52 3.4 40.0 7.0	78 5.1 60.0 9.9
(4) TOT% ROW% COL%	293 19.2	1	189 12.4 64.5 25.5	104 6.8 35.5 13.2
(5) TOT% ROW% COL%	391 25.6	1	208 13.6 53.2 28.0	183 12.0 46.8 23.3

TESTS OF INDEPENDENCE	STATISTIC	SIGNIF	DF= 4	N= 1528
MAXIMUM LIKELIHOOD	349.00	0.	CRAMER'S PHI=	.4607
CHI-SQUARE	324.34	0.	CONTINGENCY COEFF=	.4184

MEASURES PREDICTING:	VAR 2	VAR 10	COMBINED
GOODMAN-KRUSKAL LAMBDA	.3706	.1155	.2203
GOODMAN-KRUSKAL TAU	.2123	.0658	.1233

Before proceeding too far in the analysis of the data in the computer output, it is advisable to label the information so that you know what variables you are talking about. If you look at the information contained in Appendix B, you will be able to decode the output. Variable two (2) deals with the question that asked for the sex of the respondent. The codes were 1 = male, and 2 = female. You might like to write them in on the output in Figure 9–1. Likewise, variable 10 asked the major field of study of the respondents and was coded as Business Administration = 1, Education = 2, Humanities = 3, Physical Sciences/Math = 4, and Social Sciences = 5 (as you can see from the output, there were no students who were classified as being in the "Other" category).

The only problems you may have concern the numbers that seem to have little reference across the top of the table that are:

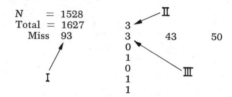

"$N = 1528$" indicates the number of persons the table computations are based on. "Total = 1627" indicates the total number of persons in the sample. The other numbers deal with missing data and represent the numbers of persons who, for whatever reasons, did not answer one or both of the questions. The number 93 (number I in the above diagram) is the number of persons who did not answer the question on their major field of study. The number three (number II on the diagram) represents the number of persons who did not answer the question on their sex. The other number three (number III in the diagram) is the number of people who did not answer either question. The other numbers in this section of the table tell us something about the respondents even though they did not answer one of the questions. The vertical line, for example, shows us how the persons who did not answer the question on sex answered the question on their major field of study—one was an education major, one a physical science/math major, and one was a social science major. Thus, even though we may not have all the information we would like to have about our respondents, we do have some, and we make use of what little we have.

We can now go back and fill in the dummy table, using the vertical percentaging from the computer output (see Table 9–2).

On the basis of this table, we would certainly be inclined to argue that our hypothesis was somewhat but not totally correct. The males clearly are more likely to be found in the major fields of Business Ad-

TABLE 9–2
First Approximation at Showing the Relationship between
Student's Sex and Major Field of Study

	Sex	
Major Field of Study	Male	Female
Business Administration	28.8%	5.5%
Education	11.5	48.1
Humanities	7.0	9.9
Physical Sciences/Math	25.5	13.2
Social Sciences	28.0	23.3
Total	100.0%	100.0%
N	(742)	(786)

ministration, Social Sciences, and Physical Sciences/Math, while the
females are more likely to be found in the areas of Education and Social Sciences. The problem for the hypothesis is that 28.0% of the
males are to be found in the social sciences. As one means for "teasing" a possible explanation from the available data, percentage the
table horizontally to see if possible explanations present themselves,
as shown in Table 9–3.

TABLE 9–3
Second Approximation at Showing the Relationship between Student's Sex and
Major Field of Study

Major Field of Study	Male	Female	Total	N
Business Administration	82.9%	17.1%	100.0	(251)
Education	18.4	81.6	100.0	(463)
Humanities	40.0	60.0	100.0	(130)
Physical Sciences/Math	64.5	35.5	100.0	(293)
Social Sciences	53.2	46.8	100.0	(391)

Percentaging the table horizontally tells us a little more than we
knew already. Males predominate in three areas and females in the
other two. We still do not know why there are more males in the Social Sciences than females. We would have to do additional analyses
of other variables to see if we could locate the reason why our hypothesis was not confirmed for the Social Sciences.

An additional example of the approach to data analysis might be
useful at this point. In Chapter 2, we asked you to interpret a table
that had as its three variables (1) how important money was in the
decision to attend the college; (2) the religion of the respondent; (3)
the marital status of the respondent. Suppose we had a hypothesis that
religion of the respondents would affect the degree to which money
was important in the choice of a college, and we also hypothesized that
the marital status of a person would affect the degree to which money

FIGURE 9–2
Computer Output Showing Relationship between Variables Five (5) and Sixty-Two (62)

TWOWAY CROSS-TABULATION

62. VAR 62		5. VAR 5 MISS	(1)	(2)	(3)	(4)	(9)
N = TOTAL = TOT% ROW% COL%	1240 1627	313	699 56.4	360 29.0	18 1.5	162 13.1	1 .1
MISS TOT% ROW% COL%	60	14	40	11	0	9	0
(1) TOT% ROW% COL%	812 65.5	210	440 35.5 54.2 62.9	242 19.5 29.8 67.2	10 .8 1.2 55.6	120 9.7 14.8 74.1	0
(2) TOT% ROW% COL%	295 23.8	67	176 14.2 59.7 25.2	86 6.9 29.2 23.9	8 .6 2.7 44.4	24 1.9 8.1 14.8	1 .1 .3 100.0
(3) TOT% ROW% COL%	14 1.1	6	9 .7 64.3 1.3	3 .2 21.4 .8	0	2 .2 14.3 1.2	0
(4) TOT% ROW% COL%	91 7.3	25	58 4.7 63.7 8.3	23 1.9 25.3 6.4	0	10 .8 11.0 6.2	0
(5) TOT% ROW% COL%	28 2.3	5	16 1.3 57.1 2.3	6 .5 21.4 1.7	0	6 .5 21.4 3.7	0

TESTS OF INDEPENDENCE	STATISTIC	SIGNIF	DF= 16	N= 1240
MAXIMUM LIKELIHOOD	23.059	.1122	CRAMER'S PHI=	.0658
CHI-SQUARE	21.493	.1603	CONTINGENCY COEFF=	.1305

MEASURES PREDICTING:	VAR 5	VAR 62	COMBINED
GOODMAN-KRUSKAL LAMBDA	0.	.0023	.0010
GOODMAN-KRUSKAL TAU	.0041	.0086	.0062

FIGURE 9–3
Computer Output Showing Relationship between Variables Seven (7) and Sixty-Two (62)

62. VAR 62		7. VAR 7 MISS	(1)	(2)	(3)	(4)
N =	1545					
TOTAL =	1627	8	507	987	9	42
TOT%			32.8	63.9	.6	2.7
ROW%						
COL%						
MISS	73	1	44	25	2	2
TOT%						
ROW%						
COL%						
(1)	1016	6	306	675	5	30
TOT%	65.8		19.8	43.7	.3	1.9
ROW%			30.1	66.4	.5	3.0
COL%			60.4	68.4	55.6	71.4
(2)	360	2	141	210	3	6
TOT%	23.3		9.1	13.6	.2	.4
ROW%			39.2	58.3	.8	1.7
COL%			27.8	21.3	33.3	14.3
(3)	20	0	6	13	0	1
TOT%	1.3		.4	.8		.1
ROW%			30.0	65.0		5.0
COL%			1.2	1.3		2.4
(4)	116	0	40	72	1	3
TOT%	7.5		2.6	4.7	.1	.2
ROW%			34.5	62.1	.9	2.6
COL%			7.9	7.3	11.1	7.1
(5)	33	0	14	17	0	2
TOT%	2.1		.9	1.1		.1
ROW%			42.4	51.5		6.1
COL%			2.8	1.7		4.8

TESTS OF INDEPENDENCE   STATISTIC   SIGNIF   DF= 12   N= 1545

	STATISTIC	SIGNIF		
MAXIMUM LIKELIHOOD	15.662	.2072	CRAMER'S PHI=	.0584
CHI-SQUARE	15.792	.2010	CONTINGENCY COEFF=	.1006

MEASURES PREDICTING: VAR 7   VAR 62   COMBINED

	VAR 7	VAR 62	COMBINED
GOODMAN-KRUSKAL LAMBDA	0.	0.	0.
GOODMAN-KRUSKAL TAU	.0066	.0056	.0061

was perceived as a problem in the choice of a college. Figures 9–2 and
9–3 show these two pairs of relationships. As a first step, you might use
the codebook from Appendix B and label the figures so that we all can
agree on what we are about. In Figure 9–2 we note, among other
things, an error in our keypunching. If you look at the codebook, you
will note that there is no code "9" for this variable, and yet our figure
includes one. This category is in error and should be excluded from
the analysis. We note by looking at the categories that there seems to
be a large amount of agreement that money is important, regardless
of one's religion. We also note at the same time that persons who list
their religion as "Other" seem to find money more important than the
other groups (at least in terms of listing it as "very important"). At
the same time, we would have to say that the table is really not very
"dramatic" in its presentation of the information.

Unfortunately, Figure 9–3 is not too dramatic in its presentation
either. While the students who are married seem to be somewhat less
concerned with money than the single students, it is the divorced persons who are the most affected. Again, we can point out that money
is important to all the students in the survey even though it may seem
of greater importance to some than to others. Even while saying this,
we are forced to also point out that the differences are not very great.

When we put all the variables into a single table, the relationships
become somewhat more clear. As you noted in Table 2–6, the married
students, regardless of religion, are less likely to point to money as
very important in their choice of a college than are the not-married
students (a category that includes not only those labeled "single" but
also those who are "widowed" and "divorced"). Had we been able to
take the analysis one step further, we might have discovered that the
married students had spouses who were employed, and thus, while
money was an important consideration for them, it was not listed as
very important as they had someone to help them with the bills. You
might also have looked at other variables that influence the choice of
money as a very important variable in the choice of a college—Are
the respondents on scholarship? Do the respondents work? Are the parents of the students in the lower echelons of the work force? and so on.
All these variables might have a bearing on the original relationships
you hypothesized above.

We can now add the final two steps to our outline of the research
process:

14. *Analyze* the data in such a way that your research questions
    (specified in suggestion number 2 in Chapter 8) are answered
    to the best of your ability.
15. *Write up* the results of your study. At the same time that you are
    writing up research results, it is useful to do a postmortem analy-

sis of the entire project. In this kind of analysis, it is always help-ful (for other, later studies) to consider what questions worked well, what questions did not work very well, and which questions did not work at all (that is, which questions were worded in such a way that they did not elicit the information you needed to an-swer your research questions). All are pieces of information we need to know for the sake of both this and future studies.

THE ANALYSIS

You are now on your own. Take the data the class gathered for the exercises in the previous two chapters (as well as for the exercise in this chapter), and conduct an analysis of them. Short of actually con-ducting an analysis of the data, you could describe how you would analyze the data from the student questionnaire. In this description you should include hypotheses to be tested as well as the dummy tables that would be filled in.

How you go about it is up to the class. We strongly suggest, how-ever, that you follow the steps outlined in this and previous chapters. It is always helpful to move back and forth between the chapters, using some information suggested in one chapter to lead you into another means for analysis suggested in another. As has been suggested be-fore, you are limited in how you analyze your data only by your own ingenuity and resourcefulness.

Interview Using a Focused Interview

THE PROBLEM

Using the techniques that you began to develop in the previous chapter, interview someone in depth, about his or her relationships with brothers and sisters. In this interview, record as completely as possible what the subject said about the relationships. The interview should be a "focused" interview rather than one in which a definite schedule must be followed. Include in your report, both your notes on the interview and your analysis of the individual's relationship with his or her siblings.

THE APPROACH

In previous chapters we have been attempting to help you develop your perception of the social situations that you have been investigating. In earlier chapters we asked that you observe social occurrences, in the last chapter we asked that you begin to question people about the aspects of social situations. For this problem you will need to combine both approaches: while you are questioning a person about his or her sibling relationships you will also have to be carefully observing what he or she is doing. The hard part is that you must be doing both of these simultaneously. In other words, not only must you be concerned with the questions you are asking, you must also be thinking about what you will ask next, and after that, the completeness of the answer just given, the relationship of the answer to the previous ones, the facial expression of the respondent as he or she answers the quesiton, the "body language" of the respondent, and so on. All of these aspects of the situation must be taken into account in understanding the answers being given.

The first problem you must deal with in deciding to question a person about his or her relationship with brothers and sisters (in fact, any interview you may choose to do) is to decide on the information you need to get (and by implication, how you will get that information). Normally, it would be up to the researcher to decide how to gather the information; that is, it would be the researcher's decision to use one particular type of interview rather than another. As you discovered in Chapter 8, one may use a structured questionnaire as an interview. In such a situation the interviewer is usually restricted to asking the questions as they are written in the questionnaire without adding explanations or interpretation. One might also have a less structured approach, in which the interviewer is allowed, by the research director, to interpret the questions for the respondent when necessary. In the unstructured interview situation, the interviewer is allowed to investigate answers the respondent provides and also to explain questions the respondent does not understand. In the unstructured interview the interviewer is allowed great latitude in the way the interview is conducted.[1] In an in-depth interview, the interviewer can pursue ideas and details more deeply than is possible in a structured interview or questionnaire situation. The focused interview is another possibility and is the least structured of the interview approaches. In the focused interview, the interviewer is sent to do an interview with a general series of topics about which he or she must ask questions.[2] Thus, there is a general notion as to what the research is looking for but there is no specific approach one should use to obtain these results. In the focused interview situation, the interviewer continues to "focus" in on the topics being investigated and continues to lead the respondent in the directions dictated by the concerns of the research project. (We will have more to say about directing and leading respondents later.)

Once the decision as to how the material is to be gathered (by focused interview) has been made, we can move to the question of what material we will look for in the interview. As a beginning, consider what information might be relevant to a discussion of a person's rela-

---

[1] It is entirely possible that even in the unstructured interview the interviewer may be restricted to asking questions as they are written on the interview schedule and in the order in which they appear.

[2] It is possible to look at this from a slightly different perspective. The focused interview can be thought of as having a need to get answers in certain areas and about certain topics. How these answers are received and the questions used to elicit these answers are immaterial to the research process.

tionships with siblings. Are there socioeconomic variables that might
be relevant? Might items such as age and sex of respondent and siblings be important? What about other information such as race, religion, and occupation and education of mother and father? Are there
any other aspects of the socioeconomic background of the respondents
you think are important? If so, be certain to include the relevant items
in the interview and gather information about them.

Before you get into the specific areas of the relationships you think
ought to be covered, you might first wish to indicate a general question
that can summarize the nature of the research project. All research
projects of this nature would probably benefit from the inclusion of a
general research question. For this example, you may want to ask the
respondent to summarize his or her relationship with siblings. What
were the respondent's feelings toward the siblings and what did the
respondent think were his or her brother's and sister's feelings? Once
you have a general idea of the area about which you will be interviewing, you can then move to design some of the more specific questions
that you want to ask during the interview. Some of the more specific
questions for the respondent might be:

1.   What sort of people did you think your brothers and sisters were
     as you were all growing up? That is, how would you have described
     them as persons? What sort of person did your siblings think you
     were?
2.   How close was the relationship between you (the respondent) and
     your siblings? Was there any sibling to whom you (the respon-
     dent) felt closer? Why? Was the relationship a warm one? Why?
3.   What sort of people did you want your siblings to be? What sort
     of person did they want you (the respondent) to be? Was there
     agreement between the members of the family on the type of peo-
     ple to be? If there was a lack of agreement did this affect the rela-
     tionship? In what ways was the relationship affected?
4.   In what respects were you (the respondent) and your siblings
     alike? In what ways were you different?
5.   Were any members of the family treated differently by the parents
     than others? How were they treated differently? Did it make a
     difference to the other siblings that some were treated differently?
6.   Were some of the siblings disciplined for different things or was
     there a constancy of discipline in the family?

While the above list does not exhaust the possible topics to be covered, it should suggest some of the directions to take. You should think
of additional topics to be covered in this interview. As you are considering the possible topics to be covered you should also be thinking of
the hypotheses that you will be testing in this particular research proj-

ect. Obviously, the general question asked above is (or can be) the basis of the hypotheses that are generated. For example, you might hypothesize that the greater the age difference between the respondent and the siblings, the less close the relationship between them. Additional hypotheses that could be dealt with are:

1. The greater the number of children in the household the more likely that the respondent will have one sibling to whom he or she felt closest.
2. All siblings will feel themselves "singled" out by parents for special punishments or "treatments," regardless of the actual situation.
3. The closer the relationship to other siblings, the more it will be seen as a "warm" relationship.

Hopefully, the list of hypotheses will suggest other hypotheses to you that you may, either alone or as a class, want to investigate in this research project.

Once you have decided what you are trying to discover and how you will discover it, the next stage is to decide how to ask the questions. The asking of the questions will be different in this project than it was in the project given in Chapter 8. In that chapter you asked structured questions in a structured situation. You went to the interview situation with a specific set of questions in mind and asked them in a specific order. In addition you probably did not do a great deal of explaining if the respondent had trouble answering the questions. In this project, on the other hand, there is little if any systematic structure to your research.

Assuming that you are able to secure permission to interview someone, the single, most important technique to master is the *probe*. Once you have settled into the interview situation and have your note pad ready on which to write the respondent's comments verbatim, you still will have to push and prod the respondent in the direction you wish him or her to go. Asking the questions, in other words, does not guarantee that you will get any answers or that you will get answers that are usable.

The technique of using the probe may be defined as using a technique that leads the respondent to elaborate answers in areas that are not clear to you, as the researcher. In order to probe an answer, the researcher has a number of possible approaches open. One of the best techniques is to sit and wait at the apparent end of an answer. For example, if you ask a respondent whether or not he enjoyed a good relationship with his siblings, you may get an answer such as: "Yes, we always got along very well." If you then go on to another question you may miss some important information. If, on the other hand, you wait without saying anything, you may get additional information, such as: "While we got along well, there were also times when I felt that my siblings took advantage of me since I was the youngest child in the family." By sitting and waiting (by acting as if you expect additional information) you are inducing the respondent to add material that he or she might not add otherwise. Another possible probe would be to take the last sentence of the respondent and turn it into a question. In the example above, you might, after the respondent had finished, ask, "In what ways did you get along very well?" You are, again, forcing the respondent to elaborate his or her answers and thus are receiving more information than you would if you did not probe.

Additional techniques involve, for example, giving a noncommittal response at the end of the respondent's statements. In the above example, you might simply sit and nod your head when the respondent was finished, or you could say "uh huh," or "yes," and so on. One final probing technique should be mentioned and this is the "negative probe." A negative probe is one that is used (1) carefully and (2) rarely. In an interview situation in which you feel that you are being tested or "put on" by the respondent, you might want to respond in a negative manner after a particularly outrageous statement. You might, to return to the above example, respond with a statement such as "Come on, nobody always gets along with his siblings." Such an approach may, if not used carefully, terminate (or cause to be terminated) the interview. On the other hand, the negative probe may show the respondent that you "mean business" and that it is time to stop fooling around and answer the questions. The decision to use a negative probe should be made carefully and, probably, only when all other techniques have failed. While it is important to use a probe carefully, it is also important to probe when you feel it is necessary.[3]

Because of the possible subjective nature of a focused interview a logical question to ask is whether the use of a probe does not ensure that the research results will be subjective. The reasoning often used by students is as follows: If you are probing for an answer, might you not also suggest possible answers for the respondent thus causing your biases to be intruded into the research? The argument suggests that the researcher, by probing, causes the respondent to answer questions the way the researcher wants them answered and thus the research compromises its objectivity. Unfortunately, if the researcher is not careful, the above scenario is likely to take place as described. However, the researcher who allows subjectivity to intrude is not the better researcher.

---

[3] For more information on probing, see Converse and Schuman (1974); Babbie (1973); Allen and Colfax (1967); and Survey Research Center (1969). Converse and Schuman (1974) also present an extended bibliography on research and particularly interview-type research.

Throughout the discussion of the techniques of asking questions, we have been stressing that the researcher must remain objective. There are, of course, problems for the researcher even when he or she tries to remain totally objective. The problem area we have in mind at this point is what might be called "unintentional" or "unconscious" bias.[4] In Chapter 8, we discussed the problems in designing questions and questionnaires and how easy it was to build bias into the questions. While it is extremely easy to bias a written questionnaire by designing questions badly, imagine for a moment how simple it would be to bias an interview. In the same way that one biases questionnaire research, one could bias an interview by asking questions in a particular way. The interviewer could ask the "spouse beating" question mentioned in the previous chapter. In the present situation, such a biased question would be even more devastating because you and the respondent are in face-to-face contact. Another way in which to assure that bias will be built into the interview situation is to ask only the questions that will elicit answers on particular topics rather than asking questions on all relevant topics. By restricting the questions to certain areas you will be able to successfully (if unconsciously) bias the results.

One can also suggest answers to the respondent by the manner in which the question is presented. The suggesting of answers in the question is more subtle than the "spouse beating question." In this instance, the interviewer asks a question and then adds, "You do agree, don't you?" Or, alternatively, the interviewer will ask the respondent, "You didn't feel hostility toward your younger brother, did you?" In these situations you are biasing the research because you are using leading questions (the same type of questions that are always being objected to in courtroom scenes on television). You as the questioner are asking a question that leads the respondent to an answer, rather than allowing the respondent to find his or her own answer.

We must add one final note on the biasing of the interview by the interviewer. While we can train interviewers and can imbue them with a strong sense of purpose about the research, we can never prevent them from interpreting answers in their own unique ways. What may seem, even to the most casual observer, as a straightforward answer, may be changed into something totally different by the interviewer as he or she writes it down during the interview situation. An interviewer may—subconsciously—find an answer too embarrassing or too hard to accept and thus, unconsciously, change the answer as it is being written down. An interviewer may on another level alter or change the wording of an answer as it is being written not out of any malice but simply in error. The interviewer might, for example, have

---

[4] Intentional bias is ignored here as not worthy of discussion.

difficulty with a person's accent or speech defect and misunderstand the words. Misunderstanding the words may lead to misrepresentation as notes are being taken. Whether the mistake is made intentionally or unintentionally, the mistake will produce biased research. Because unconscious or unintentional bias is such a great possibility in all research projects, one imperative for all interviewers is *be extremely careful when recording answers.*

Not only must researchers be extremely careful when recording answers, they must also be certain that the probes they are using are neutral, except in the obvious case of the negative probe. As we have been stressing, it is imperative that the researcher not suggest an answer to the respondent when probing for more detailed information. Possibly, at this point, you have begun to get the idea that interviewing is not simply listening and recording the answers to various questions that are put to respondents. As you are recording responses to the immediate question you, as the researcher, must be with the respondent, you must be in front of the respondent (in terms of the questions being asked) and you must be behind the respondent. You must be interested enough in the answer to the present question to probe if necessary. At the same time, you must be thinking back to previous answers to see if there is information that has already been covered, or that you want to probe more deeply. In addition, you must be thinking ahead to see if the respondent is now answering questions that you will want to deal with later in the interview.

Thinking ahead is important in all interview research, not only when the questions are structured. While a focused interview has no specific questions to be asked, there are always specific topics to be covered. If a respondent has already dealt with a topic, he or she may become insulted if you ask him to cover it again. You could, of course, preface your latest request by saying, "You have already dealt with this question to a certain extent but. . . ." As an interviewer, you must always "cover" yourself because you will not be able to extricate yourself from this somewhat (in the sense of potential termination of the interview) unfortunate situation if you have not been thinking ahead. Your way out of a potential dilemma is to be thinking in all directions at once.

The last aspect of the interview situation to be dealt with at this point concerns the "body language" of the respondent.[5] The way in which the respondent sits during the interview, the manner in which the respondent uses his or her hands, the nonverbal communication that accompanies the verbal answers to the questions you ask, all may

---

[5] On this point, the reader is urged to reread the relevant sections of Chapters 3 and 4.

be relevant to your research. In an interesting work summarizing much of the previous work on body language, Fast (1970), indicates that a person who sits with arms and/or legs crossed may be unconsciously indicating that he or she is "closed" to ideas. The crossing of the arms is an unconscious signal that the person is unwilling to accept new ideas or persons. At the same time, the person who sits in an "open" posture may be "telling" you that he or she is willing to listen to new ideas and, in fact, has not prejudged you. If you are asking questions and the respondent is sitting in a closed position, it will be important to note that position in your research notes. Suppose that the interviewer was asking questions about the relationship between the respondent and his siblings, and noticed that the responses were beginning to get into areas of the relationship that might be considered "touchy." The alert interviewer could tell a great deal about the "touchiness" of the situation by observing the body language of the respondent. If the posture of the respondent was an open one, the interviewer could infer that the subject, while "touchy," was one that the respondent was willing to talk about.[6] We note here also the existence of various forms of truth—factual and social truth being only two of many types. At what point does one choose to report or accept one type of truth rather than another?

An interviewer aware of the body language of the respondents could also make inferences about the "real" answers to questions from the nonverbal communication of the respondent. The respondent may tell you one thing in the interview and really mean something else. If you ask a question covering a sensitive area of the respondent's relationship with a relative, it is possible that the answer you receive might be a socially correct answer rather than a factually correct answer. There is no reason why the interviewer, aware of the significance of body language, could not see that the respondent's inability to look into the interviewer's eyes, tells something about the veracity of previous answers. In such a case, the researcher must determine whether or not to probe deeper for the "truth." Decisions about the probing of responses, as mentioned above, are left to the discretion of the researcher and this is part of the research task itself: What is truth and how hard should one push to find it?

On the subject of truth, we must note that not telling the truth may happen for a number of reasons. The subject of the discussion may be something about which the respondent is ashamed and thus be something about which he or she is unwilling to tell the truth. The behavior in question may also be illegal behavior and thus the respondent may

---

[6] See on this subject Fast (1970); Eisenberg and Smith (1971); and Speier (1973).

be reticent about retelling his or her part in it. The respondent may
lack information about the behavior in question and, rather than appear "stupid" in front of the interviewer, may tell an untruth—he or
she may allege some behavior in which, in fact, he or she has not engaged. The truth or falsity of a piece of information may not be something that is actually verifiable by the interviewer; it may depend on
an interpretation by the respondent, and an interpretation of that answer by the researcher. On this subject, we return to the notion first
suggested by W. I. Thomas (1928:572): "if persons define situations
as real [as factually truthful], the situations are real in their consequences." What is reality to one person may be fancy to another and
the researcher had better be extremely careful about making snap
judgements.

One individual interviewed about his participation in a particular
occupation informed us that he had recently been fired and that he was
finding it extremely difficult to be hired at other companies. The respondent was of the opinion that he was fired from the one job, and
not hired at others, because of his activities on behalf of a union, and
because he was a minority person in an occupation with few minorities. Was he being discriminated against? Was he fired because he
was a union activist, or was he fired for not being able to do the job?
Obviously, we could have pursued the information and checked into
his allegations much more deeply, but what would the research have
gained? Our opinion at the time was that it was enough for us to know
that *he* felt the way he did and that *he* acted as if the information *he*
had was correct. Much of his behavior as a member of the occupation
was due to his belief that he was being discriminated against, and
further research discovered other people who were feeling as this individual did. The activities of many persons in the occupation were
directed by the fact that they thought the owners of the companies
were acting in collusion and that a "black list" of troublemakers existed. If the members of the occupation could be controlled by the owners through the use of a supposed "black list," it matters little whether
or not the list existed.

We may summarize the approach to be taken in an interview situation as that of being a good listener: such an approach has also been
referred to as being an "active listener."[7] The good listener is one who
can bring the respondent out of his or her shell and obtain the information that is needed in that particular research project. At the same
time that one must be a good listener, the interviewer must also anticipate information to come—as well as questions to come—and must be
thinking about answers to questions already asked. The interviewer

---

[7] See Selltiz et al. (1976:563–573), "The Art of Interviewing." On the idea of
being an "active listener," see Gordon (1970), chapter 2.

must be alert to the situation, to changes in the situation, and to changes that must be made in the situation. By always being "on top" of the situation, a person has a better chance of being a good interviewer.

THE ANALYSIS

The approach to the analysis of data gathered in an interview is similar to that used in analyzing any data gathered in any research project. The researcher must take the raw data gathered in the research and apply it to the test(s) of his or her hypotheses. If the data support or decisively contradict the hypotheses, then all is well and good. If the data do not support or refute the hypotheses, it is "back to the old drawing board." All research projects face data analysis situations in a similar way.

While the situations faced are similar, the analysis of the data gathered in an interview-based project will often be somewhat different from that in a questionnaire project. In both cases, however, the data must be made amenable to analysis. In both cases, the data must be "coded" so that they can be analyzed. As we mentioned in Chapter 7, while the coding of data makes analysis easier, the coding does not change the meaning of the data. In the same way that coding a female a 1 on a questionnaire does not change the fact that the person is a female, so also coding a sentence into a category called a 4 does not change the meaning of that sentence. What is important is that the data from the interview can be coded and analyzed in a manner similar to that used for the more obviously quantitative projects.

We might also note that the information gathered in an interview does not have to be analyzed numerically. There are numerous possible approaches that can be taken, only some of which involve numerical coding. On this subject we can follow the discussion by Sjoberg and Nett (1969:257 ff) of the difference between cases and numbers. According to Sjoberg and Nett, "it is possible to classify cases according to the substantive area being studied, be it individuals, families, communities, formal organizations, or total societies" (258). The authors go on to indicate that there are many ways in which the case approach can be used in sociological analysis. Sjoberg and Nett indicate that it is possible to

> . . . examine the normal (or typical) case, the deviant (or negative) case, and the extreme case in relation to (1) the confirmation of hypotheses; (2) clarification, falsification, and discovery of hypotheses; and (3) the question of "understanding" (259).

In the case approach, one examines each case, or all cases, and concludes from it (them) how well the hypotheses fare.

By examining cases one at a time the researcher can determine if they all fit his or her hypothesis; that is, if most fit the hypothesis, or if none fit. At the same time, the researcher can examine the deviant cases—those that clearly do not fit the hypothesis—to see why they do not. While examining the deviant cases, the researcher can see how to refine his or her research objectives to better take account of cases such as those in the future. The researcher may also wish to incorporate the deviant cases into special hypotheses for later, or additional, investigation. In the problem for this chapter, for example, if the research shows that those persons with many siblings do not interact with any of them, but are "loners," such a finding may be the basis for a future study of persons in large families. Likewise, if the hypotheses are confirmed concerning respondents who feel singled out by parents, but at the same time, some of the respondents feel they were never singled out for special punishments, these "deviant cases" may warrant additional investigation.

Another use for the case approach would be to use individual cases to verify (or at least add to) numerical (statistical?) information that is also being used. For example, in the study of the truck drivers mentioned in earlier chapters, a number of drivers were interviewed at great length and their comments were included along with the statistical data. In the case of the truck drivers, the interview data were used to reinforce the statistical data that had been gathered by a questionnaire. As an example of the combined approach, the study (Runcie, 1971) found that 87.9 percent of the respondents knew someone who was a truck driver before they entered the occupation. While such a finding is significant, it becomes even more conclusive when the information from interviews is added to it. As the study (Runcie, 1971: 144–146) indicated:

> It would seem to be the relationship with another person already in the occupation that influenced drivers in the sample into becoming truck drivers. As some of the drivers have stated:
>
> "My father was a truck driver and I started by taking rides with the drivers at age fourteen—to learn my profession."
> > Tractor-trailer driver who drives both locally and over the road.
>
> "Father had a trucking business."
> > Tractor-trailer driver who drives locally.
>
> "I was out of a job and a friend suggested I tryout for a job driving a truck. I had to learn on the job how to drive a truck. I took this as a temporary job."
> > Tractor-trailer driver who drives locally.
>
> "A friend who had two tractor-trailer combos asked if I would like to drive one of them. I have been driving this type of unit ever since."
> > Tractor-trailer driver who drives locally.

Information that began as individual case studies of individual truck drivers was added to the statistical data and used to underline or reinforce the findings. The case studies were not used as evidence by themselves alone but as sources of information to "triangulate" (Denzin, 1978:28–29) the findings of other methods. By analyzing the relationship from many different angles and with many different approaches we were able to make a much stronger case for our conclusions.

One other use of the interview to bolster statistical conclusions might be helpful at this point. Curtis et al. (1970:15–16) present findings of an attitude survey conducted among Model Cities neighborhood residents concerning the residents' feeling about the neighborhood and its problems. In the analysis, comments from interviews conducted with the residents were included along with the statistical responses. As an example, one section of the study showed that 42.8 percent of all respondents indicated some type of community-oriented response when asked about neighborhood problems. The study defined the nature of a "community-oriented response" as having

> . . . one or more of the following characteristics: (1) Direct relationship to a question of public policy; (2) Involvement with the performance of public agencies, officials or employees; (3) Reflection of a generalized condition or situation in the local area. Examples of community oriented responses were:
>
> "Everything! Don't clean streets as they should."
> "Thefts and burglaries."
> "Crime rate in this area."
> "Air pollution, water pollution."
> "Speeders on the street. They run stop signs."
> "Need recreation place . . . there is a house next door which is too dangerous."
> "Some houses need repairing and painting. Rent is too high for what you get. Not enough quality rental homes. A farce on low-cost homes for low-income people. Low-cost homes are not available to others, other than ADC and welfare recipients."

Once again, by including the interview data, the researchers were able to more clearly define what the research was dealing with. While it may appear that responses are repeated verbatim in these examples, a certain amount of coding has taken place. Without an interpretation of each of the listed responses as being "community oriented" they could not have been included as relevant to the particular section of the report. The interpretation of the responses as being relevant for a particular topic, is another way of describing the coding of responses.

We can return, then, to the idea of coding the responses and the use of these coded responses in a research report. Categories of responses are constructed by the research team which have relevance for the testing of the hypotheses. Once the categories have been constructed, the researchers then go through the interview schedules, locating responses that can be placed into the appropriate categories. While it is possible that a single researcher might be able to code all responses for all interviews, a better technique is to use a number of coders all of whom have been trained in the general purposes of the research. If all the coders can agree on the category in which a particular statement belongs it is possible to be more certain that the research is discovering what it says it is discovering. The problem, of course, is to get general agreement on the part of the coders. Agreement to a great extent, is dependent on the training the coders go through and their understanding of the project's goals. Agreement is, by the way, necessary for any study (not simply an interview-based study) and is achieved basically the same way in all.

While interviewing research may seem to be substantially different from other types of research, it is not. All research, whether quantitative or qualitative, has the problems of interpreting the data once gathered. All research must somehow use the data that is gathered to test the hypotheses generated in the earliest stages of the project. The problem faced by the researcher basing his or her study on interview data is, in principle, the same as that faced by the researcher using questionnaire data. Both must interpret the raw data and, somehow, make it useful for analysis.

11

Social Experimentation and Ethnomethodology

THE PROBLEM

Using prudence and good judgment, violate certain rules that are commonly understood in social situations to see what those around you do about the violations. As an experiment you may (1) pretend for a day to be a boarder in your home, or (2) you may go to a church of a different faith than the one in which you were raised. In the first problem, the violations of the rules will be yours as they are interpreted by others and in the second, the violations of the rules will be by others as they are interpreted by you. Write up the notes of your experience(s) stressing the tactics you used, the unwritten rules that were violated, and your observations of what transpired.

THE APPROACH

When the unwritten rules of our society are violated we all, as human beings, feel uneasy. We do not realize that rules exist until they are broken and when they are, we feel a need to correct the situation. We feel a need to repair the social fabric that is torn by rule violation. We feel the need for repair even when we did not know beforehand that rules existed which might be broken.

One area where unwritten rules abound is the college classroom. Classrooms have rules and regulations many of which are outside the official guidelines. For example on the first day of any semester, the instructor enters the classroom and begins the semester by outlining the requirements of the class, by giving each student a syllabus, and by describing the books for the course. The instructor is normally dressed in something other than blue jeans and a work shirt (although this is not quite so true today as it was but a few years ago). What would happen if the instructor came to the class early and carefully seated himself or herself in a seat as if one of the students. Many instructors could "pull this off" if also dressed in jeans and a sport shirt. About the time the class became restless, the instructor could get up, walk to the front of the room and begin to discuss the requirements for the class. At the point the person walked to the front of the room, the class would at first not accept the person as the instructor. Later the class would probably be somewhat angry at the instructor for doing such a "dirty trick." Why would the class be upset? Because instructors are not supposed to do things like that![1] Instructors are supposed to "play the game" using both the written and the unwritten rules.

As suggested earlier, when persons define situations as real the situations are, for the persons doing the defining, real in their consequences. While the situations are real for persons when the situations are consciously defined, the situations are also real when the situations are unconsciously (or subconsciously) defined. When we awaken and "know" that a burglar has entered the house and is prowling on the first floor, we act as if there is a burglar there. The objective fact may be that no burglar is present but we will act as if there is one. We may pull the covers up over our heads, we may take out the old muzzle-loading shotgun and proceed to stalk the intruder, we may call the police, and so on. Whatever it is that we do, we do it because we "know" the intruder is there.

While unusual situations may be defined by us and thus cause us to act in certain ways, the routine or normal happenings of our lives lead us to the same sort of behavior. When we pass someone in the hall of a building, and the person says "Hi, how are you feeling?" We know that the person does not really want to know about the back twinge we have had for a week, or the postnasal drip that has affected our sleep for the last two nights, or the fact that we have a mosquito bite in the most sensitive of places. How do we "know" all of these things pertaining to this one minor encounter? We "know" them because we have "thought" about the consequences of our behavior at one point (or we have broken rules) and decided that such is the case.

---

[1] Instructors who lecture from the "back" of the room are also seen as being somehow deviant. There is a "wall" between the traditional area occupied by the instructor and the area occupied by the students. The instructor who crosses the line is "breaking" the rules and invading the students' territory.

By investigating the encounter, we have discovered that there are rules to behavior, both personal and interpersonal, that all members of a society must abide by. These rules exist and have a certain degree of control over our behaviors. How strong the rules are and how rigidly they control our behaviors will depend to a great extent on how great an impact will be made on the society if they are broken. While these rules are strong, and, in fact, exert great pressure on us, notice that we did not indicate that these rules are necessarily codified in any way. Nor, necessarily, are these rules written down anywhere. Written or unwritten, the rules are important and are influential in guiding our behavior.

If we might, for the moment, return to "general sociology," we might be able to determine the origin of these rules and regulations that govern our behavior. There is clear evidence that our knowledge of the rules is acquired during the socialization process. As we learn, we are given infusions of, what has come to be called, the culture of the society in which we live. The culture is the sum total of knowledge available to the "average" member of the society. The culture of the society contains information vital to our survival in terms of such items as how to build a shelter, what to wear to a formal dinner, what clothes to wear to protect ourselves in cold or wet weather, and so on. In addition, culture also is the repository of the rules and regulations that we must all abide by if we wish society to survive. On the subject of societal survival note the Hobbesian notion of the problem of social order. According to Hobbes, without some form of social order (and here we might include culture), society would be impossible and would in fact be a situation where there was the war of all against all, where life is nasty, brutish and short.[2] Rules of all kinds are necessary to create, maintain, and protect the social order.

We learn as children that there are a certain number of very strictly interpreted "thou shalt nots" and a perhaps larger number of "thou shalt nots" that are not so strictly interpreted. These commandments are rigidly laid down for us and we are told that we have broken the rules whenever we do so. At the same time, there are a number of rules we never speak about and which we never realize are there but which are important and must not be broken. What are these rules? We will never know until the rule is broken and either (1) we break the rule, (2) we see the rule broken, or (3) we are told about the broken rule *and* we somehow are made aware of the reactions to both the violation and the violator.

Where the more traditional sociological interest has been in the written and codified rules of society, the interest of the ethnomethod-

---

[2] See Hobbes, 1961.

ologist has been in the unwritten and often unknown rules of social order.[3] According to Jonathan Turner (1974:324) the methods of ethnomethodology are not new or refined techniques for examining human behavior. Rather,

> For the ethnomethodologist, emphasis is on the *methods employed by those under study* in creating, maintaining, and altering their presumption that a social order, forcing certain kinds of behavior, actually exists "out there" in the "real" world. (Emphasis in original.)

In the same way, Douglas (1970:x) argues that sociology must not impose an "as if" science on everyday life, instead

> . . . we must seek to understand everyday life. Rather than explicitly adopting the common-sense understandings of everyday life . . . we must begin all sociological understandings of human existence with an understanding of everyday life gained from a systematic and objective study of the commonsense meanings and actions of everyday life.

While we may begin the study by looking at commonsense explanations, we must not stop there. As Douglas argues (1970:x), we must go further because we must be

> . . . true to our goal of creating a science of man's existence, we must seek an ever more general, trans-situational (objective) understanding of everyday life.

The understanding of the commonsense[4] meanings that persons attach to everyday life experiences is the province of the ethnomethodologist.

As a social scientist, the ethnomethodologist is concerned with the rules that are part of the commonsense knowledge of the persons involved in situations. As previously mentioned, people do not realize the rules exist until the rules are somehow violated. The rules, in other words, remain unwritten and unspoken, until they are broken. Once the rules are broken they can be dealt with scientifically because it is at this point that the participants in the social situation become aware of the rules. Once people are aware that they possess certain values, or that they play according to certain rules, we can then ask them what the rules are and how the rules affect social life. In trying to understand the meaning of behavior to persons doing that behavior we are brought back to a discussion of *verstehen:* we try to understand the other's behavior on the level of meaning to this other. We do not impose our meanings on the behavior in question, rather, we let the participants tell us what the meaning is for them.

---

[3] See on this subject: Garfinkel (1967); Schutz (1963, 1970); and Roy Turner (1974).

[4] For another view of the sociological analysis of everyday life, see Berger and Luckmann (1966), chapter 2.

Understanding on the level of meaning implies that the person of whom we ask questions, actually understands what has occurred. As suggested above, in order for a person to understand, it is necessary for something to be brought to the conscious level.[5] Thus, we must first cause the meaning of the act to become conscious and then we can examine why someone does the act. Suppose for a moment, that we observe a person engaged in some type of social behavior. We note that the person walks down the right side of a shopping mall aisle rather than down the left side of the aisle. Has our person thought out beforehand the behavior that he or she is doing? To what degree is the behavior of walking down one side of an aisle, rather than another, a conscious decision on the part of the participant? Why bother to walk on one side or the other anyway? Why not simply stroll where one pleases? What social pressures are brought to bear on the people who we discover violating the "rules" in a mall? Is there any sort of social sanctioning process in a mall when the rules were disobeyed?

Because we are able to question the existence and the importance of these commonsense explanations of everyday occurrences, we can also suggest that commonsense explanations are part of the sociologist's domain. As part of the domain of the sociologist, the commonsense explanations must be understood (would this also be a commonsense explanation of behavior?)[6] Can we make any sociological sense out of people's commonsense explanation of behavior?

THE ANALYSIS

In answer to the question asked above, we can say that we hope we can make sense out of the explanation. It is important for the sociologist to understand and interpret all forms of human behavior, even those that are left unsaid or unconscious. The question facing the researcher in a relatively uncharted area is: Where should one begin?

While we may be accused of being heretical, we would think that one should start at the beginning; that is, with what might be considered a "standard research design." An appropriate place from which to start is to decide what you want to look for in a situation that is based on unconscious rules and regulations. In other words, what can you as the researcher hypothesize about the unwritten rules and regulations that you will (may) find in the experiment you are about to perform?

What does it mean to the performers in the situation if all of a sud-

---

[5] We may assume, for the moment, that we are not here involved in an exercise in imaginative reconstruction but in empirical research on real social behaviors.

[6] On this subject, see Zimmerman and Pollner (1970).

den you choose not to perform in the "standard" manner? If you attend a church you are unfamiliar with, what happens when you perform the religious practices incorrectly? A story that had great popularity many years ago indicated the problems a person might encounter when attending a church that is unfamiliar. The story dealt with two American sailors on leave in a foreign country and while on leave they decided to attend a Sunday service in the local church. The two decided beforehand they would, since they did not know the language, follow the lead of the people sitting near them so they would be "more at home." A young gentleman sat in front of them during the service and everytime he knelt down, they knelt down; every time he stood up, they stood up, and so on. At one point in the service, the gentleman stood up and when they stood up the action was greeted by laughter from the members of the congregation. After the service, a resident of the town approached the sailors and asked in halting English if they were foreigners and if they understood the language of the service. When the two sailors indicated their origins, the towns-person said that all was then explained. When the laughter occurred in the service, the two sailors had stood with the gentleman sitting in front of them as the minister asked the father of the child about to be baptized to stand.

The two sailors were simply following someone they thought was the "perfect" role model under the circumstances. The laughter, of course, occurred when the two sailors "broke the rules." Interestingly enough, the sailors would never have understood the rule breaking if they had not talked with the gentleman from the town. The sailors would never have understood the reasons for the laughter and would never have understood that they had violated the commonsense understandings of the people living in the town. The same problem may be faced by any person in an unusual surrounding. How does one ever "know" whether the behavior that one does is appropriate? One learns correct behavior through trial and error in social situations.

We may suggest that one way to begin would be to examine the many possible aspects of behavior in situations that could be problematic. By doing a bit of thinking before venturing into the situation, one may be able to anticipate the things one will "do wrong." By anticipating what one might do incorrectly, one has the basis for some hypotheses that are then testable in the research.

What might some of the hypotheses be for this project? What might you expect to happen when you break rules? One might hypothesize that the people whose rules you break will feel angry with you. At the same time, if the people whose rules you are breaking are your parents or your spouse, they may view the breaking of the rules as a form of rejection and thus be more hurt than angry. People whose rules you break will also, we can hypothesize further, argue that all persons know what the rules are so you cannot legitimately say you did not know that you were not supposed to do what you did. In other words, people whose rules are broken assume that you are in agreement about the rules in the first place and they will have difficulty understanding why you, of all people, did not know the rules.[7] In Chapter 1, we discussed the classic example of the rule breaker in the discussion of the "tic-tac-toe" game. What reaction do you imagine you would get if you erased a person's mark and put yours in its place? We can imagine that you would get a comment such as: "Hey, don't you know the rules?"

Once you have set down what you think you will find in your experiment, you may then proceed to the experiment. The best approach is to carefully plan out what you are doing and what you think will happen so that the situation does not get "out of hand" later on. Occasionally, students plan out experiments with great care only to find out that they have overlooked some important factor which causes the experiment to malfunction.

One student, in attempting to experiment with the unwritten rules, decided to act (1) as if he were drunk, and (2) as if he thought he was visiting a house of ill-repute, while knocking at his own front door.[8] The student's wife, as one might expect was none too thrilled at her husband's loud banging on the door and his offers of money. At the same time, the violation of many unwritten rules and commonsense understandings was accomplished. We must add here, however, that the student overlooked one very important factor in setting up the experiment. The student failed to take into account the fact that his wife would reject his explanations and would, in fact, not speak to him for quite awhile, and would also threaten to divorce him for his behavior. To argue that it was all done for a sociology class did no good. It took a long time for the spouse to "forgive and forget." Be extremely careful when you set up your experiment—try to foresee any and all possible situations that might come up so that you will be prepared for them. If you anticipate the possible problems you may have, you should come out of this experiment with better results than if you leave things to chance.

One of the major differences between this research project and others you have done is that here you will probably experience some

---

[7] There are always legitimate ways around "the rules" in any situation. See Toby (1964, 11–15).

[8] The student experimenter was extremely creative in his projects and it always amazed me that he did not get himself arrested with his "experiments." He did, however, demonstrate that he was learning research techniques. I do not think students have to go quite this far to show how much they are learning.

difficulty during the conduct of the research. If the other participants in the experiment saw that you were taking notes as you were breaking the rules and regulations it is possible they would think something was wrong. The other participants might not believe that you were doing all the things you were doing "for real." Other actors in the situation might see your note taking as an indication of a "sham" and not accept your "unusual behavior." In a situation where the other actors see your behavior as sham, your attempts to break rules (and thus to make them appear on the conscious level) will cause nothing. All you will get for your troubles are comments about how "out of sorts" you are today.

Another example of rule-breaking behavior was undertaken by a student while studying behavior in the shopping center as you did earlier. In the experimentation, the student chose to see what would happen if one violated the unwritten rules concerning the water fountains that we find in so many malls today. While many shopping malls have fountains, the general rule is that we are to use the mall's fountain to look at and nothing more. The student who investigated the enforcement of this rule, conducted his experiment on a particularly warm day. He went to the mall in bermuda shorts, t-shirt, and sandals and carrying a lawn chair. He proceeded to the fountain, shed his sandals, and placed the chair in the fountain. He then waded to the chair and sat in it. His main purpose was to see whether people would look at him if they knew he (a "deviant") was looking at them. Would they, in other words, stare at him while he was staring at them. Would they maintain eye contact when they knew he was trying to stare at them?[9]

As his research showed, the other shoppers in the mall would not look at the deviant sitting in the fountain if they thought he was looking at them. It became obvious, however, that as long as they thought he was not looking at them, they would stare at him, shake their heads, and comment about his behavior among themselves. As soon as they realized he was looking at them, however, the shoppers would look away as if they did not see him, almost as if he was not there. The student concluded that people, while they are repulsed by and concerned about extreme deviance, are willing to do little about it. At the same time, the student found that the security forces in this mall were also unwilling to do much about what was clearly a "deviant act." Soon after taking his place in the fountain, a security guard arrived to ask if the student was comfortable in his chair and to see if he needed anything. The student, while not revealing the purpose for the occupa-

---

[9] One question you might wish to answer for yourselves is whether this "experiment" is an example of useful "deviant behavior" or whether it is simply a copy of what one might find on "Candid Camera" on television?

tion of the fountain, indicated that he was quite comfortable and did not require any assistance from the guard. The guard then offered to make certain that the fountain was turned off for the duration of the student's occupation so that it would not "erupt" and drench him. When the student indicated that this would be very nice of the guard, the guard left and the fountain was turned off for the duration of the experimenter's stay. Occasionally the guard would come by on his rounds and pass the deviant, without any additional conversation.

While this experiment was somewhat questionable in terms of legality, there is no question that it was able to examine a great deal of unspoken social behavior that goes on in public. The hesitance on the part of both the guard and the shoppers to "do anything" is interesting in light of the literature on the "I don't want to get involved" syndrome. In addition, the hesitance on the part of the shoppers to be seen staring at the person sitting in the fountain suggests a reticence on the shoppers' part to be thought of as accepting this behavior; that is, if the deviant could have held eye contact with the other patrons of the mall, he might have been able to get them to smile and thus tacitly "go along" with this deviant act. By staring only when they thought he was not looking, the patrons could indulge themselves in sanctioning the behavior without interacting with the person doing it.

Your attempts at breaking the rules must appear legitimate and, consequently, you will have to find alternative means than obvious recording of data. You may have to retire often to another room in order to record important information. You may have to try to remember important information if your experiment continues over a long period of time. If you are pretending to be a boarder in your own home, you may be able to retreat to your "rented room" occasionally and then record your observations. However you choose to record what transpires, you should attempt to include as much data as possible, including verbatim comments by the other actors in the situation. Verbatim comments by other actors will be extremely helpful in your analysis of the experiment as you begin to show who said what about the broken rules. While you can say that unwritten rules were broken, a much better approach is to show what the other persons in the situation said about your breaking of the unwritten rules.

Before completing the discussion of the ethnomethodological experiment, one additional observation is important. While we have called the present problem "an experiment," in fact, it is not. What we have here is similar to what Denzin (1970a:169) has called the "one-group pre-test post-test design."

In a research project using such a design, one group has all observations made on it. By using only one group, the approach leaves out a control group and according to Denzin (1978:162)

> . . . this restricts inference because the investigator has no way of knowing what would have occurred had the sample not been exposed to the critical event. It also suffers from loss of observers and subjects between observations—that is, differential mortality rates.

The problems inherent in losing subjects or observers for various reasons are not the only problems one confronts when using such an "experimental" approach. Denzin adds (1978:162) that

> Reactive effects of repeated observations are also present, as are changes in the subject and observer. Last, changes in the measuring instrument can also distort the causal analysis.

While we can grant the problems mentioned by Denzin, we might also note there are few other techniques that are available to test the assumptions that human beings make about "normal" behavior. Unless we can cause the questionable behavior in a semistructured situation we are in no position to examine the participants and their reactions. In a sense, then, the problem for the present chapter is a semiexperiment entailing the introduction of the experimental stimuli and the observation of the resulting behavior.

The observation of behavior resulting from the breaking of unwritten rules and regulations could no doubt, be accomplished without formal (or even informal) controls over the situation. In your "experiment" for this problem, we hope that you will impose certain controls on the introduction of the behavioral stimuli as well as in the formulation of the problem and the analysis. By carefully controlling the various factors in the research problem, you should be gaining an understanding of the commonsense explanations of everyday behavior.

Bibliography

Adams, R. N., and Jack J. Preiss (eds)
    1960   Human Organization Research. Homewood, Illinois: Dorsey Press.

Allen, Irving L., and J. David Colfax
    1967   Urban Sample Survey Field Procedures: Materials and Strategies. Storrs, Connecticut: Institute of Urban Research of the University of Connecticut.

Allen, Michael Patrick
    1974   "The structure of interorganizational elite cooptation: Interlocking corporate directorates." American Sociological Review 39(3) (June):393–406.

Altman, Irwin
    1975   The Environment and Social Behavior. Monterey, California: Brooks/Cole Publishing Company.

Babbie, Earl R.
    1973   Survey Research Methods. Belmont, California: Wadsworth Publishing Company.

Bales, Robert F.
    1952   "Some uniformities of behavior in small social systems." Pp. 146–159 in Guy Swanson, Theodore M. Newcomb, and Eugene L. Hartley (eds), Readings in Social Psychology. Revised edition. New York: Holt, Rinehart and Winston.

    1958   "Task roles and social roles in problem-solving groups." Pp. 437–447 in Eleanor E. Maccoby, Theodore M. Newcomb and Eugene L. Hartley (eds), Readings in Social Psychology. New York: Holt, Rinehart and Winston.

1965   "The equilibrium problem in small groups." Pp. 444–476 in
        A. Paul Hare, Edgar F. Borgatta, and Robert F. Bales (eds),
        Small Groups. Revised edition. New York: Alfred A. Knopf.

1979   The SYMLOG Kit, Unpublished Manuscript. New York: © 1979,
        The Free Press, a division of Macmillan Publishing Co., Inc.

Bales, Robert F., and Stephen P. Cohen, with Stephen A. Williamson
1979   SYMLOG: A Manual for the Case Study of Groups, Unpublished
        Manuscript. New York: © 1979 The Free Press, a division of
        Macmillan Publishing Co., Inc.

Ball, Donald W.
1973   Microecology: Social Situations and Intimate Space. Indianap-
        olis, Indiana: The Bobbs-Merrill Company.

Bart, Pauline, and Linda Frankel
1971   The Student Sociologist's Handbook. Cambridge, Massachu-
        setts: Schenkman Publishing Company.

Berger, Peter L.
1963   Invitation to Sociology: A Humanistic Perspective by Peter L.
        Berger. Copyright © 1963 by Peter L. Berger. Reprinted by per-
        mission of Doubleday & Company, Inc., and Penguin Books Ltd'.

Berger, Peter L., and Thomas Luckmann
1966   The Social Construction of Reality. New York: Doubleday.

Bierstadt, Robert
1963   The Social Order. New York: McGraw-Hill Book Company.

Birdwhistle, Ray L.
1960   Kinesics and Context. Philadelphia, Pennsylvania: University
        of Pennsylvania Press.

Bjerstedt, Ake
1956   The Methodology of Preferential Sociometry. Lund, Sweden:
        Sociometry Monographs, Number 37.

Blalock, Hubert M.
1970   An Introduction to Social Research. Englewood Cliffs, New
        Jersey: Prentice-Hall.

1972   Social Statistics. Second edition. New York: McGraw-Hill.

Bodmer, Walter F., and Luigi Luca Cavalli-Sforza
1970   "Intelligence and race." Scientific American 223(4) (October):
        19–29.

Brown, Roger
1965   Social Psychology, New York: © 1965 The Free Press, a division
        of Macmillan Publishing Co., Inc.

Converse, Jean M., and Howard Schuman
1974   Conversations at Random: Survey Research as Interviewers See
        It. New York: John Wiley & Sons.

Cooley, Charles Horton
1956   Human Nature and the Social Order. Glencoe, Illinois: Free
        Press.

Curtis, Theodore T., W. G. Marston, E. Perlman, J. F. Runcie, and G. D.
Bishop
1970   Perceptions of Problems and Priorities in the Genesee County
        Model Cities Neighborhood. Flint, Michigan: Genesee County
        Model Cities Agency.

Denzin, Norman K.
    1970   Sociological Methods: A Sourcebook. Chicago: Aldine-Atherton.
    1978   The Research Act. Second edition. Chicago: Aldine-Atherton.
Dial, O. Eugene
    1968   Computer Programming and Statistics for Basic Research. New York: American Book Company.
Douglas, Jack D. (ed)
    1970   Understanding Everyday Life. Chicago: Aldine-Atherton.
Edney, Julian J., and Nancy L. Jordan-Edney
    1974   "Territorial spacing on a beach." Sociometry 37(1) (March): 92–104.
Eisenberg, Abne M., and Ralph H. Smith, Jr.
    1971   Nonverbal Communication. Indianapolis: The Bobbs-Merrill Company.
Fast, Julius
    1970   Body Language. New York: Evans.
Filstead, William J.
    1970   Qualitative Methodology. Chicago: Markham Publishing Company.
Frank, Harry
    1974   Introduction to Probability and Statistics: Concepts and Principles. New York: John Wiley & Sons.
Garfinkel, Harold
    1967   Studies in Ethnomethodology. Englewood Cliffs, New Jersey: Prentice-Hall.
Goffman, Erving
    1963   Behavior in Public Places. New York: Free Press.
Gold, Raymond L.
    1969   "Roles in sociological field observations." Social Forces 36 (1958):217–223. As quoted on pages 30–38 in George J. McCall and J. L. Simmons (eds), Issues in Participant Observation. Reading, Massachusetts: Addison-Wesley.
Gordon, Thomas
    1970   P.E.T.: Parent Effectiveness Training. New York: Peter H. Wyden.
Hagedorn, Robert, and Sanford Labovitz
    1973   An Introduction into Sociological Orientations. New York: John Wiley & Sons.
Hall, Edward T.
    1959   The Silent Language. New York: Doubleday.
    1966   The Hidden Dimension. New York: Doubleday.
Hammond, Peter B.
    1967   Sociologists at Work. New York: Anchor Books.
Hays, William L.
    1963   Statistics. New York: Holt, Rinehart and Winston.
Herrnstein, Richard
    1971   "I.Q." The Atlantic 228(3) (1971):43–64.
Hobbes, Thomas
    1961   "Of the natural conditions of mankind." Pp. 99–101 in Talcott Parsons, Edward Shils, Kasper D. Naegle, and Jesse R. Pitts (eds), Theories of Society. Volume I. New York: Free Press.

Hyman, Herbert H.
    1955   Survey Design and Analysis. Glencoe, Illinois: Free Press.
Jacobs, Glenn (ed)
    1970   The Participant Observer. New York: George Braziller.
Jennings, Helen H.
    1950   Leadership and Isolation. New York: Longmans, Green and Company.
    1965   "Individual differences in the social atom." Pp. 258–266 in A. Paul Hare, Edgar F. Borgatta, and Robert F. Bales (eds), Small Groups. Revised edition. New York: Alfred A. Knopf.
Kaplan, Abraham
    1964   The Conduct of Inquiry. San Francisco: Chandler Publishing Company.
Kaufman, Bel
    1964   Up the Down Staircase. Englewood Cliffs, New Jersey: Prentice-Hall.
Kerlinger, Fred N.
    1964   Foundations of Behavioral Research. New York: Holt, Rinehart and Winston.
Kish, Leslie
    1965   Survey Sampling. New York: © 1965 John Wiley & Sons. Material reprinted by permission of John Wiley & Sons.
Knop, Edward
    1967   "Suggestions to aid the student in systematic interpretation and analysis of empirical sociological journal presentations." The American Sociologist 2:90–92.
Knowles, Eric S.
    1972   "Boundaries around social space: Dyadic responses to an invader." Environment and Behavior 4(4) (December):437–445.
Levine, Joel H.
    1972   "The sphere of influence." American Sociological Review 37(1) (February):14–27.
Lofland, John
    1971   From Analyzing Social Settings: A Guide to Qualitative Observation and Analysis by John Lofland. © 1971 by Wadsworth Publishing Company, Inc., Belmont, California 94002. Reprinted by permission of the publisher.
Lundberg, George A.
    1961   Can Science Save Us? Second edition. New York: David McKay.
Mann, Leon
    1969   "Queue culture: The waiting line as a social system." American Journal of Sociology 75(3) (November):340–354. © 1969 by The University of Chicago. All rights reserved.
McCall, George J., and J. L. Simmons (eds)
    1969   Issues in Participant Observation. Reading, Massachusetts: Addison-Wesley.
Mendenhall, William, Lyman Ott, and Richard L. Schaeffer
    1971   Elementary Survey Sampling. Belmont, California: Wadsworth Publishing Company.

Miller, Delbert C.
    1977   Handbook of Research Design and Social Measurement. Third
            edition. New York: David McKay.

Mitroff, Ian I.
    1974   "Norms and counter-norms in a select group of the Apollo moon
            scientists: A case study of the ambivalence of scientists." Amer-
            ican Sociological Review 39(4) (August):579–595.

Moreno, Jacob L.
    1947   "Contributions of sociometry to research methodology in soci-
            ology." American Sociological Review 12:287–292.

    1953   Who Shall Survive? Beacon, New York: Beacon House.

Moser, C. A.
    1967   Survey Methods in Social Investigation. London: Heinemann
            Educational Books.

Nie, Norman H., C. Hadlai Hull, Jean G. Jenkins, Karen Steinbrenner, and
Dale H. Brent
    1975   SPSS: Statistical Package for the Social Sciences. Second edi-
            tion. New York: McGraw-Hill Book Company.

Northway, Mary L.
    1967   A Primer of Sociometry. Second edition. Toronto, Canada: Uni-
            versity of Toronto Press.

Olsen, Marvin E.
    1968   The Process of Social Organization. New York: Holt, Rinehart
            and Winston.

Parsons, Talcott
    1962   "The institutionalization of scientific investigation." Pp. 7–15 in
            Bernard Barber and Walter Hirsch, The Sociology of Science.
            New York: Free Press of Glencoe.

Parsons, Talcott, and Robert F. Bales (eds)
    1955   Family, Socialization and Interaction Process. New York: Free
            Press of Glencoe.

Phillips, Bernard S.
    1971   Social Research: Strategy and Tactics. Second edition. New
            York: Macmillan.

RAND Corporation
    1955   A Million Random Digits with 100,000 Normal Deviates. Glen-
            coe, Illinois: Free Press.

Robinson, John P., Robert Athanasiou, and Kendra B. Head
    1969   Measures of Occupational Attitudes and Occupational Charac-
            teristics. Ann Arbor, Michigan: Institute for Social Research,
            University of Michigan.

Roethlisberger, Fritz J., and William J. Dickson
    1939   Management and the Worker. Cambridge, Massachusetts: Har-
            vard University Press.

Runcie, John F.
    1971   "Group formation in an occupation: A case study of the truck
            driver." Doctoral dissertation, Rutgers University, New Bruns-
            wick, New Jersey.

    1973   "Group formation: Theoretical and empirical approaches."
            Small Group Behavior 4(2) (May):181–205.

1974   "Occupational communication as boundary mechanism." Sociology of Work and Occupations 1(4) (November):419–441.
Schutz, Alfred
1963   "Concept and theory formation in the social sciences." Pp. 231–249 in Maurice Natanson (ed), Philosophy of the Social Sciences: A Reader. New York: Random House.
1970   "The problem of rationality in the modern world." Pp. 89–114 in Dorothy Emmet and Alasdair MacIntyre (eds), Sociological Theory and Philosophical Analysis. New York: Macmillan.
Schwartz, Morris S., and Charlotte Green Schwartz
1955   "Problems in participant observation." American Journal of Sociology 60:343–353.
Selltiz, Claire, Marie Jahoda, Morton Deutsch, and Stuart W. Cook
1959   Research Methods in Social Relations. Revised one-volume edition. New York: Holt, Rinehart and Winston.
Selltiz, Claire, Lawrence S. Wrightsman and Stuart W. Cook
1976   Research Methods in Social Relations. Third edition. New York: Holt, Rinehart and Winston.
Simon, Julian L.
1978   Basic Research Methods in Social Science. Second Edition. New York: Random House.
Sjoberg, Gideon
1967   "Project Camelot: selected reactions and personal reflections." Pp. 141–161 in Gideon Sjoberg (ed), Ethics, Politics and Social Research. Cambridge, Massachusetts: Schenkman Publishing Company.
Sjoberg, Gideon, and Roger Nett
1969   A Methodology for Social Research. New York: Harper and Row.
Sommer, Robert
1969   Personal Space. Englewood Cliffs, New Jersey: Prentice-Hall.
1974   Tight Spaces. Englewood Cliffs, New Jersey: Prentice-Hall.
Southwick, Jessie C. (ed.)
1975   Survey Data for Trend Analysis. Washington, D.C.: Roper Public Opinion Research Center and the Social Science Research Council.
Speier, Matthew
1973   How to Observe Face-to-Face Communication: A Sociological Introduction. Pacific Palisades, California: Goodyear Publishing.
Survey Research Center
1969   Interviewer's Manual. Ann Arbor, Michigan: Institute for Social Research, University of Michigan.
Thomas, W. I.
1928   The Child in America. New York: Alfred A. Knopf.
Thompson, Hunter S.
1967   Hell's Angels: A Strange and Terrible Saga. New York: Random House.
Toby, Jackson
1964   "Role conflict: Competing commitments of the individual to several systems of interaction." Pp. 11–15 in Jackson Toby, Contemporary Society. New York: John Wiley & Sons.

Tumin, Melvin
    1961   Social Class and Social Change in Puerto Rico. Princeton, New
            Jersey: Princeton University Press.
Turner, Jonathan H.
    1974   The Structure of Sociological Theory. Homewood, Illinois:
            Dorsey Press.
Turner, Roy (ed)
    1974   Ethnomethodology. Baltimore: Penguin Books.
Volkhart, Edmund H.
    1951   "Introduction: Social behavior and the defined situation." Pp.
            1–32 in Edmund H. Volkhart (ed), Social Behavior and Per-
            sonality. New York: Social Science Research Council.
Wallace, Walter L.
    1971   The Logic of Science in Sociology. Chicago: Aldine-Atherton.
Warwick, Donald P., and Charles A. Lininger
    1975   The Sample Survey: Theory and Practice. New York: McGraw-
            Hill Book Company.
Weber, Max
    1947   The Theory of Social and Economic Organization. Trans. by A.
            M. Henderson and Talcott Parsons. New York: Free Press.
Weisberg, Herbert F., and Bruce D. Bowen
    1977   An Introduction to Survey Research and Data Analysis. San
            Francisco: W. H. Freeman and Company.
Zimmerman, Don H., and Melvin Pollner
    1970   "The everyday world as phenomenon." Pp. 80–103 in Jack
            Douglas (ed), Understanding Everyday Life. Chicago: Aldine-
            Atherton.

Appendix A:
Tables of
Random Numbers

The tables of random numbers included here are for your use when attempting to choose samples. You can use them in the same way as in the example in the text. Open the book to one of the pages and just let your finger determine the first place from which to begin. After that you simply record the identification numbers of the persons who will then be in your sample.

71131	39128	95364	14727	10903	14016	73378	73765	73564	41904
48082	18514	87749	69360	64239	00120	00199	44073	74187	78050
59444	84054	20287	28000	66522	50656	25138	42750	09950	66181
69574	76618	00681	29041	92022	40538	41542	40554	21805	65977
10237	44584	45648	59357	52663	67344	99850	53830	15063	23415
31770	72568	60266	85384	51489	99722	27063	17044	28926	45293
34864	73275	25376	11083	40891	12974	98504	73725	14548	16700
18584	23107	24383	02719	25904	82780	18475	59151	07796	02192
55044	56911	70596	73282	40779	75352	71518	06624	12410	57365
26097	18143	19772	57959	61179	34405	46311	37956	66790	92272
62038	78396	60265	31583	73227	18344	82914	63778	07816	45858
38643	06928	72877	86706	10548	86960	27422	56683	56998	96123
21634	41351	60577	24488	05987	08012	91962	07432	09941	23982
47678	74956	89815	55105	05321	03465	57445	65558	09516	21658
10485	76044	20363	16215	69787	48078	73806	02982	94813	10102
89123	19256	90275	07057	13893	70080	95104	16639	17764	40307
46359	68231	11524	14318	97823	69012	32960	79903	01137	38377
11111	13337	36367	27259	46555	74875	64260	60114	23164	34802
21949	93827	82947	33658	40010	67437	22544	90635	48751	88964
22012	76425	49624	53979	11287	90676	14287	36716	25004	85773
04225	99832	11280	85155	36501	94641	97504	62713	01915	09828
85631	93047	25635	32590	46206	84704	56808	21889	87226	61443
88624	55002	26962	70607	83487	62949	30169	17506	12354	83559
41335	13788	98115	75291	35037	28469	90041	35047	42844	24797
81723	77495	79342	19732	10147	30990	86065	04117	41789	69301
64942	93767	78750	14299	02267	48169	86917	28947	26618	82875
30041	02318	19121	58187	48588	59568	29961	49295	11136	43713
05575	35926	30140	70875	43761	66167	21498	72601	84322	26416
93017	73741	51603	14682	00019	47573	83801	53070	56398	73362
75691	52259	88040	31398	42421	58251	74177	69216	61422	68331
04064	47683	08971	85035	12581	56098	58658	08267	59736	85113
33186	57637	53859	26598	48053	79563	82120	72303	60663	31510
91192	31534	82091	36005	82121	71464	41357	82235	80610	43314
79721	91243	94728	52907	31722	48608	82767	02325	09283	32498
43121	98232	32656	98888	39736	11805	86488	38394	07200	60514
66165	67460	65172	30579	19725	93874	02872	95548	60952	82308
86909	35793	09159	80879	25397	26504	18295	57163	12877	46340
71009	31458	14747	34669	77710	97403	12262	42828	11547	61803
95065	12882	73788	46666	86274	91095	22522	37651	77291	22267
17351	61443	48925	52664	30121	36134	09430	08319	31524	55207
63664	34333	62872	74118	33144	71880	63904	52070	79899	82522
58640	63682	41818	48686	66859	41673	44145	25598	61587	30221
32618	46635	20341	79686	94857	17799	02913	11642	32158	67960
77114	73442	74497	10823	33578	50383	34998	92090	63278	04436
00132	89119	56338	30217	18925	88656	94649	13334	81817	36299
30649	97885	61933	11291	03467	27803	65427	39956	27929	91878
20968	72973	45125	07174	70441	72318	37021	71260	98233	70064
34659	62241	20011	03492	53195	02590	72610	28687	94585	56839
89477	06185	65869	04520	40521	19653	43815	97642	49677	29257
32858	61877	14348	55412	07166	91481	92648	31946	42710	99584

Tables reprinted from: The RAND Corporation, *A Million Random Digits with 100,000 Normal Deviates* (Glencoe, Ill.: Free Press, 1955), pp. 156–157.

30447	44742	78438	51717	25340	90286	89923	61387	18381	24589
44164	60665	85334	67983	99039	73068	51501	85941	68216	08583
16162	09880	18418	62739	17851	73417	79074	82789	35664	21417
26377	20006	41013	78658	14849	93134	97777	27858	56950	14630
61754	27716	27351	36419	04590	03692	21245	23480	20888	42321
26707	58185	61655	17448	65235	51859	48190	81975	58536	00275
11822	72949	38411	32667	63884	75230	93241	26698	21308	76164
59952	15580	94599	40735	74690	08262	12017	41062	05448	98236
19173	42725	65401	54228	22385	69500	27082	03143	40304	85498
64305	93656	08263	59652	52011	56034	33883	77628	76539	12777
31954	41564	23252	06551	96574	25211	77567	73836	61517	22243
77417	26361	54644	55599	08640	77348	77834	21399	68846	30162
40449	94534	35704	01974	14878	78755	69649	65965	67603	47536
57906	89889	23993	06666	89949	32940	80120	62294	55155	54891
58168	18717	29162	87814	57105	09655	66331	55497	48332	78790
21855	62199	76917	94673	85922	85118	03534	15996	52249	72058
82365	51412	32023	24529	88845	08082	67834	02719	76821	28396
00322	24456	64702	95843	64623	49324	87883	87627	15125	00874
55410	86219	24971	41576	60358	94374	08459	14126	25909	75683
92993	30649	44001	66442	31043	90736	62692	20250	97869	21664
06920	20918	19686	96926	68127	72138	81604	88236	01447	58703
41175	74374	62223	84351	36660	22981	89296	99302	63148	22380
57722	07619	45268	43628	13513	47258	50724	41764	58440	89329
27865	04935	68065	27224	34062	02585	49201	58111	52225	86916
05602	17997	77191	51183	31776	56866	98464	93899	26914	41391
86924	40584	34346	91017	24793	97388	81775	64342	69217	29316
99944	24070	73258	20746	73078	11600	42296	34701	53709	78466
00773	92937	27362	04108	87224	87138	96033	04880	89704	02418
24142	96876	31647	34761	67265	68955	37562	90795	01582	92743
10749	59762	44628	15182	69326	77861	30967	62882	16526	65288
43999	42878	34480	22884	55486	34432	05305	33353	21428	74944
05522	79960	64251	43762	37615	12825	63660	04268	69205	14016
15149	68345	28032	09358	11471	80169	50298	63288	68366	26528
53510	56715	23351	60928	50021	84031	14220	42336	15133	15031
22958	91979	60487	68841	35384	51908	72586	08181	57770	23357
12172	82875	72670	77920	83226	06557	91626	56495	75134	17065
97485	41986	98946	54943	58163	73073	46597	24120	41173	26391
06429	17190	32768	94805	47754	71958	57896	23781	40427	06479
61152	76267	62201	65171	07337	82622	26188	71393	35101	41465
44386	45787	73359	16972	66820	31020	96866	71153	60731	94020
07275	55585	90711	18179	36327	61738	33289	07412	61923	56387
73746	87131	73706	30784	18651	13686	28451	32681	69172	21099
83266	21104	49554	26849	34233	96817	99961	98295	69252	70875
23676	44187	81852	61523	59395	29411	36507	44110	18831	70096
87537	80583	52191	30359	06303	90660	41529	25966	53002	39505
20216	78312	25185	85110	75504	85557	94823	08803	11683	34890
81439	25397	83613	26459	86574	71952	47189	81974	95511	64809
99126	36900	42473	68507	74692	97542	58847	52905	00341	76322
21317	84609	36024	88040	25242	46032	84016	28125	70249	72604
22756	01473	87039	83837	05328	59321	68440	51121	87534	88506

Appendix B: Code Book for Student Questionnaire

The following pages represent what might be used as a coding manual or guide for the questionnaire that was discussed in Chapter 8. It may be the case that you will want to add categories to some of the questions, particularly some of the open-ended questions. You may also, of course, choose to leave some aspects of information included here, out of your analysis. There is no reason to assume that information relevant to one campus will always be relevant to another; consequently you should feel free to modify the coding manual as is necessary.

As you can see, some of the response categories have been left blank. We have left the categories blank for two reasons: (1) adding categories will give you practice in deciding what is the important material that must be included in a code book (and by implication that which must be left out); and (2) some information that you will need will be different from that which other campuses need. For example, in variable number 8, class standing of the respondent may be altered to take account of: those students who are graduate students, those who are extension students, those who are simply taking courses, and so on. The same sort of additions can be made in variable number 12, where the respondents are asked what they plan to do after graduation from college. We have left a number of columns blank so that you can fill them in if you find any additional categories that apply. We feel that when you do an analysis of data, the following rule should apply: If you need to add a code to better explain your results, then add the code.

The code book is designed so that the data from the questionnaire can easily be transferred to data cards and analyzed by electronic means. You will notice that the number of variables does not equal the number of columns allotted on the data cards. The two do not equal the same number because very often a variable will require more than one column in which to show the data. The variable mentioned above, that of the student's plan after graduation, is one of those categories that requires more than one column. Thus, any time a student mentioned that he or she was planning to enter a seminary after graduation, we have to code it number 11. Such a coding takes two adjacent columns on the data card though it is considered only one variable. Look also at the identification number that can be assigned to the questionnaire when it is coded. While the identification number is considered a single variable, it takes up four columns on the data card. Thus, each questionnaire, when it is returned, is given a specific and unique identification number which may be anywhere from 0001 to 9999. On this same subject, if it becomes necessary to increase the space allotted for a variable (if, for example, a variable must be enlarged from one to two columns), the adjustment is relatively easy. All that must be done is to move all other variables over, across the columns in the same way. For example, if a variable in column 22 of the first data card must be enlarged, this means that it now will take up columns 22–23. The next variable that used to be in column 23, must now be moved to column 24, that which used to be in column 24 must now be moved to column 25, and so on.

STUDENT STUDY
Card Number 1

Column	Variable Number	Question Number	Code
1–4	1		Student ID for Questionnaire
5	2	1	1. Male 2. Female
6–7	3	2	00–99 Age
8	4	2	AGE COLLAPSE[1] 1. 18–19 (less than 20) 2. 20–23 3. 24–27 4. 28–34 5. 35 and over 6. 7. 8. 9. No Answer

Card Number 1 (continued)

Column	Variable Number	Question Number	Code	
9	5	3	1.	Protestant
			2.	Catholic.
			3.	Jewish
			4.	Other
10	6	4	1.	White
			2.	Black
			3.	Native American
			4.	Mexican-American/ Chicano
			5.	Oriental
			6.	Puerto Rican-American
			7.	Other
11	7	5	1.	Married
			2.	Single
			3.	Widowed
			4.	Divorced
				COLLEGE CLASS[1]
12	8	6	1.	Freshman
			2.	Sophomore
			3.	Junior
			4.	Senior
			5.	Other
			6.	
			7.	
			8.	
			9.	
13	9	7	1.	Full-time (12 credit hours or more)
			2.	Part-time (less than 12 hours)
14	10	8	1.	Business Administration
			2.	Education
			3.	Humanities
			4.	Physical Science/Math
			5.	Social Sciences
			6.	Other
15	11	8(a)	1.	Yes
			2.	No
16–17	12	8(b)	01	Teaching elementary
			02	Teaching high school
			03	Teaching other
			04	Teaching (but not specified)
			05	Graduate study
			06	Medical-dental school
			07	Law school

Card Number 1 *(continued)*

Column	Variable Number	Question Number	Code
			08 Working-business
			09 Nursing
			10 Medical technologist
			11 Seminary
			12 U.S. Woman's Army Corps
			13
			14
			15
			16
			17
			18
			19
			20 Not specified
			99 No answer
18–20	13	9	000–999 Use Census Occupation Code[2] as included below.
21	14	9	Collapse of Occupational Code

21 / 14 / 9:

Code
1. 000–299
2. 300–399
3. 400–599
4. 600–799
5. 800–810
6. 811–899
7. 900–959
8. 960–990
9. 995

Column	Variable Number	Question Number	Code
22–24	15	9	000–999 Use Census Industry Code[2] as included below.
25	16	9(a)	Collapse of Industry Code

25 / 16 / 9(a):

Code
1. 000–199
2. 200–299
3. 300–499
4. 500–599
5. 600–629
6. 630–799
7. 800–849
8. 850–936
9. Automotive Manufacturing = 267 = 9

997–8–999   No answer = Blank

Card Number 1 *(continued)*

Column	Variable Number	Question Number	Code
26–27	17	10	01–21 Father's education in years completed
28	18	10	Collapse of Father's Education 1. Less than 8 2. 8 years 3. 9–11 years 4. 12 years (high school graduate) 5. Some college 6. College graduate 7. Professional education (more than 16) 8. 9. No answer
29–31	19	11	000–999 Father's occupation Use Census Code[2]
32	20	11	Collapse of Occupational Code (see Variable No. 14)
33–35	21	11(a)	000–999 Father's industry Use Census Code[2]
36	22	11(a)	Collapse of Industry Code (See Variable No. 16)
37–38	23	12	00–21 Mother's education in years completed
39	24	12	Collapse of Mother's Education 1. Less than 8 years 2. 8 years 3. 9–11 years 4. 12 years (high school graduate) 5. Some college 6. College graduate 7. Professional education (more than 16) 8. 9. No answer
40	25	13	1. Yes 2. No
41–43	26	13(a)	000–999 Mother's occupation Use Census Code[2]

Card Number 1 *(continued)*

Column	Variable Number	Question Number	Code
44	27	13(a)	Collapse of Occupation Code (See Variable No. 14)
45–47	28	13(b)	000–999 Mother's industry Use Census Code[2]
48	29	13(b)	Collapse of Mother's Industry (See Variable No. 16)
49	30	Sex of Spouse	1. Male Code by 2. Female Elimination
50–51	31	14	00–21 Spouse's education in years completed
52	32	· 14	Collapse of Spouse's Education 1. Less than 8 2. 8 years 3. 9–11 years 4. 12 years (high school graduate) 5. Some college 6. College graduate 7. Professional education (more than 16) 8. 9. No answer
53–55	33	15	000–999 Spouse's occupation Use Census Code[2]
56	34	15	Collapse of Spouse's Occupation (See Variable No. 14)
57–59	35	15(a)	Spouse's Industry Use Census Code[1]
60	36	15(a)	Collapse of Spouse's Industry (See Variable No. 16)
61	37	16	1. $000–$ 2,999 2. $ 3,000–$ 4,999 3. $ 5,000–$ 6,999 4. $ 7,000–$ 8,999 5. $ 9,000–$10,999 6. $11,000–$12,999 7. $13,000–$14,999 8. $15,000 and over 9.
62	38	17	1. $000–$ 2,999 2. $ 3,000–$ 4,999 3. $ 5,000–$ 6,999 4. $ 7,000–$ 8,999 5. $ 9,000–$10,999

Card Number 1 (continued)

Column	Variable Number	Question Number	Code		
			6.	$11,000–$12,999	
			7.	$13,000–$14,999	
			8.	$15,000 and over	
			9.		
63	39·	17(a)	1.	Yes	
			2.	No	
64–67	40	17(b)	$0,000–$9,999	Amount of scholarship money	
68	41	17(b)	Scholarship Money Collapse		
			1.	$0–$ 499	
			2.	$ 500–$ 699	
			3.	$ 700–$ 999	
			4.	$1,000–$1,499	
			5.	$1,500–$2,499	
			6.	$2,500 and over	
			7.		
			8.		
			9.	Not specified	
69	42	18(a)	1.	Yes	
			2.	No	
70	43	18(b)	1.	Resident	
			2.	Nonresident	
71	44	19(a)	1.	Yes	
			2.	No	
72	45	19(b)	1.	Resident	
			2.	Nonresident	
73	46	20(a)	1.	Car	
			2.	Truck	
			3.	Motorcycle	
			4.	Camper	
			5.	Other	
			6.	1–3	
			7.		
			8.		
			9.		
74	47	20(b)	1.	Regularly	
			2.	Occasionally	
			3.	Split with others	
75–76	48	21(a)	00–99	Distance in miles from home to university	
77–79	49	21(b)	Time (in minutes) for trip		
80	50	—	1.	Card number	

Card Number 2

Column	Variable Number	Question Number	Code
1–4	51		Respondent ID Number Time Collapse
5	52	21(b)	1.　0–10 2.　11–15 (10–15) 3.　16–20 (15–20) 4.　21–30 (20, 25, 20–30) 5.　31–60 6.　More than 60 minutes 7. 8. 9.　Not specified
6	53	22	1.　This town 2.　This county 3.　Outside county, less than 50 miles from campus 4.　More than two hours 5.　Other
7	54	23(a)	1.　Yes 2.　No
8	55	23(b)	1.　1 child 2.　2 children 3.　3 children 4.　4 children 5.　5 children 6.　6 chidlren 7.　7 children 8.　8 or more children 9.　No answer
9	56	23(c)	1.　1 child 2.　2 children 3.　3 children 4.　4 children 5.　5 children 6.　6 children 7.　7 children 8.　8 or more children 9.　No answer
10	57	23(d)	1.　1 child 2.　2 children 3.　3 children 4.　4 children 5.　5 children 6.　6 children 7.　7 children 8.　8 or more children 9.　No answer

Card Number 2 *(continued)*

Column	Variable Number	Question Number	Code
11	58	24	1. 1 brother or sister 2. 2 brothers and sisters 3. 3 brothers and sisters 4. 4 brothers and sisters 5. 5 brothers and sisters 6. 6 brothers and sisters 7. 7 brothers and sisters 8. 8 brothers and sisters 9. 9 or more brothers and sisters
12	59	25(a)	1. Own home 2. Parents' home 3. With relatives 4. In apartment 5. In college housing 6. Other 7. 8. 9.
13	60	25(b)	1. Own home 2. Parents' home 3. With relatives 4. In apartment 5. In college housing 6. Other 7. 8. 9.
14	61	25(c)	1. Own home 2. Parents' home 3. With relatives 4. In apartment 5. In college housing 6. Other 7. 8. 9.
15–22	62–69	26	Each question is to be coded. (Note: Order of codes different from questionnaire.) 1. Very important 2. Important 3. Undecided 4. Unimportant 5. Very unimportant
23–30	70–77	27	Each category is to be scored from 1–8.

Card Number 2 *(continued)*

Column	Variable Number	Question Number	Code
31	78	28	1. Yourself 2. Friend 3. Parents 4. Relative 5. Other
32	79	29(a)	1. Very good 2. Good 3. 50–50 4. Not good 5. Very bad 6. No chance
33	80	29(b)	Reasons for changing 01. Independence, to be on own 02. To get away from home 03. Getting married 04. College atmosphere—social opportunities 05. Privacy 06. Money 07. Transferring—moving 08. 09. Not specified
34	81	30	1. Began here as freshman 2. Transfer from junior college 3. Transfer from public 4-year college 4. Transfer from private 4-year college 5. Other
35	82	31	Reasons for transferring in: 1. Location, closeness, convenience 2. Money, cost 3. Close to work 4. Reputation, good school, associate with other schools 5. Aspects of college small, friendly, good courses 6. Has good teachers 7. Did not like other possible school 8. 9. Not specified

Card Number 2 *(continued)*

Column	Variable Number	Question Number	Code	
36	83	32	1.	State university
			2.	Another state college
			3.	Private college in this state
			4.	Other
			5.	
37–38	84	32	01.	Other school better
			02.	Change major—better class selection
			03.	Friends there—better social life
			04.	Better jobs after graduating
			05.	College atmosphere— larger campus
			06.	Get away from parents
			07.	Want to live there
			08.	Prefer a private college
		(Reasons	09.	I like other school better
		for trans-	10.	Wouldn't lose credits
		ferring	11.	Major not offered
		out)	12.	
			13.	
			14.	
			15.	
			16.	
			17.	
			18.	
			19.	
			20.	Other general
			⋮	
			99.	No answer

Card Number 2 *(continued)*

Column	Variable Number	Question Number		Code		Code (Combined reasons)
39–40	85	33	01.	Academic reasons	51.	8 & 21
			02.	Size of school	52.	37 & 3
			03.	Academic rating	53.	1 & 20
		(What liked	04.	Good classes	54.	7 & 11
		about UMF)	05.	Teaching—grading	55.	7 & 18
				system	56.	6 & 13
			06.	Good instructors	57.	31 & 6 & 12
			07.	Student-teacher	58.	7 & 14
				relationships	59.	6 & 13 & 18
			08.	Student-teacher	60.	
				communication	61.	
			09.	Types of classes	62.	
			10.	Nonacademic reasons	63.	
			11.	The building	64.	
			12.	Registration	65.	
			13.	The cost	66.	
			14.	Good food	67.	
			15.		68.	
			16.		69.	
			17.		70.	
			18.	Class size	71.	
			19.		72.	
			20.	Locational reasons	73.	
			21.	Proximity to home	74.	
			22.	Locale	75.	1 & 31
			23.		76.	
			24.		77.	
			25.	Security measures	78.	
			26.		79.	
			27.		80.	
			28.		81.	
			29.		82.	
			30.	Attitudinal reasons	83.	
			31.	Friendly atmosphere	84.	
			32.	Friendly people	85.	
			33.	Friendly teachers	86.	
			34.	Peoples' enthusiasm	87.	
			35.	Peoples' dedication	88.	
			36.	Peoples' interest	89.	
			37.	Personal contacts	90.	
			38.	Teacher's enthusiasm	91.	
			39.	Campus spirit	92.	
			40.	Other reasons	93.	
			41.	Social activities	94.	
			42.		95.	
			43.		96.	
			44.		97.	
			45.		98.	
			46.		99.	Not specified
			47.			
			48.			
			49.			
			50.			

Card Number 2 *(continued)*

Column	Variable Number	Question Number	Code		Code	
41–42	86	34	01.	Academic reasons	42.	Major sports
			02.	Size of school		(lack)
			03.	Academic departments	43.	Gym (lack)
					44.	
			04.	The courses	45.	
			05.	Teaching—grading system	46.	
					47.	
			06.	Instructors not good	48.	
			07.	Teachers too advanced	49.	
					50.	Everything (Combined reasons)
			08.	Loss of student-teacher contact		
			09.	Too few types of classes	51.	14 & 41
					52.	14 & 42
			10.	Nonacademic reasons	53.	14 & 15 & 41
			11.	The building—air conditioning	54.	3 & 14
					55.	9 & 43
			12.	Registration	56.	33 & 39
			13.	The cost	57.	Lecture test
			14.	Parking facilities	58.	5 & 57
			15.	Student housing	59.	5 & 9
			16.	Lack of adequate study area	60.	16 & 27
					61.	
			17.	Class hours not good	62.	
			18.	Class size	63.	
			19.	Classes not offered enough	64.	
					65.	
			20.	Locational reasons	66.	
			21.	Proximity to home	67.	
			22.	Locale	68.	
			23.	Being near to Junior College	69.	
					70.	
			24.		71.	
			25.	Security measures	72.	
			26.	Security police	73.	
			27.	Locked doors	74.	
			28.	Too "high scholarship"	75.	14 & 26 & 27
					76.	
			29.		77.	
			30.	Attitudinal reasons	78.	
			31.	Unfriendly atmosphere	79.	
					80.	
			32.	Student apathy	81.	
			33.	Conservatism	82.	
			34.	Professors' attitudes	83.	
			35.		84.	
			36.		85.	
			37.		86.	
			38.		87.	
			39.	No campus spirit	88.	
			40.	Other reasons		
			41.	Social activities (lack)	89.	
					90.	

Card Number 2 *(continued)*

Column	Variable Number	Question Number	Code		Code	
			91.		96.	
			92.		97.	
			93.		98.	
			94.		99.	Not
			95.			specified
43–44	87	35	01.	Academic changes	35.	
			02.	Raise academic standards	36.	
					37.	
			03.	Academic departments curriculum	38.	Eliminate student cliques
			04.	Give wider choice of classes	39.	Create campus spirit
			05.	Teaching—grading system	40.	Other changes
			06.	Remove some instructors	41.	Increase social activities
			07.	Improve student-teacher relationships	42.	Music in cafeteria
			08.	Improve student-teacher communication	43.	
			09.	Improve types of classes	44.	Add a better music program
			10.	Nonacademic changes	45.	Females not accepted in game room
			11.	College expansion	46.	Increase public relations
			12.	Improve registration procedures		
			13.	The cost	47.	
			14.	Parking facilities	48.	
			15.	Add student housing	49.	
			16.	Add adequate study area	50.	No changes needed
			17.	Add evening division		(Combined reasons)
			18.	Change class size	51.	14 & 44
			19.	Offer all classes each semester	52.	4 & 18
			20.	Locational changes	53.	8 & 38
			21.		54.	6 & 14
			22.	Improve the locale	55.	3 & 30
			23.	Add more trees	56.	3 & 5 & 6
			24.	Move college to suburbs	57.	14 & 23
			25.	Security measures	58.	Change in semester length
			26.	Security police		
			27.	Locked doors		
			28.			
			29.		59.	4 & 5 & 58
			30.	Attitudinal changes	60.	15 & 30
			31.		61.	
			32.		62.	
			33.		63.	
			34.		64.	

Card Number 2 *(concluded)*

Column	Variable Number	Question Number	(Combined reasons) Code	(Combined reasons) Code
			65.	77.
			66.	78.
			67.	79.
			68.	80.
			69.	81.
			70.	82.
			71.	83.
			72.	84.
			73.	85.
			74.	99. Not
			75. 14 & 26 & 27	specified
			76.	

OCCUPATIONAL CLASSIFICATION[3]

(The 3-digit number in the left margin is the code symbol for the occupation category; "n.e.c." means not elsewhere classified.)

Professional, Technical, and Kindred Workers

005   Accountants and auditors
010   Actors and actresses
012   Airplane pilots and navigators
013   Architects
014   Artists and art teachers
015   Athletes
020   Authors
021   Chemists
022   Chiropractors
023   Clergymen

College presidents, professors, and instructors (n.e.c.)
030   College presidents and deans
031   Professors and instructors, agricultural sciences
032   Professors and instructors, biological sciences
034   Professors and instructors, chemistry
035   Professors and instructors, economics
040   Professors and instructors, engineering
041   Professors and instructors, geology and geophysics
042   Professors and instructors, mathematics
043   Professors and instructors, medical sciences
045   Professors and instructors, physics
050   Professors and instructors, psychology
051   Professors and instructors, statistics
052   Professors and instructors, natural sciences (n.e.c.)
053   Professors and instructors, social sciences (n.e.c.)
054   Professors and instructors, nonscientific subjects
060   Professors and instructors, subject not specified

070	Dancers and dancing teachers
071	Dentists
072	Designers
073	Dietitians and nutritionists
074	Draftsmen
075	Editors and reporters
080	Engineers, aeronautical
081	Engineers, chemical
082	Engineers, civil
083	Engineers, electrical
084	Engineers, industrial
085	Engineers, mechanical
090	Engineers, metallurgical, and metallurgists
091	Engineers, mining
092	Engineers, sales
093	Engineers (n.e.c.)
101	Entertainers (n.e.c.)
102	Farm and home management advisors
103	Foresters and conservationists
104	Funeral directors and embalmers
105	Lawyers and judges
111	Librarians
120	Musicians and music teachers
	Natural scientists (n.e.c.)
130	Agricultural scientists
131	Biological scientists
134	Geologists and geophysicists
135	Mathematicians
140	Physicists
145	Miscellaneous natural scientists
150	Nurses, professional
151	Nurses, student professional
152	Optometrists
153	Osteopaths
154	Personnel and labor relations workers
160	Pharmacists
161	Photographers
162	Physicians and surgeons
163	Public relations men and publicity writers
164	Radio operators
165	Recreation and group workers
170	Religious workers
171	Social and welfare workers, except group
	Social scientists
172	Economists
173	Psychologists
174	Statisticians and actuaries
175	Miscellaneous social scientists
180	Sports instructors and officials
181	Surveyors
182	Teachers, elementary schools

183	Teachers, secondary schools
184	Teachers (n.e.c.)
185	Technicians, medical and dental
190	Technicians, electrical and electronic
191	Technicians, other engineering and physical sciences
192	Technicians (n.e.c.)
193	Therapists and healers (n.e.c.)
194	Veterinarians
195	Professional, technical, and kindred workers (n.e.c.)

Farmers and Farm Managers

| 200 | Farmers (owners and tenants) |
| 222 | Farm managers |

Managers, Officials, and Proprietors, Except Farm

250	Buyers and department heads, store
251	Buyers and shippers, farm products
252	Conductors, railroad
253	Credit men
254	Floor men and floor managers, store
260	Inspectors, public administration
262	Managers and superintendents, building
265	Officers, pilots, pursers, and engineers, ship
270	Officials and administrators (n.e.c.), public administration
275	Officials, lodge, society, union, etc.
280	Postmasters
285	Purchasing agents and buyers (n.e.c.)
290	Managers, officials, and proprietors (n.e.c.)

Clerical and Kindred Workers

301	Agents (n.e.c.)
302	Attendants and assistants, library
303	Attendants, physician's and dentist's office
304	Baggagemen, transportation
305	Bank tellers
310	Bookkeepers
312	Cashiers
313	Collectors, bill and account
314	Dispatchers and starters, vehicle
315	Express messengers and railway mail clerks
320	File clerks
321	Insurance adjusters, examiners, and investigators
323	Mail carriers
324	Messengers and office boys
325	Office machine operators
333	Payroll and timekeeping clerks
340	Postal clerks
341	Receptionists
342	Secretaries
343	Shipping and receiving clerks

345	Stenographers
350	Stock clerks and storekeepers
351	Telegraph messengers
352	Telegraph operators
353	Telephone operators
354	Ticket, station, and express agents
360	Typists
370	Clerical and kindred workers (n.e.c.)

Sales Workers

380	Advertising agents and salesmen
381	Auctioneers
382	Demonstrators
383	Hucksters and peddlers
385	Insurance agents, brokers, and underwriters
390	Newsboys
393	Real estate agents and brokers
394	Salesmen and sales clerks (n.e.c.)
395	Stock and bond salesmen

Craftsmen, Foremen, and Kindred Workers

401	Bakers
402	Blacksmiths
403	Boilermakers
404	Bookbinders
405	Brickmasons, stonemasons, and tile setters
410	Cabinetmakers
411	Carpenters
413	Cement and concrete finishers
414	Compositors and typesetters
415	Cranemen, derrickmen, and hoistmen
420	Decorators and window dressers
421	Electricians
423	Electrotypers and stereotypers
424	Engravers, except photoengravers
425	Excavating, grading, and machinery operators
430	Foremen (n.e.c.)
431	Forgemen and hammermen
432	Furriers
434	Glaziers
435	Heat treaters, annealers, and temperers
444	Inspectors, scalers, and graders, log and lumber
450	Inspectors (n.e.c.)
451	Jewelers, watchmakers, goldsmiths, and silversmiths
452	Job setters, metal
453	Linemen and servicemen, telegraph, telephone, and power
454	Locomotive engineers
460	Locomotive firemen
461	Loom fixers
465	Machinists
470	Mechanics and repairmen, air conditioning, heating, and refrigeration

471   Mechanics and repairmen, airplane
472   Mechanics and repairmen, automobile
473   Mechanics and repairmen, office machine
474   Mechanics and repairmen, radio and television
475   Mechanics and repairmen, railroad and car shop
480   Mechanics and repairmen (n.e.c.)
490   Millers, grain, flour, feed, etc.
491   Millwrights
492   Molders, metal
493   Motion picture projectionists
494   Opticians, and lens grinders and polishers
495   Painters, construction and maintenance
501   Paperhangers
502   Pattern and model makers, except paper
503   Photoengravers and lithographers
504   Piano and organ tuners and repairmen
505   Plasterers
510   Plumbers and pipe fitters
512   Pressmen and plate printers, printing
513   Rollers and roll hands, metal
514   Roofers and slaters
515   Shoemakers and repairers, except factory
520   Stationary engineers
521   Stone cutters and stone carvers
523   Structural metal workers
524   Tailors and tailoresses
525   Tinsmiths, coppersmiths, and sheet metal workers
530   Toolmakers, and die makers and setters
535   Upholsterers
545   Craftsmen and kindred workers (n.e.c.)
555   Members of the armed forces, and former members of the armed
       forces

Operatives and Kindred Workers

601   Apprentice auto mechanics
602   Apprentice bricklayers and masons
603   Apprentice carpenters
604   Apprentice electricians
605   Apprentice machinists and toolmakers
610   Apprentice mechanics, except auto
612   Apprentice plumbers and pipe fitters
613   Apprentices, building trades (n.e.c.)
614   Apprentices, metalworking trades (n.e.c.)
615   Apprentices, printing trades
620   Apprentices, other specified trades
621   Apprentices, trade not specified
630   Asbestos and insulation workers
631   Assemblers
632   Attendants, auto service and parking
634   Blasters and powdermen
635   Boatmen, canalmen, and lock keepers
640   Brakemen, railroad

641	Bus drivers
642	Chainmen, rodmen, and axmen, surveying
643	Checkers, examiners, and inspectors, manufacturing
645	Conductors, bus and street railway
650	Deliverymen and routemen
651	Dressmakers and seamstresses, except factory
652	Dyers
653	Filers, grinders, and polishers, metal
654	Fruit, nut, and vegetable graders and packers, except factory
670	Furnacemen, smeltermen, and pourers
671	Graders and sorters, manufacturing
672	Heaters, metal
673	Knitters, loopers, and toppers, textile
674	Laundry and dry cleaning operatives
675	Meat cutters, except slaughter and packing house
680	Milliners
685	Mine operatives and laborers (n.e.c.)
690	Motormen, mine, factory, logging camp, etc.
691	Motormen, street, subway, and elevated railway
692	Oilers and greasers, except auto
693	Packers and wrappers (n.e.c.)
694	Painters, except construction and maintenance
695	Photographic process workers
701	Power station operators
703	Sailors and deck hands
704	Sawyers
705	Sewers and stitchers, manufacturing
710	Spinners, textile
712	Stationary firemen
713	Switchmen, railroad
714	Taxicab drivers and chauffeurs
715	Truck and tractor drivers
720	Weavers, textile
721	Welders and flame-cutters
775	Operatives and kindred workers (n.e.c.)

Private Household Workers

801	Baby sitters, private household
802	Housekeepers, private household
803	Laundresses, private household
804	Private household workers (n.e.c.)
805	Housewife

Service Workers, Except Private Household

810	Attendants, hospital and other institutions
812	Attendants, professional and personal service (n.e.c.)
813	Attendants, recreation and amusement
814	Barbers

815	Bartenders
820	Bootblacks
821	Boarding and lodging house keepers
823	Chambermaids and maids, except private household
824	Charwomen and cleaners
825	Cooks, except private household
830	Counter and fountain workers
831	Elevator operators
832	Housekeepers and stewards, except private household
834	Janitors and sextons
835	Kitchen workers (n.e.c.), except private household
840	Midwives
841	Porters
842	Practical nurses
843	Hairdressers and cosmetologists

Protective service workers

850	Firemen, fire protection
851	Guards, watchmen, and doorkeepers
852	Marshals and constables
853	Policemen and detectives
854	Sheriffs and bailiffs
860	Watchmen (crossing) and bridge tenders

874	Ushers, recreation and amusement
875	Waiters, and waitresses
890	Service workers, except private household (n.e.c.)

Farm Laborers and Foremen

901	Farm foremen
902	Farm laborers, wage workers
903	Farm laborers, unpaid family workers
905	Farm service laborers, self-employed

Laborers, Except Farm and Mine[4]

960	Carpenters' helpers, except logging and mining
962	Fishermen and oystermen
963	Garage laborers, and car washers and greasers
964	Gardeners, except farm, and groundskeepers
965	Longshoremen and stevedores
970	Lumbermen, raftsmen, and woodchoppers
971	Teamsters
972	Truck drivers' helpers
973	Warehousemen (n.e.c.)
985	Laborers (n.e.c.)

| 995 | *Occupation not Reported or Persons Deceased or Retired* |

Industrial Classification

(The 3-digit number in the left margin is the code symbol for the industry category.)

Agriculture, Forestry, and Fisheries

016   Agriculture
017   Forestry
018   Fisheries

Mining

126   Metal mining
136   Coal mining
146   Crude petroleum and natural gas extraction
156   Nonmetallic mining and quarrying, except fuel
196   Construction

Manufacturing Durable Goods

Lumber and wood products, except furniture
206   Logging
207   Sawmills, planing mills, and mill work
208   Miscellaneous wood products
209   Furniture and fixtures

Stone, clay, and glass products
216   Glass and glass products
217   Cement, and concrete, gypsum, and plaster products
218   Structural clay products
219   Pottery and related products
236   Miscellaneous nonmetallic mineral and stone products

Metal industries
237   Blast furnaces, steel works, rolling and finishing mills
238   Other primary iron and steel industries
239   Primary nonferrous industries
246   Cutlery, hand tools, and other hardware
247   Fabricated structural metal products
248   Miscellaneous fabricated metal products
249   Not specified metal industries

Machinery, except electrical
256   Farm machinery and equipment
257   Office, computing and accounting machines
258   Miscellaneous machinery
259   Electrical machinery, equipment, and supplies

Transportation equipment
267   Motor vehicles and motor vehicle equipment
268   Aircraft and parts
269   Ship and boat building and repairing
276   Railroad and miscellaneous transportation equipment

Professional and photographic equipment, and watches
286   Professional equipment and supplies
287   Photographic equipment and supplies
289   Watches, clocks, and clockwork-operated devices
296   Miscellaneous manufacturing industries

Nondurable Goods

Food and kindred products
306   Meat products
307   Dairy products
308   Canning and preserving fruits, vegetables, and sea foods
309   Grain-mill products
316   Bakery products
317   Confectionery and related products
318   Beverage industries
319   Miscellaneous food preparations and kindred products
326   Not specified food industries
329   Tobacco manufactures

Textile mill products
346   Knitting mills
347   Dyeing and finishing textiles, except wool and knit goods
348   Floor covering, except hard surface
349   Yarn, thread, and fabric mills
356   Miscellaneous textile mill products

Apparel and other fabricated textile products
359   Apparel and accessories
367   Miscellaneous fabricated textile products

Paper and allied products
386   Pulp, paper, and paperboard mills
387   Paperboard containers and boxes
389   Miscellaneous paper and pulp products

Printing, publishing, and allied industries
396   Newspaper publishing and printing
398   Printing, publishing, and allied industries, except newspapers

Chemicals and allied products
406   Synthetic fibers
407   Drugs and medicines
408   Paints, varnishes, and related products
409   Miscellaneous chemicals and allied products

Petroleum and coal products
416   Petroleum refining
419   Miscellaneous petroleum and coal products

Rubber and miscellaneous plastic products
426   Rubber products
429   Miscellaneous plastic products

Leather and leather products
436   Leather: Tanned, curried, and finished
437   Footwear, except rubber

438   Leather products, except footwear
459   Not specified manufacturing industries

Transportation, Communication, and Other Public Utilities

Transportation
506   Railroads and railway express service
507   Street railways and bus lines
508   Taxicab service
509   Trucking service
516   Warehousing and storage
517   Water transportation
518   Air transportation
519   Petroleum and gasoline pipe lines
526   Services incidental to transportation

Communications
536   Radio broadcasting and television
538   Telephone (wire and radio)
539   Telegraph (wire and radio)

Utilities and sanitary services
567   Electric light and power
568   Gas and steam supply systems
569   Electric-gas utilities
576   Water supply
578   Sanitary services
579   Other and not specified utilities

Wholesale and Retail Trade

Wholesale trade
606   Motor vehicles and equipment
607   Drugs, chemicals, and allied products
608   Dry goods and apparel
609   Food and related products
616   Farm products—raw materials
617   Electrical goods, hardware, and plumbing equipment
618   Machinery, equipment, and supplies
619   Petroleum products
626   Miscellaneous wholesale trade
629   Not specified wholesale trade

Retail trade
636   Food stores, except dairy products
637   Dairy products stores and milk retailing
638   General merchandise retailing
639   Limited price variety stores
646   Apparel and accessories stores, except shoe stores
647   Shoe stores
648   Furniture and housefurnishings stores
649   Household appliances, TV, and radio stores
656   Motor vehicles and accessories retailing
657   Gasoline service stations
658   Drug stores

659	Eating and drinking places
666	Hardware and farm equipment stores
676	Lumber and building material retailing
678	Liquor stores
679	Retail florists
686	Jewelry stores
687	Fuel and ice dealers
689	Miscellaneous retail stores
696	Not specified retail trade

Finance, Insurance, and Real Estate

706	Banking and credit agencies
716	Security and commodity brokerage and investment companies
726	Insurance
736	Real estate (including real estate-insurance-law offices)

Business and Repair Services

806	Advertising
807	Miscellaneous business services
808	Automobile repair services and garages
809	Miscellaneous repair services

Personal Services

816	Private households
826	Hotels and lodging places
828	Laundering, cleaning, and dyeing services
829	Dressmaking shops
836	Shoe repair shops
838	Barber and beauty shops
839	Miscellaneous personal services

Entertainment and Recreation Services

846	Theaters and motion pictures
848	Bowling alleys, and billiard and pool parlors
849	Miscellaneous entertainment and recreation services

Professional and Related Services

867	Medical and other health services, except hospitals
868	Hospitals
869	Legal services
876	Educational services
879	Welfare and religious services
888	Nonprofit membership organizations
896	Engineering and architectural services
897	Accounting, auditing, and bookkeeping services
898	Miscellaneous professional and related services
899	Philanthropic Foundation

Public Administration

906   Postal service
916   Federal public administration
926   State public administration
936   Local public administration
997   Retired
998   Unemployed
999   Industry not reported

---

[1] Some categories are left empty in order to allow for differences between schools. If necessary at your school, simply add categories.

[2] See as source for the codes: U.S. Bureau of the Census; U.S. Census of Population and Housing, 1960. "1/1,000–1/10,000, Two National Samples of the Population of the United States, Description and Technical Documentation" (Washington, D.C.: U.S. Government Printing Office, 1964), pp. 41–52. The material may also be found in U.S. Bureau of the Census, 1960 Census of Population. Alphabetical Index of Occupations and Industries. Revised edition (Washington, D.C.: U.S. Government Printing Office, 1960), pp. xv–xxiv.

[3] The codes for occupations and industry are reprinted from the U.S. Bureau of the Census (1960 Census of Population. Alphabetical List of Occupations and Industries, Rev. ed. (Washington, D.C.: U.S. Government Printing Office, 1960), pp. xv–xxiv).

[4] Mine laborers are included in the main group "Operatives and Kindred Workers."

SOCIOLOGY QUESTIONNAIRE

My name is _____. I am a member of the Sociology research class in the department of Sociology. Because there is so little known about the students here at _____ University, we thought it important to design a questionnaire to get some information. The Sociology Department and the research methods class are conducting the research and we would appreciate it if we could ask you a few questions. The responses you give will be completely anonymous and confidential. The responses will be used by the Sociology Department for statistical purposes and will not be connected with the statements of any individual.

ID Number _____

1. What is your sex? Male _____ Female _____

2. What is your age (at your last birthday)? _____

3. You do not have to answer this, but what religion are you?
   Protestant _____ Catholic _____ Jewish _____ Other (please specify) _____

4. You do not have to answer this, but what race are you (please mark all that apply)?
   White _____
   Black _____
   Native American _____
   Mexican-American/Chicano _____
   Oriental _____
   Puerto Rican-American _____
   Other (please specify) _____

5. Are you: Married _____ Single _____ Widowed _____ Divorced _____

6. Are you: Freshman _____ Sophomore _____ Junior _____ Senior _____ Other (please specify) _____

7. Are you full-time student (12 credit or more hours)? _____
   Part-time student (less than 12 hours)? _____

8. What is your major (or what do you plan to major in)?
   Business Administration _____
   Education _____
   Humanities _____
   Physical Science/Math _____
   Social Sciences _____
   Other (please specify) _____

8(a). Do you have a specific plan for what you wish to do upon graduation?
    Yes _____ No _____

 (b). If yes, what is your plan? _____

9(a). If you are working, what is your occupation (please be specific)? _____
    _____

 (b). For what company do you work? _____

10. What is the amount of your father's education?

Grade School	High School	College	Graduate
1 2 3 4 5 6 7 8	9 10 11 12	13 14 15 16	17 18 19 20 more

11(a). What is your father's occupation (please be specific)? _____

(b). For what company does your father work? _____

12. What is the amount of your mother's education?

Grade School	High School	College	Graduate
1 2 3 4 5 6 7 8	9 10 11 12	13 14 15 16	17 18 19 20 more

13(a). Does your mother have an occupation outside the home?   Yes _____ No _____

(b). If yes, what is your mother's occupation (please be specific)? _____

(c). For what company does your mother work? _____

14. If you are married, what is the level of your spouse's education?

Grade School	High School	College	Graduate
1 2 3 4 5 6 7 8	9 10 11 12	13 14 15 16	17 18 19 20 more

15(a). What is your spouse's occupation (please be specific)? _____

(b). For what company does your spouse work? _____

16. Answer only if you are married: What is your approximate total family income going to be for this year from all sources (parents, spouse's job, etc.)?

$0-$2,999 _____	$9,000-$10,999 _____	
$3,000-$4,999 _____	$11,000-$12,999 _____	
$5,000-$6,999 _____	$13,000-$14,999 _____	
$7,000-$8,999 _____	$15,000 and over _____	

17. Answer only if you are not married: What is your approximate total personal income going to be for this year from all sources (parental, scholarship, work-study, jobs, etc)?

$0-$2,999 _____	$9,000-$10,999 _____	
$3,000-$4,999 _____	$11,000-$12,999 _____	
$5,000-$6,999 _____	$13,000-$14,999 _____	
$7,000-$8,999 _____	$15,000 and over _____	

17(a). Do you get scholarship or work-study money?   Yes _____ No _____

(b). If yes, how much per year do you receive? _____

18(a). Do you pay city income tax?   Yes _____ No _____

(b). If yes, what rates do you pay?   Resident _____ Nonresident _____

19(a). If married, does your spouse pay city income tax?   Yes _____ No _____

(b). If yes, what rates does he/she pay?   Resident _____ Nonresident _____

20(a). Do you own: Car _____ Truck _____ Motorcycle _____ Camper _____ Other _____

(b). Do you drive to school?   Regularly _____ Occasionally _____ Split with others _____

21(a). What is the distance, in miles (one way), from your home to the university? _____

(b). How long does the trip take?   Hours _____ Minutes _____

22. Where do your parents live?
    In this town _____
    In this county _____
    Outside of the county but within 50 miles of campus _____
    More than two hours from campus _____
    Other (please specify) _____

23(a). If married, do you have children? Yes _____ No _____

(b). If yes, how many? _____

(c). How many are in public schools (grades Kindergarten – 12)? _____

(d). How many are in private schools (grades Kindergarten – 12)? _____

24. How many brothers and sisters do you have? _____

25(a). Where do you live?
    Own home _____
    Parents' home _____
    With relatives _____
    In apartment _____
    In college housing _____
    Other (please specify) _____

(b). Where would you prefer to live?
    Own home _____
    Parents' home _____
    With relatives _____
    In apartment _____
    In college housing _____
    Other (please specify) _____
    Why? _____

(c). Where would you prefer not to live?
    Own home _____
    Parents' home _____
    With relatives _____
    In apartment _____
    In college housing _____
    Other (please specify) _____.
    Why? _____

26. How important were the following factors in the decision you made to attend this school?

	Very Important	Important	Unimportant	Very Unimportant	Undecided
The amount of money you have available					
Distance to class					
Distance to work					
Distance to movies and other entertainment					
Distance to go for dates					
Lack of campus social life					
Studying atmosphere					
Other (specify) _____					

27. Please put in order from 1 (like) to 8 (dislike) the following aspects of where you live <u>now</u>:

Studying atmosphere _____   Distance to work _____
Distance to school _____   The people _____
Cost _____   Distance to entertainment _____
Parents like it _____   Other (specify) _____

28. Who was most important in helping you make the decision to live where you now live?

Yourself _____   Relative _____
Friend _____   Other (specify) _____
Parents _____

29(a). What are your chances of living next year in the same place you now live?

Very good _____   Not good _____
Good _____   Very bad _____
50-50 _____   No chance _____

(b). If you expect to change, why do you think you will change? _____
_____

30. Did you:

Begin here as a freshman _____
Transfer from a junior college _____
Transfer from a public 4-year college _____
Transfer from a private 4-year college _____
Other (specify) _____

31. Why did you pick this college? _____

32. If you were to transfer from this college, where would you go?

State university _____
Another state college _____
Private college in this state _____
Other (specify) _____
Why? _____

33. What are the things you like about this college? _____

34. What are the things you dislike about this college? _____
_____

35. If you had the power, what would you change about this college? _____
_____

Please use the remaining space to add any comments you might have.

SOCIOLOGY QUESTIONNAIRE

My name is _____. I am a member of the Sociology research class in the department of Sociology. Because there is so little known about the students here at _____ University, we thought it important to design a questionnaire to get some information. The Sociology Department and the research methods class are conducting the research and we would appreciate it if we could ask you a few questions. The responses you give will be completely anonymous and confidential. The responses will be used by the Sociology Department for statistical purposes and will not be connected with the statements of any individual.

ID Number _____

1. What is your sex? Male _____ Female _____

2. What is your age (at your last birthday)? _____

3. You do not have to answer this, but what religion are you?
   Protestant _____ Catholic _____ Jewish _____ Other (please specify) _____

4. You do not have to answer this, but what race are you (please mark all that apply)?
   White _____
   Black _____
   Native American _____
   Mexican-American/Chicano _____
   Oriental _____
   Puerto Rican-American _____
   Other (please specify) _____

5. Are you: Married _____ Single _____ Widowed _____ Divorced _____

6. Are you: Freshman _____ Sophomore _____ Junior _____ Senior _____ Other
   (please specify) _____

7. Are you full-time student (12 credit or more hours)? _____
   Part-time student (less than 12 hours)? _____

8. What is your major (or what do you plan to major in)?
   Business Administration _____
   Education _____
   Humanities _____
   Physical Science/Math _____
   Social Sciences _____
   Other (please specify) _____

8(a). Do you have a specific plan for what you wish to do upon graduation?
   Yes _____ No _____

(b). If yes, what is your plan? _____

9(a). If you are working, what is your occupation (please be specific)? _____
   _____

(b). For what company do you work? _____

10. What is the amount of your father's education?

Grade School	High School	College	Graduate
1 2 3 4 5 6 7 8	9 10 11 12	13 14 15 16	17 18 19 20 more

11(a). What is your father's occupation (please be specific)? _____

(b). For what company does your father work? _____

12. What is the amount of your mother's education?

Grade School	High School	College	Graduate
1 2 3 4 5 6 7 8	9 10 11 12	13 14 15 16	17 18 19 20 more

13(a). Does your mother have an occupation outside the home? Yes _____ No _____

(b). If yes, what is your mother's occupation (please be specific)? _____

(c). For what company does your mother work? _____

14. If you are married, what is the level of your spouse's education?

Grade School	High School	College	Graduate
1 2 3 4 5 6 7 8	9 10 11 12	13 14 15 16	17 18 19 20 more

15(a). What is your spouse's occupation (please be specific)? _____

(b). For what company does your spouse work? _____

16. Answer only if you are married: What is your approximate total family income going to be for this year from all sources (parents, spouse's job, etc.)?

$0-$2,999 _____	$9,000-$10,999 _____
$3,000-$4,999 _____	$11,000-$12,999 _____
$5,000-$6,999 _____	$13,000-$14,999 _____
$7,000-$8,999 _____	$15,000 and over _____

17. Answer only if you are not married: What is your approximate total personal income going to be for this year from all sources (parental, scholarship, work-study, jobs, etc)?

$0-$2,999 _____	$9,000-$10,999 _____
$3,000-$4,999 _____	$11,000-$12,999 _____
$5,000-$6,999 _____	$13,000-$14,999 _____
$7,000-$8,999 _____	$15,000 and over _____

17(a). Do you get scholarship or work-study money? Yes _____ No _____

(b). If yes, how much per year do you receive? _____

18(a). Do you pay city income tax? Yes _____ No _____

(b). If yes, what rates do you pay? Resident _____ Nonresident _____

19(a). If married, does your spouse pay city income tax? Yes _____ No _____

(b). If yes, what rates does he/she pay? Resident _____ Nonresident _____

20(a). Do you own: Car _____ Truck _____ Motorcycle _____ Camper _____ Other _____

(b). Do you drive to school? Regularly _____ Occasionally _____ Split with others _____

21(a). What is the distance, in miles (one way), from your home to the university? _____

(b). How long does the trip take? Hours _____ Minutes _____

22. Where do your parents live?
    In this town_____
    In this county_____
    Outside of the county but within 50 miles of campus_____
    More than two hours from campus_____
    Other (please specify)_____

23(a). If married, do you have children? Yes____ No_____

(b). If yes, how many? _____

(c). How many are in public schools (grades Kindergarten – 12)? _____

(d). How many are in private schools (grades Kindergarten – 12)? _____

24. How many brothers and sisters do you have?_____

25(a). Where do you live?
    Own home_____
    Parents' home_____
    With relatives_____
    In apartment_____
    In college housing_____
    Other (please specify)_____

(b). Where would you prefer to live?
    Own home_____
    Parents' home_____
    With relatives_____
    In apartment_____
    In college housing_____
    Other (please specify)_____
    Why?_____

(c). Where would you prefer not to live?
    Own home_____
    Parents' home_____
    With relatives_____
    In apartment_____
    In college housing_____
    Other (please specify)_____
    Why?_____

26. How important were the following factors in the decision you made to attend this school?

	Very Important	Important	Unimportant	Very Unimportant	Undecided
The amount of money you have available					
Distance to class					
Distance to work					
Distance to movies and other entertainment					
Distance to go for dates					
Lack of campus social life					
Studying atmosphere					
Other (specify) _____					

4

27. Please put in order from 1 (like) to 8 (dislike) the following aspects of where
you live <u>now</u>:

Studying atmosphere _____	Distance to work _____
Distance to school _____	The people _____
Cost _____	Distance to entertainment _____
Parents like it _____	Other (specify) _____

28. Who was most important in helping you make the decision to live where you now
live?

Yourself _____	Relative _____
Friend _____	Other(specify) _____
Parents _____	

29(a). What are your chances of living next year in the same place you now live?

Very good _____	Not good _____
Good _____	Very bad _____
50-50 _____	No chance _____

(b). If you expect to change, why do you think you will change? _____
_____

30. Did you:
Begin here as a freshman _____
Transfer from a junior college _____
Transfer from a public 4-year college _____
Transfer from a private 4-year college _____
Other (specify) _____

31. Why did you pick this college? _____

32. If you were to transfer from this college, where would you go?
State university _____
Another state college _____
Private college in this state _____
Other (specify) _____
Why? _____

33. What are the things you like about this college? _____

34. What are the things you dislike about this college? _____

35. If you had the power, what would you change about this college? _____
_____

Please use the remaining space to add any comments you might have.

SOCIOLOGY QUESTIONNAIRE

My name is _____. I am a member of the Sociology research class in the

department of Sociology. Because there is so little known about the students here at _____

University, we thought it important to design a questionnaire to get some information. The

Sociology Department and the research methods class are conducting the research and we would

appreciate it if we could ask you a few questions. The responses you give will be completely

anonymous and confidential. The responses will be used by the Sociology Department for

statistical purposes and will not be connected with the statements of any individual.

ID Number _____

1. What is your sex? Male _____ Female _____

2. What is your age (at your last birthday)? _____

3. You do not have to answer this, but what religion are you?
   Protestant _____ Catholic _____ Jewish _____ Other (please specify) _____

4. You do not have to answer this, but what race are you (please mark all that apply)?
   White _____
   Black _____
   Native American _____
   Mexican-American/Chicano _____
   Oriental _____
   Puerto Rican-American _____
   Other (please specify) _____

5. Are you: Married _____ Single _____ Widowed _____ Divorced _____

6. Are you: Freshman _____ Sophomore _____ Junior _____ Senior _____ Other
   (please specify) _____

7. Are you full-time student (12 credit or more hours)? _____
   Part-time student (less than 12 hours)? _____

8. What is your major (or what do you plan to major in)?
   Business Administration _____
   Education _____
   Humanities _____
   Physical Science/Math _____
   Social Sciences _____
   Other (please specify) _____

8(a). Do you have a specific plan for what you wish to do upon graduation?
   Yes _____ No _____

(b). If yes, what is your plan? _____

9(a). If you are working, what is your occupation (please be specific)? _____
   _____

(b). For what company do you work? _____

10. What is the amount of your father's education?

Grade School	High School	College	Graduate
1 2 3 4 5 6 7 8	9 10 11 12	13 14 15 16	17 18 19 20 more

11(a). What is your father's occupation (please be specific)? _____
_____

(b). For what company does your father work? _____

12. What is the amount of your mother's education?

Grade School	High School	College	Graduate
1 2 3 4 5 6 7 8	9 10 11 12	13 14 15 16	17 18 19 20 more

13(a). Does your mother have an occupation outside the home? Yes _____ No _____

(b). If yes, what is your mother's occupation (please be specific)? _____
_____

(c). For what company does your mother work? _____

14. If you are married, what is the level of your spouse's education?

Grade School	High School	College	Graduate
1 2 3 4 5 6 7 8	9 10 11 12	13 14 15 16	17 18 19 20 more

15(a). What is your spouse's occupation (please be specific)? _____
_____

(b). For what company does your spouse work? _____

16. Answer only if you are married: What is your approximate total family
income going to be for this year from all sources (parents, spouse's job, etc.)?

$0-$2,999 _____	$9,000-$10,999 _____
$3,000-$4,999 _____	$11,000-$12,999 _____
$5,000-$6,999 _____	$13,000-$14,999 _____
$7,000-$8,999 _____	$15,000 and over _____

17. Answer only if you are not married: What is your approximate total personal
income going to be for this year from all sources (parental, scholarship,
work-study, jobs, etc)?

$0-$2,999 _____	$9,000-$10,999 _____
$3,000-$4,999 _____	$11,000-$12,999 _____
$5,000-$6,999 _____	$13,000-$14,999 _____
$7,000-$8,999 _____	$15,000 and over _____

17(a). Do you get scholarship or work-study money? Yes _____ No _____

(b). If yes, how much per year do you receive? _____

18(a). Do you pay city income tax? Yes _____ No _____

(b). If yes, what rates do you pay? Resident _____ Nonresident _____

19(a). If married, does your spouse pay city income tax? Yes _____ No _____

(b). If yes, what rates does he/she pay? Resident _____ Nonresident _____

20(a). Do you own: Car _____ Truck _____ Motorcycle _____ Camper _____ Other _____

(b). Do you drive to school? Regularly _____ Occasionally _____ Split with others _____

21(a). What is the distance, in miles (one way), from your home to the university? _____

(b). How long does the trip take? Hours _____ Minutes _____

22. Where do your parents live?
    In this town _____
    In this county _____
    Outside of the county but within 50 miles of campus _____
    More than two hours from campus _____
    Other (please specify) _____

23(a). If married, do you have children? Yes _____ No _____

 (b). If yes, how many? _____

 (c). How many are in public schools (grades Kindergarten – 12)? _____

 (d). How many are in private schools (grades Kindergarten – 12)? _____

24. How many brothers and sisters do you have? _____

25(a). Where do you live?
    Own home _____
    Parents' home _____
    With relatives _____
    In apartment _____
    In college housing _____
    Other (please specify) _____

 (b). Where would you prefer to live?
    Own home _____
    Parents' home _____
    With relatives _____
    In apartment _____
    In college housing _____
    Other (please specify) _____
    Why? _____

 (c). Where would you prefer not to live?
    Own home _____
    Parents' home _____
    With relatives _____
    In apartment _____
    In college housing _____
    Other (please specify) _____.
    Why? _____

26. How important were the following factors in the decision you made to attend this school?

	Very Important	Important	Unimportant	Very Unimportant	Undecided
The amount of money you have available					
Distance to class					
Distance to work					
Distance to movies and other entertainment					
Distance to go for dates					
Lack of campus social life					
Studying atmosphere					
Other (specify) _____					

27. Please put in order from 1 (like) to 8 (dislike) the following aspects of where you live <u>now</u>:

Studying atmosphere _____   Distance to work_____
Distance to school _____   The people _____
Cost _____   Distance to entertainment _____
Parents like it _____   Other (specify) _____

28. Who was most important in helping you make the decision to live where you now live?

Yourself_____   Relative _____
Friend_____   Other(specify) _____
Parents _____

29(a). What are your chances of living next year in the same place you now live?

Very good _____   Not good _____
Good _____   Very bad _____
50-50 _____   No chance _____

(b). If you expect to change, why do you think you will change?_____
_____

30. Did you:

Begin here as a freshman_____
Transfer from a junior college_____
Transfer from a public 4-year college_____
Transfer from a private 4-year college _____
Other (specify)_____

31. Why did you pick this college?_____

32. If you were to transfer from this college, where would you go?

State university_____
Another state college _____
Private college in this state_____
Other (specify)_____
Why?_____

33. What are the things you like about this college?_____
_____

34. What are the things you dislike about this college?_____
_____

35. If you had the power, what would you change about this college?_____
_____

Please use the remaining space to add any comments you might have.

SOCIOLOGY QUESTIONNAIRE

My name is _____. I am a member of the Sociology research class in the department of Sociology. Because there is so little known about the students here at _____ University, we thought it important to design a questionnaire to get some information. The Sociology Department and the research methods class are conducting the research and we would appreciate it if we could ask you a few questions. The responses you give will be completely anonymous and confidential. The responses will be used by the Sociology Department for statistical purposes and will not be connected with the statements of any individual.

ID Number _____

1. What is your sex? Male _____ Female _____

2. What is your age (at your last birthday)? _____

3. You do not have to answer this, but what religion are you?
   Protestant _____ Catholic _____ Jewish _____ Other (please specify) _____

4. You do not have to answer this, but what race are you (please mark all that apply)?
   White _____
   Black _____
   Native American _____
   Mexican-American/Chicano _____
   Oriental _____
   Puerto Rican-American _____
   Other (please specify) _____

5. Are you: Married _____ Single _____ Widowed _____ Divorced _____

6. Are you: Freshman _____ Sophomore _____ Junior _____ Senior _____ Other
   (please specify) _____

7. Are you full-time student (12 credit or more hours)? _____
   Part-time student (less than 12 hours)? _____

8. What is your major (or what do you plan to major in)?
   Business Administration _____
   Education _____
   Humanities _____
   Physical Science/Math _____
   Social Sciences _____
   Other (please specify) _____

8(a). Do you have a specific plan for what you wish to do upon graduation?
   Yes _____ No _____

(b). If yes, what is your plan? _____

9(a). If you are working, what is your occupation (please be specific)? _____
_____

(b). For what company do you work? _____

10. What is the amount of your father's education?
     Grade School   High School   College   Graduate
     1 2 3 4 5 6 7 8   9 10 11 12   13 14 15 16   17 18 19 20 more

11(a). What is your father's occupation (please be specific)? _____

  (b). For what company does your father work? _____

12. What is the amount of your mother's education?
     Grade School   High School   College   Graduate
     1 2 3 4 5 6 7 8   9 10 11 12   13 14 15 16   17 18 19 20 more

13(a). Does your mother have an occupation outside the home? Yes _____ No _____

  (b). If yes, what is your mother's occupation (please be specific)? _____

  (c). For what company does your mother work? _____

14. If you are married, what is the level of your spouse's education?
     Grade School   High School   College   Graduate
     1 2 3 4 5 6 7 8   9 10 11 12   13 14 15 16   17 18 19 20 more

15(a). What is your spouse's occupation (please be specific)? _____

  (b). For what company does your spouse work? _____

16. Answer only if you are married: What is your approximate total family income going to be for this year from all sources (parents, spouse's job, etc.)?
     $0-$2,999 _____ $9,000-$10,999 _____
     $3,000-$4,999 _____ $11,000-$12,999 _____
     $5,000-$6,999 _____ $13,000-$14,999 _____
     $7,000-$8,999 _____ $15,000 and over _____

17. Answer only if you are not married: What is your approximate total personal income going to be for this year from all sources (parental, scholarship, work-study, jobs, etc)?
     $0-$2,999 _____ $9,000-$10,999 _____
     $3,000-$4,999 _____ $11,000-$12,999 _____
     $5,000-$6,999 _____ $13,000-$14,999 _____
     $7,000-$8,999 _____ $15,000 and over _____

17(a). Do you get scholarship or work-study money? Yes _____ No _____

  (b). If yes, how much per year do you receive? _____

18(a). Do you pay city income tax? Yes _____ No _____

  (b). If yes, what rates do you pay? Resident _____ Nonresident _____

19(a). If married, does your spouse pay city income tax? Yes _____ No _____

  (b). If yes, what rates does he/she pay? Resident _____ Nonresident _____

20(a). Do you own: Car _____ Truck _____ Motorcycle _____ Camper _____ Other _____

  (b). Do you drive to school? Regularly _____ Occasionally _____ Split with others _____

21(a). What is the distance, in miles (one way), from your home to the university? _____

  (b). How long does the trip take? Hours _____ Minutes _____

22. Where do your parents live?
In this town_____
In this county_____
Outside of the county but within 50 miles of campus_____
More than two hours from campus_____
Other (please specify)_____

23(a). If married, do you have children? Yes_____No_____

(b). If yes, how many? _____

(c). How many are in public schools (grades Kindergarten – 12)? _____.

(d). How many are in private schools (grades Kindergarten – 12)? _____

24. How many brothers and sisters do you have? _____

25(a). Where do you live?
Own home_____
Parents' home_____
With relatives_____
In apartment_____
In college housing_____
Other (please specify)_____

(b). Where would you prefer to live?
Own home_____
Parents' home_____
With relatives_____
In apartment_____
In college housing_____
Other (please specify)_____
Why?_____

(c). Where would you prefer not to live?
Own home_____
Parents' home_____
With relatives_____
In apartment_____
In college housing_____
Other (please specify)_____.
Why?_____

26. How important were the following factors in the decision you made to attend this school?

	Very Important	Important	Unimportant	Very Unimportant	Undecided
The amount of money you have available					
Distance to class					
Distance to work					
Distance to movies and other entertainment					
Distance to go for dates					
Lack of campus social life					
Studying atmosphere					
Other (specify) _____					

27. Please put in order from 1 (like) to 8 (dislike) the following aspects of where you live _now_:

Studying atmosphere _____   Distance to work_____
Distance to school _____   The people _____
Cost _____   Distance to entertainment_____
Parents like it _____   Other (specify) _____

28. Who was most important in helping you make the decision to live where you now live?

Yourself_____   Relative _____
Friend_____   Other(specify) _____
Parents _____

29(a). What are your chances of living next year in the same place you now live?

Very good _____   Not good_____
Good _____   Very bad _____
50-50 _____   No chance _____

(b). If you expect to change, why do you think you will change?_____
_____

30. Did you:

Begin here as a freshman_____
Transfer from a junior college_____
Transfer from a public 4-year college_____
Transfer from a private 4-year college _____
Other (specify)_____

31. Why did you pick this college?_____

32. If you were to transfer from this college, where would you go?

State university_____
Another state college _____
Private college in this state_____
Other (specify)_____
Why?_____

33. What are the things you like about this college?_____
_____

34. What are the things you dislike about this college?_____
_____

35. If you had the power, what would you change about this college?_____
_____

Please use the remaining space to add any comments you might have.